Cyprus

Bernard Mc Donagh
and Ian Robertson

BLUE GUIDE

A&C Black • London
WW Norton • New York

4th edition © Bernard Mc Donagh and Ian Robertson 1998

1st edition © Ernest Benn, by Ian Robertson, 1981
2nd edition © A&C Black (Publishers) Ltd, by Ian Robertson, 1987
3rd edition © A&C Black (Publishers) Ltd, by Ian Robertson, 1990

Published by A & C Black (Publishers) Limited
35 Bedford Row, London WC1R 4JH

Maps and plans drawn by Robert Smith, RJS Associates; sketch maps drawn by Tony Mills, ©
A&C Black

Illustrations © Lorna Bernard

A CIP catalogue record of this book is available from the British Library.

ISBN 0–7136–3986–5

Published in the United States of America by
WW Norton and Company Inc.
500 Fifth Avenue, New York, NY 10110

Published simultaneously in Canada by
Penguin Books Canada Limited
10 Alcorn Avenue, Toronto
Ontario M4V 3B2

ISBN 0–393-30730-1 USA

The authors and the publishers have done their best to ensure the accuracy of all the information
in Blue Guide Cyprus; however, they can accept no responsibility for any loss, injury or inconve-
nience sustained by any traveller as a result of information or advice contained in the guide.

Cover photograph the cloistered courtyard of Ayia Napa Monastery by Edmund Nägele, FRPS.

Since his retirement from the Civil Service **Bernard Mc Donagh** has been able to indulge in full
his passions for travelling and writing. He may have got his taste for travelling from postings to the
British Embassy in Kinshasa (where he was awarded the Order of Zaire by the Congolese
Government), and to Hamburg, Stuttgart and Munich, where he was British Consul. His *Blue
Guide Turkey, Aegean and Mediterranean Coasts* received the Thomas Cook Award for the best guide
book in 1989. He is also author of *Blue Guide Belgium and Luxembourg, Blue Guide Turkey*, which
covers the whole country, and a book for children *Turkish Village*. He is currently writing an
archaeological guide to Tunisia.

Ian Robertson was the original author of *Blue Guide Cyprus*. He currently lives in France and is
the author of *Blue Guide France*.

Printed and bound in England by William Clowes Ltd., Beccles and London.

Contents

Preface 7

Introduction to Cyprus 8

**Practical information
Southern Cyprus** 12
Planning your trip ~ Formalities 12,
Sources of information 12, Tour
operators 12, Currency 12; **Getting
to Southern Cyprus** ~ By air 13;
Arriving in Southern Cyprus
Airports 13, Customs regulations
13; **Travelling around** ~ By bus 14,
By car 14, Hitchhiking 15, Coach
tours 15, Boat trips 15, Marinas 16;
Where to stay ~ Hotels 16, Youth
hostels 16, Camp sites 17; **Where to
eat** ~ Restaurants and tavernas 17,
Cafés and bars 17, Water 17

General Information 18
Best time to visit 18; Changing
money 18; Credit cards 18; Electric
current 18; Embassies and consulates
18; Emergencies 18; Festivals 18;
Green Line 19; Medical services 19;
Monasteries and churches 19;
Museums and archaeological sites
20; National parks 20; Photography
20; Postal services 20; Press, radio
and television 20; Public holidays
21; Returning home 21; Shopping
21; Sports 21; Telephones 21;
Tourist offices 22; Weights and
measures 22

**Practical information
Northern Cyprus** 23
Planning your trip ~ Formalities 23,
Sources of information 23, Tour
operators 23, Currency 23; **Getting
to North Cyprus** ~ By air 24;
Arriving in North Cyprus ~ Airports
24, Customs regulations 24;
Travelling around ~ By bus 24, By
car 25, Hitchhiking 25, Coach tours
25, Boat tours 26; **Where to stay** ~
Hotels 26, Camp sites and picnic
areas 26; **Where to eat** ~ Restaurants
26, Cafés and bars 26, Turkish
Cypriot food 26

General information 28
Beaches 28; British Resident's Society
28; Diplomatic representation 28;
Disabled travellers 28; Electric
current 29; Emergencies 29; Green
Line 29; Medical services 29;
Mosques 29; Museums and archaeological sites 29; Opening hours 30;
Photography 30; Postal and telephone services 30; Public holidays
30; Returning homes 30; Shopping
30; Sports 31; Toilets 31; Tourist
offices 31; Weights and measures 31

Introduction to the food and wine of Cyprus by Sir David and Iro Hunt 32
Introduction to the monuments and early history of Cyprus by Nicolas
Coldstream 39

Chronology 49

Glossary 53

Further reading 56

The guide

Larnaca 57
  Southern Sector 63
  Northern Sector & Kition 64

East of Larnaca 67

North and north west of Larnaca 72

West of Larnaca 76

Limassol 80

East of Limassol ~ Amathus and beyond 87

South west of Limassol ~ The Akrotiri Peninsula, Kolossi Castle and beyond 91

East of Paphos 102

Paphos 108

North west of Paphos 125

North of Paphos ~ the hill villages of Akamas 129

North east of Paphos ~ Polemi to Amargeti 132

North of Limassol 134

North west of Limassol 135

The Mountain Villages I 137

The Mountain Villages II 146

Nicosia 152
  Southern Nicosia 158
  South east and south west of Nicosia 168
  Northern Nicosia 172

Girne ~ Kyrenia 181

South of Girne ~ Kyrenia 188

Girne ~ Kyrenia to the Karpas 191

West of Girne~Kyrenia ~ To Güzelyurt (Morphou), Soloi and Vouni 200

Castles of the Gothic Mountain Range 209

Around Northern Nicosia 215

Gazimağusa ~ Famagusta 216

North and west of Gazimagusa ~ Famagusta 228
  Salamis 228
  Enkomi 234

Maps and plans
Gazimağusa 220–221
Girne ~Kyrenia 185
Kato Paphos 116
Kourion 97
Larnaca 61
Limassol 84
Nicosia 156–157
Paphos 113
Salamis 229
Saranda Kolones 119

Area maps
Around Gazimagusa ~ Famagusta 227
Around Girne ~ Kyrenia (east) 192
Around Girne ~Kyrenia (west) 202–203
Around Larnaca 68–69
Around Limassol 90–91
Around Nicosia 169
Around Paphos 128
Castles of the Gothic Mountain Range 209
The Karpas 196–197
Troodos Hill resorts 139

Index 237

Preface

Writing the fourth edition of *Blue Guide Cyprus* has been both a joy and a challenge! A joy, because it gave me the opportunity to visit a beautiful island and, as a result, brought me into contact with a wonderfully kind and hospitable people. A challenge, because it was not easy to put within two covers the rich, varied culture and the complicated history of the Cypriot people.

The book contains a number of innovations. We have abandoned the old structure of routes and substituted chapters which describe individual towns, eg, Paphos, and, where appropriate, the places around them. There is a good deal of new material like the information on hotels, restaurants, and methods of transport. The expanded description of the flora and fauna of the island will, I hope, be of interest to all readers and not just to naturalists. In most of the chapters the history section has been greatly increased. The legends and stories that lie behind the icons and wall paintings in churches and monasteries and the mosaics and frescoes in ancient buildings are told in full. There are new maps and revised plans of the towns and ancient sites. Each chapter begins with a list of 'highlights', places or buildings that the visitor should not miss. There is a chronology that sets out the principal events in the island's history and an expanded glossary that explains the archaeological, architectural, religious and mythological terms used in the text.

I hope the book will be of help to all who visit Cyprus and that it will increase their enjoyment of that

> 'Fairest inle, all isles excelling
> Seat of pleasures, and of loves;'

where, indeed, Venus still makes her dwelling.

May I thank all those in Cyprus and Britain who helped me in a multitude of ways with my research and my travels. This book could not have been written without their interest and assistance.

Bernard Mc Donagh
London, June 1998

Per la Famiglia Rufolo

Introduction to Cyprus

Topography

Cyprus, Kypros in Greek, Kibris in Turkish, is, after Sicily and Sardinia, the third largest and the most easterly island in the Mediterranean. It lies between latitudes 34° 33° and 35° 42° north and longitudes 32° 17° and 34° 35° east. Its total area is 9251sq. km, 3572 sq. miles, slightly larger than the two English counties of Norfolk and Suffolk combined. Its greatest length, from the Akamas peninsula in the west to the tip of the Karpas Peninsula in the east, is 222km, 138 miles. Its greatest breadth, from Cape Kormakiti in the north to Cape Gata in the south, is 95km or 59 miles.

The south coast of Turkey is only 70km, 44 miles to the north. On most days it is possible to see Anamur Burnu, which towers over the ancient city of Anemurium, from Kyrenia. Syria lies 103km, 64 miles, to the east and Egypt is some 340km, 211 miles to the south. The nearest Greek territory, the island of Rhodes, is 386km, 240 miles, to the west.

Near the north coast of the island is the long, narrow Kyrenia range of mountains which is sometimes called Pentadaktylos in Greek and Beşparmak in Turkish. Incidentally, both words have the same meaning, the 'Five Fingers'. The range rises to1024m, 3360ft, at Mt Kyparissovouno near Lapta (Lapithos) and then runs parallel to the northern coast to form the area that has acquired the bizarre and incorrect soubriquet of 'the panhandle'. To the south is the fertile plain of the Mesaoria. Its name means 'between the mountains' and is derived from its position between the Kyrenia range and the Troodos massif to the south west. The Troodos Mts., which cover a large part of the island, rise to1951m, 6401ft. at Mt Olympos. The island's coastline measures some 782km, 486 miles. There are no perennial freshwater lakes or rivers. The many watercourses, dry during summer and autumn, often become torrents in winter. Reservoirs have been constructed to store as much water as possible.

South and North Cyprus

Since July 1974 the island has been divided by the Attila Line, sometimes called the Green Line, into two parts, the Republic of Cyprus (South Cyprus) and North Cyprus, which later adopted the title, Turkish Republic of North Cyprus. The Attila Line is manned by United Nations troops, the UNFICYP force. The Republic of Cyprus occupies about two thirds of the island. If you visit North Cyprus, you will not be allowed to cross into the Republic. If you visit South Cyprus, you may cross into North Cyprus at the Ledra Palace hotel checkpoint in Nicosia, but you must return to the Republic each evening.

There are two British Sovereign Bases on the island. Both are in the Republic of Cyprus. They occupy an area of 256sq.km, 99 sq. miles.

Population

During its long history the population of Cyprus has fluctuated considerably. It has been estimated that in 50 BC it was as high as 450,000, but it dropped dramatically in the 4C AD to c 50,000 largely through war and famine. It later climbed to 300,000 before falling again again because of the Black Death. In

1489 at the end of the Lusignan period and the beginning of the Venetian occupation, the figure was c 106,000. By the third quarter of the 16C it had risen to between 180,000 and 197,000. The population of the Turkish province of Cyprus was c 200,000, but it varied considerably during the next three centuries. Even though the ratio of Moslems to Christians increased, this may have been due to the fact that some Christians ostensibly changed their religion to avoid the kharaj or tax. These were the Linobambakoi, crypto Christians who paid lip service to Islam. In the early 18C the population again decreased to between 80,000 and 84,000, with 47,000 to 60,000 claiming to be Moslem and 20,000 to 37,000 Christians. During the late 18C and early decades of the 19C it continued to fluctuate between 60,000 and 100,000.

The last official census of the whole island was held in 1960, the first year of independence. Out of a total population of 577,615 there were some 442,521 Greek Cypriots and 104,350 Turkish Cypriots. The remaining 30,744 was made up of 3628 Armenians, 2708 Maronites ie Lebanese and Syrian Christians in communion with the Roman Catholic Church, and 2796 Latins, mostly Roman Catholic descendants of Italian merchants. The rest were described as 'British, Gypsies, Other and Not Stated'.

At present it is virtually impossible to obtain any precise figure for the population of the the island. This state of affairs is likely to continue until an entente is reached between the two communities and another island wide census made.

Climate

The best time to visit Cyprus is between March and mid June and from September to November. It has a dry, healthy climate. Some visitors may find the summer heat difficult to bear even though its effect is somewhat mitigated in the coastal resorts by sea breezes. The island enjoys sunshine for much of the year. Rain rarely falls outside the period from October to February. The driest and hottest place is Nicosia. This has an average rainfall of 14.72 inches. Girne (Kyrenia) is the wettest place on the island with 21.15 inches. Troodos has an annual average precipitation of 48.95 inches. Most of this falls between late October and early May, but between January and March it is largely in the form of snow. Woollen clothing is desirable during the winter months. In the evenings there is often a sudden drop in temperature.

The table below gives the average air and sea temperatures and the average

Month	Air	Sea	Mountain	Sunshine
Jan.	16.6	16.4	6.3	57
Feb.	16.0	16.9	5.9	63
March	18.4	17.3	10.4	67
April	22.8	18.6	14.3	71
May	27.2	21.0	18.8	79
June	30.5	24.0	24.1	87
July	33.3	26.3	26.3	90
Aug.	33.6	27.7	26.9	88
Sept.	30.8	26.6	23.2	88
Oct.	27.3	25.1	18.4	80
Nov.	22.9	21.9	14.1	71
Dec.	19.2	18.9	9.6	59

maximum day temperatures in the hill resorts in degrees Centigrade, also the percentage of sunny days in each month.

July and August are the hottest months with a maximum temperature of 44.5°C. December to February are the coolest with a minimum of minus 5.5°C.

Because of its geographical position darkness falls suddenly and comparatively early during the winter months in Cyprus. At that time of the year make an early start if you are planning a long journey.

Flora and fauna

In antiquity Cyprus was almost as famous for its forests as it was for its deposits of copper. With Lycia in Asia Minor it was the sources of much of the timber used for shipbuilding in the Eastern Mediterranean. Unfortunately, in the course of centuries large parts of the island were denuded of their trees. The forests were particularly badly damaged during the intercommunal troubles of 1974. However, **conservation** is being undertaken in both South and North Cyprus and it still possible to see specimens of the trees that figure in its history. They include the Aleppo Pine, *Pinus halepensis*, which was much used for shipbuilding; the Cypress, *Cupressus sempervivens*, whose shape is said to resemble the fire of a funeral pyre; the cedar, *Cedrus brevifolia*, which is found in the highest parts of the Troodos Mountains; the Oriental Plane, *Platanus orientalis*, which, it is said, was brought to Cyprus by the Persians; the Strawberry Tree, *Arbutus andrachne*, which is found all over the Eastern Mediterranean; the Carob, *Ceratonia siliqua*, whose pods were shipped from Kyrenia and other places on the north coast until the end of the 19C; and the olive, *Olea europaea*, Athena's precious gift to mankind.

Among the many **wild plants** and **herbs** used as food or for curative purposes are wild sage, *Salvia fruticosa*, from which an infusion good for sore throats is made; fennel, *Foeniculum vulgare*, which may be eaten and used medicinally; sweet marjoram, *Oreganum majorana*, from which an aromatic oil is produced; and myrtle, *Myrtus communis*, whose oil is used to clear blocked breathing passages.

In springtime the fields are covered with **anemonies**, **poppies**, **Cyprus cyclamens**, **irises**, **gladioli**, **grape hyacinths**, **Cyprus crocus** and the yellow flowers of **oxalis**, while the roadside verges are crowned with the pale, ghostly blooms of **asphodel**, the flower of the Elysian Fields, the flower of death, the flower of Persephone. On rocky hillsides look for the pink and white flowers of **rock roses**, genus *Cistus*, and on the slopes of the Kyrenia range search for orchids—*Orchis simia*, whose pink flowers resemble a monkey, *Ophrys kottschyi*, the **Anatolian orchid** and the yellow **Roman orchid**. In summer **convolvulus** in several colours cascades over lime washed walls and **marshmallows** grow between the cracks in the pavement of village streets. The purple flowers of the **Judas tree** celebrate the Easter festival and the flowers of the **Jacaranda** carpet the pavements in imperial purple.

Cyprus is a staging post for many **migrating birds**. Flamboyantly coloured **Bee eaters** spend a month or two here and **Golden orioles** stop long enough to gorge themselves on mulberries. Among the residents species are the **Cyprus warbler** and the **Black francolin**. The **Greater flamingos** winter in the Larnaca and Akrotiri salt marshes. **Kestrels** are not uncommon and ,if you are lucky, you may glimpse the rare **Bonelli's eagle** floating over the higher peaks of the Kyrenia range. In the Karpas Peninsula look out for the **Red footed falcon** and the **Hobby**. There are colonies of **Eleanora's falcons** on the cliff faces of Akrotiri.

Cyprus was formerly the home of pygmy elephants, pygmy hippotamoi, ibex and wild boar. Now the **Cyprus moufflon**, *Ovis musimon*, is the largest mammal on the island. Protected from hunters, its habitat is restricted to the forests on the southern side of the island. There are **foxes** in the Akamas and in the Karpas Peninsula and the **long eared hedgehog** is making a comeback after years of persecution. It was believed that this animal invaded hen houses in order to copulate with the inmates! In the Kyrenia range and in the Akamas **fruit eating bats** live in the caves.

The harmless **worm snake**, **whip snake** and **grass snake** are not uncommon. The **Montpellier snake** and the **cat snake** produce venom, but are not considered a danger to humans. The very poisonous **blunt nosed viper** has a distinctive yellow horn like tail and will not retreat, if disturbed. Its bites need **immediate** treatment. The **European tarantula** lives in burrows on open, sloping ground and is harmless. **Scorpions** may be found in old stone walls.They and the large **black millipedes** can inflict a painful sting. Both have been found occasionally in tents and camping equipment.

Loggerhead turtles and **green turtles** lay their eggs on the sandy beaches of the Akamas and Karpas Peninsula. Fishermen land catches of **red** and **grey mullet**, **peacock** and **rainbow wrasse**, **parrot fish**, and **red soldier fish**. In the deep water there are **sharks** and **sting ray**. Bathers should look out for the **weever fish** whose spines inject a highly toxic venom. If stung, **seek medical help without delay**.

Languages

Greek and Turkish are the official languages of the Republic of Cyprus, Turkish the official language of the Turkish Republic of Northern Cyprus. However, English is widely understood and is used all over the island. Visitors are unlikely to meet any language problems, but a knowledge, however slight, of Greek and/or Turkish will greatly increase the pleasure of their stay and will be much appreciated by their hosts. The BBC's courses, *Get By in Greek*, *Get By in Turkish* and the *BBC Turkish Travel Pack* are strongly recommended. By means of tapes and text books they provide an easy and interesting introduction to these languages.

Practical information

The Republic of Cyprus

Planning your trip

Formalities
Nationals of Great Britain, the Republic of Ireland, the United States of America, Canada, Australia and many other countries—a full list may be obtained from the Cyprus Tourist Organisation—need just a **valid passport** for a stay of up to 90 days in the Republic of Cyprus. No visa is required. Applications for permits to stay for more than 90 days should be addressed to the Chief Immigration Officer, Nicosia.

Sources of information
Information on all aspects of southern Cyprus can be obtained from the Cyprus Tourism Organisation at the following addresses.
In the UK: **Cyprus Tourist Office**, 213 Regent St., London, W1R 8DA.☎: 0171 734 9822/2593, fax: 0171 287 6534. email: ctolon@demon.co.uk
In the US: **Cyprus Tourist Organisation**, 13 East 40th Street, New York, New York 10016. ☎: 212 683 5280,fax: 212 683 5282. email: gocyprus@aol.com
    The CTO does not appear to have offices in Canada and Australia.

Tour operators
More than 60 companies offer holidays in South Cyprus. They include:
Airglobe Holidays, 63 Gray's Inn Road London WC1X 8TL. ☎ 0171 813 1122, fax: 0171 813 2277.
British Airways Holidays, Astral Towers, Betts Way, London Rd, Crawley, West Sussex RH10 2XA. ☎ 01293 723 131, fax: 01293 722 702.
Cosmos Holidays, Tourama House, 17 Homesdale Rd, Bromley, Kent BR2 9LX. ☎ 0181 464 3444, fax: 0181 290 0714.
Cyprair Tours Ltd, 23 Hampstead Rd, Euston Centre, London NW1 3JA, ☎ 0181 359 1234, fax: 0181 359 1310.
First Choice Cyprus, 2nd Floor, Astral Towers, Betts Way, Crawley, West Sussex RH10 2GX, ☎ 0161 742 2262, fax:0161 745 4533.
Odyssey Holidays, Interaction Ltd, 3rd Floor, 1 Torrington Park London N12 9SU. ☎ 0181 343 9090, fax: 0181 343 7444.
Skytours Holidays, Thomson Tour Operations Ltd, Greater London House, Hampstead Road, London NW1 7SD, ☎ 0990 502 552, fax: 0121 236 7030.
A full list may be obtained from any CTO office and brochures for many of the companies are available at travel agents.

Currency
Visitors may import any amount of Cypriot or foreign bank notes. They should be declared to Customs on form D.(N.R.). Visitors may export any amount of

Cypriot or foreign bank notes they have declared on form D.(N.R.) and certain other amounts of currency. Further information is available from the Customs authorities and the banks in Cyprus and from CTO offices in Cyprus and abroad.

The **monetary unit** is the Cyprus pound, C£. This is divided into 100 cents. There are coins of 1 cent, 2 cents, 5 cents, 10 cents, 20 cents and 50 cents and notes for C£1, C£5, C£10 and C£20.

Getting to Southern Cyprus

By air

There are frequent **scheduled flights** by **Cyprus Airways** and **British Airways** from London to Larnaca. There are also services by Cyprus Airways from London and Manchester to Paphos. Charter flights to Cyprus operate from Gatwick, Stanstead, Luton, Manchester and Birmingham. For details of these consult your travel agent or advertisements in the national press. The flight time from London is four hours 30 minutes. Further information may be obtained from the **Cyprus Airways**, 29–31 Hampstead Road, Euston Centre, London NW1 3JA, ☎ 0171 388 5411; New York, ☎ 212 714 2190 and from any **British Airways** office ☎ 0181 759 2525 for details of local offices. Information is also available from the **Cyprus Tourism Organisation** offices in the UK and US (see *Sources of Information* above for addesses and telephone numbers).

Ferry boats operate between Piraeus (the port of Athens), the Greek islands, Haifa, Port Said, some other Middle East ports and Limassol and Larnaca. There are reduced services during the winter. Schedules may be obtained from any CTO office.

Arriving in Southern Cyprus

Airports

Most visitors to Southern Cyprus arrive at Larnaca International Airport. This is 5km (3 miles) from Larnaca town. The other airport in the Republic is Paphos International Airport which is located 15km (9 miles) east of the town.

At Larnaca and Paphos there are the following **facilities**: tourist information; foreign exchange; hotel reservation; duty-free shops; cafés; card and coin-operated telephones; car rental offices; car park; special facilities for handicapped passengers—truck lifts for disembarkation and embarkation, wheelchairs, special washrooms and automatic doors. **Note**. The airlines do **not** provide transport to and from the airports. Transportation for independent travellers is by metered taxis.

Customs regulations

Visitors are allowed to bring in 250grs of tobacco or 200 cigarettes, one bottle (0.75 lit) of wine, one litre of spirits, perfume (0.30 lit) and other articles, except jewellery, up to a total value of C£50. These allowance do not apply to transit passengers. The importation, possession and use of narcotic drugs and psychotropic substances is **forbidden**.

The export of antiquities is prohibited.

Travelling around

By bus

There are no trains in Cyprus. **Private bus companies** provided safe, inexpensive transport. The following companies link the principal towns at specified intervals:

Nicosia—Limassol: Kemek Transport Ltd, ☎ (02) 463 989, (05) 747 532.

Nicosia—Paphos: Nea Amoroza Transport Co. Ltd, ☎ (06) 236 740, (06) 236 822.

Nicosia—Larnaca: Kallenos Buses, ☎ (04) 654 890.

Limassol—Larnaca: Kallenos Buses, ☎ (04) 654 890.

Buy your tickets at the appropriate company's bus office before departure.

Nearly all the villages are linked to the nearest town by **rural buses** once or twice every day. For details of pick up points, departure times and fares, ask at the Tourist Information Offices.

Urban buses provide frequent services during the day. In summer these are extended to midnight in tourist areas. Buy your ticket on the bus. For further information telephone the following numbers:

Nicosia (02) 473 414; **Limassol** (05) 370 592, (05) 355 273; **Larnaca** (04) 650 477; **Paphos** (06) 234 410; **Ayia Napa** (03) 721 321.

Transurban taxis link the main towns every half hour. Carrying between four and seven passengers they can be booked through your hotel reception. They operate between 05.45 and 18.30 (19.00 in the summer), Monday to Saturday, and 07.00 to 17.30 (18.30 in the summer). Passengers can be collected and dropped off anywhere within the town boundaries. This means that, for no extra charge, you get an extended tour of the suburbs! Advantages: they are inexpensive and flexible. Disadvantages: they are sometimes driven at breakneck speed; they are not airconditioned, and if full, they are not very comfortable.

Urban metered taxis provide a 24 hour service in all towns.

By car

A car is necessary if you wish to explore the island fully and visit those archaeological sites, churches and monasteries which are off the beaten track. **Note**. Motorists may not cross the Green Line.

Car hire firms with offices in all the principal towns and at Larnaca airport are listed in the CTO's free *Guide to Hotels, Travel Agencies and other Tourist Services*. Visitors need a National or International Driving Licence valid for the type of vehicle they wish to drive. The Green Insurance Card is not accepted in Cyprus. Drivers must have an insurance certificate valid for Cyprus or obtain cover on arrival. Third party cover is required by law. Fully comphrensive cover is recommended.

The use of **seat belts** by front seat passengers is compulsory. Traffic is on the left side of the road as in the UK. Distances and speed limits are in kilometres and kilometres per hour. It is advisable to stay away from town centres during the rush hour periods, ie, 0.7.30 to 08.00, 13.00 to 13.30 and 18.00 to 19.00 in summer, 17.00 to 18.00 in winter.

Four lane **motorways** link Nicosia with Limassol and Larnaca and there are fairly good roads between the towns and villages. The main roads are mostly well-cambered and in good condition, but the hard shoulder often ends abruptly and may have broken edges. **Many minor** and **forest roads** have rough surfaces. When using these roads, care should be taken, especially during wet weather. Sufficient time should always be given to cover the ground when off the main roads particularly towards dusk. The narrow, winding mountain tracks often have vertiginous, unprotected drops on one side. At dusk or after dark keep a sharp look out for unlit carts, bicycles and straying animals.

The **maximum speed limit** on motorways is 100km/h and the lower speed limit 65km/h. On all other roads the speed limit is 80km/h, unless a lower speed is indicated. Regrettably, many Cypriots still drive too fast and too recklessly.

If possible, avoid driving due west in the late afternoon, as the glare from the setting sun is both unpleasant and dangerous. Wear sunglasses. Driving or being in charge of a motor vehicle or pedal cycle with an alcohol concentration in breath or blood above the prescribed limit is an offence. The limits are 39 microgrammes of alcohol per 100 millilitres of breath and in blood 90 milligrams of alcohol per 100 millilitres of blood.

Petrol stations are normally open from 06.00 to 18.00 from Monday to Friday and to 16.00 on Saturdays. In rural areas petrol stations may open on Sundays and public holidays from 06.00 to 18.00. It is advisable to keep the petrol tank topped up when driving off the beaten track. Petrol and diesel oil are sold by the litre. At the time of writing unleaded petrol costs the same as premium grade.

International road signs are used. Place names are usually given in Greek and in English. The Kummerly & Frey 1.275000 tourist map is recommended.

The office of the **Cyprus Automobile Association** is at Chr. Mylona 12, CY Lefkosia (Nicosia), ☎ (02) 313 233, fax: (02) 313 482.

Private companies offer a 24 hour breakdown service. A list is obtainable from any CTO office. Use the emergency telephones on the motorway to call for assistance.

Motorcycles, mopeds and **scooters** can be hired in most towns. Approximate charges per day are: moped C£2.50–C£4; scooter C£3.00–C£14.00; Euduro C£5.50–C£24. Insurance is extra. Helmets must be worn by the driver and pillion passenger.

Hitchhiking
Hitchhiking is not forbidden but public transport is cheap and distances between villages and towns relatively short so that you probably will not need to do it. If you do decide to hitch, it would be wise to observe the common sense precautions, as you would take in any country. Wear a sun hat and sunglasses in summer and stand on the left hand side of the road.

Coach tours
Details of coach tours, which usually operate during the holiday season only, may be obtained from hotel reception desks and offices of the CTO.

Boat trips
Weather permitting, there are one day return boat trips between May to October along the coast from Limassol to Lady's Mile Beach, from Paphos to Coral Bay

and the Pegeia area, from Ayia Napa to Paralimni and the Protaras area, from Larnaca to Ayia Napa and Protaras and from Polis along the Akamas coast.

Cruises to Egypt and Israel. There are two and three day cruises from Limassol to Egypt and Israel. Visitors may visit the Cairo Museum, the Pyramids, Jerusalem and Bethlehem, depending on the cruise chosen.

Marinas

There are yacht marinas at Larnaca and Limassol. They offer all the usual facilities—water, electricity, telephone, telex and fax, fuel, repairs, laundry, dry cleanering, chandlery, toilets, showers and coin operated washing machines.

Where to stay

Information about accommodation, which is offered in good faith, is given in the chapters on each resort. The hotels listed in this guide are given as a general indication only of the range of accommodation available and should **not** be regarded as the personal recommendation of the author. The Cyprus Tourist Organisation produces a comprehensive guide to the hotels, hotel apartments etc registered with and classified by it each year. This can be obtained, free of charge, from any office of the CTO. Note: accommodation in private houses is not available.

Accommodation is available in hotels; hotel apartments; tourist villages; tourist villas; campsites; tourist apartments; furnished apartments; guest houses and youth hostels.

Hotels

Hotels are graded from five star to one star; **hotel apartments** from A to C. Most have air-conditioning, swimming pools, tennis courts, sports facilities etc. Rates vary from C£71 to C£92 for a single and C£100 to C£130 for a double per day in a five star hotel to C£8.65 for a single and C£14 for a double in a one star hotel. A **studio apartment**, A class, costs C£42.50, while a C class studio apartment costs C£20 to C£22 per day. All prices have been approved by the Cyprus Tourist Organisation. **Note**: they may vary from resort to resort and are given here as an indication only. In hotels prices include breakfast, taxes and VAT (currently at 8%).

Hotels are clean, comfortable and well maintained. Many hotel rooms have air-conditioning, television and a minibar. Hotel restaurants have good, if sometimes rather unimaginative, menus. There are hotel snack bars and pool bars which offer light refreshments and snacks throughout the day and most of the night.

Youth hostels

There are **youth hostels** in **Nicosia** (1, Hadjidaki 5, ☎ (02) 444 808); **Larnaca** (Nikolaou Rossou 27, ☎ (04) 621 188); **Paphos** (Leoforos Eleftheriou Venizelou 37. ☎ (06 232 588); **Ayia Napa** (Dionysiou Solomou 23. ☎ c/o (02) 442 027 or (03) 723 113); **Troodos Mountains** (open April to October— weather permitting) c 400m from Troodos Hill Resort on the Troodos— Kakopetria road ☎ (05) 422 400.

Youth Hostels are open to members of the International Youth Hostels Association. Non members are also accepted. On arrival they are issued with a guest card. Further information from the Cyprus Youth Hostel Association, PO Box 1328, CY Lefkosia, Cyprus or Mrs. Poly Monti, Secretary General of the Association, Th. Theodotu 34, Flat 22, Lefkosia, Cyprus. ☎ (02) 442 027, fax: 442 896.

Camp sites
There are camp sites licensed by the CTO at Ayia Napa, Larnaca, Limassol, Paphos and in the Troodos Mountains. Further information and current charges may be obtained from any CTO office.

Where to eat

Restaurants and tavernas
One need never go hungry in South Cyprus! There are restaurants, tavernas, cafés and snack bars to suit all tastes and pockets. There are some suggestions at the beginning of each chapter. Some tavernas specialise in traditional Cypriot dishes. A meal for two of meze with a bottle of wine costs from C£15.00 upwards. There are many fish tavernas which serve produce from local marine farms. Prices in these tavernas are somewhat higher. Dinner for two, with a bottle of wine, in a restaurant costs a minimum of C£18. These prices include VAT and a 10% service charge. It is not usually necessary to tip. However, good service may be rewarded by a further small amount.

Lunch is served in restaurants from 12.00 to 14.30 and dinner from 19.00 onwards. In addition to establishments serving Cypriot dishes, there are French, Italian, Lebanese, Arab, Chinese, Indian, Thai, Mexican, Russian and Armenian restaurants in South Cyprus.

For information about Cypriot cooking and wine see pp 32–38

Cafés and bars
Cafés play an important part in Cypriot life. Open during the day and late into the night, they are male dominated social centres where the patrons play cards, backgammon, read newspapers, exchange gossip or just watch the world go by. They are useful sources of information about local places of interest and they welcome foreign visitors. Eschew all forms of powder coffee and drink the real thing. This is brewed, usually with sugar, in a traditional copper pot. Ask for *sketos*, without sugar, *metrios*, medium sweet or *glykos*, sweet. It will be accompanied by a glass of cold water. Coffee is often served to visitors in offices and shops. If you are invited to a Cypriot house, you will offered preserves, *glyko*, with coffee and water. These refreshments should never be refused.

Snacks bars abound. They include Mc Donalds and Wimpys as well as many locally owned establishments.

Water
It is safe to drink water from the tap. However, many visitors prefer bottled mineral water which only costs a few cents and is available everywhere.

General information

Best times to visit

March and April are the best months to visit the coastal resorts. Then the spring flowers carpet the hillsides and the sea is warm enough for bathing. Avoid the summer months when the temperature can rise to 32°C on the coast and 44.5°C inland. The resorts are also very crowded at that time. By September and October the great heat of summer has diminished, but it is warm enough to picnic out of doors and the sea still tempts bathers. Winter sports enthusiasts can expect some snow on Mt. Olympos from the beginning of January to the end of March.

Changing money

Banks are open from 08.30 to 12.30 from Monday to Friday; from 15.15 to 16.45 on Monday afternoon and from 08.15 to 12.30 during July and August. Some centrally located banks offer an afternoon tourist service. At Larnaca and Paphos airports banks are open throughout the day and provide a service at night for most flights. Banking facilities are also available at Limassol harbour. There are automatic exchange machines in most towns.

Rates of exchange are given every day in the press and are broadcast on the 10.00 news bulletin of the CyBC from Monday to Saturday.

Banks are closed on public holidays and on some religious feast days.

Credit cards

Where the appropriate symbol is shown, the following cards are accepted: Visa, Mastercard, Eurocard, Diners Club, Carte Blanche, American Express and JCB (National Bank of Greece).

Electric current

The electricity supply is 240 volts AC 50Hz. Sockets are usually 13 amp. square pin. The use of adaptors for high current rated appliances, eg, heaters, toasters is not recommended.

Embassies and consulates

Information about diplomatic representation in Cyprus is given in the chapter on Nicosia. The office of the **High Commission of the Republic of Cyprus** in the **UK** is at 93 Park St, London W1, ☎ 0171 499 8272/4, telex: 0171 491 0691. The **Embassy of the Republic of Cyprus** in the **USA** is at 2211 R. St NW, Washington, DC 20008, ☎ 202 462 5772, telex: 202 483 6710.

Emergencies

For an ambulance dial 199; for the fire service or the police 199 or 112; for night pharmacies 192.

Festivals

Travellers, who like to time their visits with a local festival, are lucky. Southern Cyprus is a land of festivals. A full list is published each year by the CTO.

The Green Line

The **only** crossing point to North Cyprus is by the Ledra Palace hotel in Nicosia. In times of tension this may be closed. It is only possible to make a day trip. You will be told your return time. This is usually before 19.00. Bring your passport. Warning notices on the Green Line are in Greek and English.

Medical services

Emergency medical treatment is available to visitors at the Ambulatory and Emergency Departments of Government Hospitals. This is free of charge, but tourists may use their holiday insurance if it covers medical expenses and the length of their stay on the island.

Nicosia General Hospital, ☎ (02) 451 111, 452 760 (ambulance).

Limassol General Hospital ☎ (05) 330 777, 330 333.

Larnaca General Hospital, ☎ (04) 630 312, 630 300.

Paphos General Hospital ☎ (06) 240 111.

Paralimni Hospital, ☎ (03) 821 211.

Polis Hospital ☎ (06) 321 431.

Kyperounta Hospital ☎ (05) 532 021.

Hotels can usually arrange medical services for their guests. They will contact private doctors and private clinics and hospitals as well as the state services. To call a private doctor at weekends or holidays use the following numbers:

Nicosia, ☎ 1422.

Limassol, ☎ 1425.

Larnaca, ☎ 1424.

Paphos, ☎ 1426

Ammochostos, ☎ 1423.

Private doctors' weekday visiting hours are 09.00 to 13.00 and 16.00 to 19.00. Most doctors speak English.

Although malaria has been virtually eradicated, **mosquitos** abound. Take a spray or repellent cream like 'Mosquito Milk', wear long sleeved shirts or dresses and long trousers in the evenings to reduce the chance of being bitten. Some hotels supply appliances which keep mosquitos at bay. **Midges** can be a problem in the Troodos Mountains. If bitten by a dog or scratched by a cat, seek medical attention. The venomous **viper** is now rarely encountered.

Monasteries and churches

Most monasteries can be reached by public transport. Further information is provided in the relevant chapters. Because they often house valuable icons and wall paintings, some churches are locked. Ask for the priest or enquire at the nearest village coffee shop. Observe the following code of behaviour. Shorts, short dresses and backless tops should not be worn. Women are not allowed to pass beyond the iconostasis into the sanctuary. Men may usually do so by using the side openings in the icon screen. Ask if photography is allowed. Do not use flash. Behave in a respectful manner. A donation for the upkeep of the church or monastery is frequently expected. A pocket torch and binoculars are useful adjuncts.

Some monasteries and convents have set visiting hours. Most do not allow group visits on Saturday and Sunday. Accommodation is **not** provided. Food is sometimes on sale.

Note: women may not visit Stavrovouni Monastery. If dressed properly, men are admitted. Cameras and video cameras are prohibited.

Museums and archaeological sites

Museums and archaeological sites are closed on Christmas Day, New Year's Day and Greek Orthodox Easter Sunday. On other public holidays the major sites are open from 07.30 to 17.00 (09.00 to 18.00), and the principal museums from 10.00 to 13.00. Note, however, all opening times, and entrance fees, are subject to alteration. Check with the local CTO office on the current situation. There is usually a small charge for entrance to museums and archaeological sites in South Cyprus. This may vary from time to time and from place to place. Special entry cards are available for one day at C£2.50 and for seven days at C£5.00. A special permit is usually required for photography in museums. Apply for this well in advance.

National parks

The **Troodos Forest**, **Cavo Gkreko** and **Potamos tou Liopetriou** have been declared National Forest Parks. The A**thlassa National Park** is near Nicosia. A Forest Nature Reserve has been established at **Tripilos**. This includes the Cedar Valley. The **Akamas Peninsula** will become a National Park. Under consideration for ecological conservation are the **Salt Lake** at Larnaca, the **Platys Valley**, the **Akrotiri Salt Lake** and the **Phassouri Marsh** near Limassol.

Photography

Photography is forbidden near military camps and other military installations (there are warning notices in Greek and English), in museums where special permission must be obtained and in churches, where there are icons and /or wall paintings, if flash is required.

Postal services

Main post offices are open from 07.30 to 13.30, 15.00 to 18.00 (except Wednesday) and on Saturday from 09.00 to 11.00. Other Post Offices are open from 07.30 to 13.30 and on Thursday afternoon from 15.00 to 18.00. All post offices are closed on Sunday and Public Holidays. A poste restante service is offered by the following offices: Nicosia, Plateia Eleftherias; Limassol, Gladstone 3; Larnaca, Plateia Vasileos Pavlou and Paphos, Nikodimou Mylona. Stamps may be purchased at all post offices, in hotels, at news stands and kiosks. Pillarboxes are painted yellow.

Press, radio and television

There are two English language **papers**, the *Cyprus Mail*, which is published daily, and the *Cyprus Weekly*. British and foreign papers are available the day after publication in the large towns. They carry a surcharge.

The **Cyprus Broadcasting Corporation** transmits three programmes on AM and FM. There are broadcasts in English, Turkish and Armenian on Radio Two, 91-1 Mhz FM, at 10.00, 13.30 and 20.00. During the summer a special programme, *Welcome to Cyprus*, is broadcast in English, French, German and Russian between 19.00 and 20.00.

The **British Forces Broadcasting Service** is on the air 24 hours a day.

There are several **television channels**. CyBC Channel 2 has a news bulletin in English at 21.00 every day. SSVC provides a television service for the British Forces. Many hotels receive CNN, BBC, SKY, NBC and SUPER CHANNEL.

Public holidays

1 January	New Year's Day
6 January	Epiphany
Variable	Green Monday—50 days before Greek Orthodox Easter
25March	Greek National Day
1 April	Greek Cypriot National Day
Variable	Greek Orthodox Good Friday
Variable	Greek Orthodox Easter Monday
1 May	Labour Day
Variable	Pentecost—Kataklysmos, Feast of the Flood
15 August	Assumption of the Blessed Virgin
1 October	Cyprus Independence Day
28 October	Greek National Day—Ochi Day
24 December	Christmas Eve
25 December	Christmas Day
26 December	Boxing Day

Returning home

For confirmation of flights contact Cyprus Airways, Nicosia, ☎ (02) 44 30 54 and (02) 44 19 96; British Airways, ☎ (02) 44 21 88/9 or your travel representative.

Shopping

Best buys are leather and woven goods, ceramics, copper and silverware, handmade baskets, lace, wine and spirits and spectacles. There is no charge for the eye test! In tourist centres shops and supermarkets remain open until late in the evening. Prices shown should include VAT at the standard rate of 8%.

Sports

Among the many sports available are sea angling, diving, sub aqua activities, sailing, yachting, swimming, shooting, skiing (January to March), tennis, golf, cycling, forest walking and fishing in dams. Further details from the CTO.

Telephones

The telephone service is provided by the Cyprus Telecommunication Authority, the CYTA, and 220 countries may be accessed automatically from the island. For information about subscribers in Cyprus dial 192, for subscribers abroad dial 194. Most operators speak English. Telephone cards cost C£3, C£5 and C£10. Coin operated telephones accept 2, 5, 10 and 20 cent coins.

The Call Direct Service allows you to charge a telephone call to a foreign number. This is cheaper than calls made through the operator in Cyprus. Dial the following numbers to be connected with an operator in the destination country: United Kingdom, for a BT number, 080 90044 or 080 99044 with a telephone card, for a Mercury number, 080 90004; Republic of Ireland, 080 90053; United States, for an AT & T number 080 90010, MCI operator 080 90000, for a SPRINT operator, 080 90001; Australia, for a TELSTRA operator 080 90061, for an OPTUS operator, 080 90002; Canada, 080 90012. This service is also available to other countries. A full list may be obtained from the CTO. The International Dialling Code for Great Britain is 0044, for the Republic of Ireland 00353, United States 001, Australia 0061 and Canada 001. The CYTA also operates Fax, Telex, Telegraph and Mobile Telephony services.

Tourist offices

The **CTO**'s head office, which deals with telephone and postal enquiries only, is at Leoforos Lemesou 19, PO Box 4535, CY 1390, Nicosia. ☎ (02) 337 715; telex: 2165 CYTOUR; Fax (02) 331 644 or 334 696.

Weights and Measures

The metric system is used in Southern Cyprus.

Practical information

Turkish Republic of North Cyprus

Planning your trip

Formalities
Visitors to North Cyprus need a **valid passport**. A visa is not required by visitors from the United Kingdom, the United States of America, Canada, Australia, New Zealand and a number of other countries.

Sources of information
Information on all aspects of North Cyprus can be obtained from the North Cyprus Tourist Office Representatives at the following addresses.
In the UK. North Cyprus Tourist Office Representatives, 29 Bedford Square, London, WC1B 3EG, ☎ 0171 631 1920, fax: 0171 631 1873.
In the US. 1667 K Street, Suite 590, Washington DC 20006 USA, ☎ 001 202 887 6198, fax: 001 202 467 0685
In Canada. 328 Highway 7, East Suite, Mr. Ezel Orfi, 308, Richmond Hill, Ontario, L4B 3P7, ☎ 001 416 731 4000, fax: 001 416 731 1458.
   The Turkish Republic of North Cyprus (TRNC) does not have an office in Australia.

Tour operators
Companies offering inclusive holidays in North Cyprus include
Prospect Music & Arts Tours, 454/458 Chiswick High Rd., London W4 5TT, ☎ 0181 995 2151, fax: 0181 742 1969.
Regent Holidays (UK) Ltd, 31A High Street, Shanklin, Isle of Wight, PO37 6JW, ☎ 01983 866670, fax: 01983 866620.
President Holidays, 92 Park Lane, Croydon, Surrey, CR0 1JF, ☎ 0181 688 7555, fax: 0181 760 0555.
Noble Caledonia Ltd, 11 Charles St., Mayfair, London, W1X 8LE (7HB), ☎ 0171 409 0376 or 491 4752, fax: 0171 409 0834.
Andante Travel, Grange Cottage, Salisbury SP4 6ER, ☎ 01980 610555, fax: 0190 610002. A full list may be obtained from the North Cyprus tourist office.

Currency
The Turkish Lira (TL) is the currency used in North Cyprus. However, there are no restrictions on the importation of foreign currency and pounds sterling, dollars and Cypriot pounds are often accepted by shops, restaurants and hotels. Master Card, Eurocard, Visa and Diners' Club cards may be used in many establishments, though a surcharge is sometimes added to the bill.
   Banking hours are from 08.30 to 12.00, Monday to Friday, in the summer and from 08.30 to 12.00 and 14.00 to 16.00 in the winter. In the resorts there

are many exchange offices which are open for most of the day. Shop around for the best rates and the lowest commission charges.

Getting to Northern Cyprus

By air

Cyprus Turkish Airlines and **Turkish Airlines** operate regular flights from the UK to North Cyprus. For details of schedules and fares contact **Cyprus Turkish Airlines** at 11–12 Pall Mall, London, SW1Y 5JG, ☎ 0171 930 4851/2/3/4, fax: 0171 930 1046 and **Turkish Airlines**, 125 Pall Mall, London, SW1Y 5EA. ☎ 0171 766 9333, fax: 0171 976 1733.

There are also frequent flights by **Istanbul Airlines** and **Onur Air**. Details of these and general information may be obtained from the **North Cyprus Tourist Office Representatives**, 29 Bedford Square, London, WC1B 3EG, ☎ 0171 631 1930, fax: 0171 631 1873. **In the US**. 1667 K Street, Suite 590, Washington DC 20006 USA, ☎ 001 202 8876198, fax: 001 202 4670685. **In Canada**. 328 Highway 7, East Suite, Mr. Ezel Orfi, 308, Richmond Hill, Ontario, L4B 3P7, ☎ 001 416 7314000, fax: 00 1416 7311458.

Note. All flights call at either Istanbul, Izmir or Antalya in Turkey en route to Ercan Airport.

There are no direct flights to North Cyprus from the Republic of Ireland, the US, Canada or Australia. Nationals of those countries may pick up a connecting flight in Britain, Germany or Austria.

Ferry services. An overnight ferry service operates throughout the year between Mersin in Turkey and Gazimağusa (Famagusta). This is often very crowded. It is essential to book a cabin well in advance. During the summer months there is a quicker, daytime service between the port of Taşucu near Silifke in Southern Turkey and Girne (Kyrenia). A hydrofoil operates between Alanya and Girne during the holiday season.

Arriving in North Cyprus

Airports

Flights to northern Cyprus land at **Ercan** airport. Ercan is c 24km east of Nicosia. It is named after a Turkish pilot, who was killed during the 1974 landings. It is served by Cyprus Turkish Airways, Turkish Airlines, Istanbul Air, Onur Air and a number of other companies. There are the usual facilities including duty free shops, souvenir shops. There is a Cyprus Turkish Airlines bus service to Nicosia and Girne.

Customs regulations

The allowances for North Cyprus are the same as those for South Cyprus.

Travelling around

By bus

Buses and **minibuses** operate between the main towns and there are frequent *dolmuş* services to the villages and to some beaches. A *dolmuş* is a minibus which leaves when full. (*Dolmuş* is Turkish for 'stuffed' or 'full'). Both buses and *dolmuş* services leave from the *otogar* which is usually located on the outskirts of the town. You pay for your ticket on the bus and for your journey in the *dolmuş*.

For details of bus and *dolmuş* services apply to the local tourist office. Your hotel reception may also be able to supply the required information and make a booking on your behalf. Some hotels located outside the town centre operate a courtesy minibus service.

Taxis have fixed tariffs for specific journeys, eg, from Girne to Bellapais. Charges for these journeys are displayed on a notice board at the central taxi pick point which in the case of Girne is near the Dome Hotel.

By car

As there are fewer cars than in South Cyprus, visitors find driving in the North a pleasant and efficient way of getting around. The main roads are in good condition and are well maintained, but some side roads are narrow and twisting and have abruptly shelving verges. Keep a sharp lookout, particularly at dusk, for unlit vehicles and straying animals. Most petrol stations are on the main roads and are open seven days a week. Before exploring some of the fascinating byways, top up the tank. Petrol is cheaper than in South Cyprus.

You will need a valid British or International Driving Licence. Many car hire firms operate in North Cyprus. These include **Budget Car Rental, Deniz Kızı Rent-A-Car, Riverside Rent A Car** and **Atlantic Rent A Car** in Girne; **Fly Rent-A-Car** and **Tab Rent-A-Car** in Gazimağusa, and **Budget Car Rental** and **Sun Rent A Car** in Nicosia (Lefkoşa). A list of car hire firms may be obtained from hotels and the local tourist office. Some hotels will arrange your car hire for you. Check the insurance provisions carefully, as an additional premium may be charged for fully comphrensive cover.

Traffic circulates on the left. The speed limits, which are 60 mph on the main highways, 40mph on minor roads and 30mph in built up areas, are rigorously enforced. Infringements of the speed limits and of parking regulations may result in heavy fines which can be levied on the spot. International traffic signs are used. Place names are in Turkish. Note the following mandatory directions:

Dikkat!	Attention
Dur!	Stop
Yavaş Surunuz	Drive Slowly
Durmak Yasaktır	No Stopping

As in the South, some local motorists treat driving as a competitive activity. If someone indicates his intention to overtake, they accelerate! They are also rather sparing with signals and frequently use the horn to greet their friends.

If you wish to import a car, information and advice about the regulations may be obtained from the British Residents' Society (see below).

Hitchhiking

Hitchhiking is not forbidden and often provides interesting and informative contact with the local people.

Coach tours

During the holiday season there are full day tours from Kyrenia to Famagusta and Salamis, to the Karpas Peninsula and to Nicosia and Güzelyurt, and from Famagusta to Kyrenia, to the Karpas Peninsula and Kantara Castle and to Nicosia and Güzelyurt.

Boat trips
For details of boat tours from Kyrenia see the relevant chapter.

Where to stay

Hotels
There is a wide range of hotels—from five star to one star—in Northern Cyprus. At the five star **Palm Beach** in Mağosa a double room with sea view costs US $90, a single $70; a double with town view $80, a single $65. In Girne a double room in the four star **Deniz Royal** costs $58, a single $43 with a 10% discount between November and March. At the one star **Hotel British** in Girne a double room costs $40, a single $30 with a 35% discount between November and March. Room prices are per day and include breakfast. A complete list of hotels and other establishments providing accommodation is available from the offices of the North Cyprus Tourist Organisation, and there are some recommendations at the beginning of each of the relevant chapters. The hotels listed in this guide are given as a general indication only of the range of accommodation available and should **not** be regarded as the personal recommendation of the author.

Hotels in North Cyprus are clean and well maintained. Air conditioning, television and a minibar are standard in the more expensive establishments.

Camp sites and picnic areas
There is a campsite to the west of Girne (Kyrenia) and another near Salamis. There are picnic areas in the Kyrenia mountains and at Salamis.

Where to eat

Restaurants
Visitors eat well in North Cyprus. A full list of restaurants is available from the local tourist offices and there are recommendations at the beginning of each chapter.

Cafés and bars
As in South Cyprus, cafés and bars play an important part in the social life of Turkish Cypriots. Spend a little time in the Tree of Idleness café in Bellapais or in the simpler establishments in some of the other small villages. Watch the world go by, play *tavla* and gossip with the locals.

Turkish Cypriot food
The following list of dishes may be found useful:
Soup, *Çorba*
Domates Çorbasi, tomato soup
Et Suyu, Consommé
Sebse Çorbasi, vegetable soup
Tavuk Suyu, chicken soup
Yayla Çorbasi, mutton soup with yogurt

Hors d'oeuvres, *Mezes*
Arnavut Ciğeri, spiced liver
Börek, pastry filled with soft white cheese and herbs. Sometimes deep-fried
Cacık, yogurt flavoured with grated cucumber, garlic and olive oil
Fava, board bean paste
Pilaki, white beans and onion with vinegar
Sardalya, sardines
Tarama, a paste of red caviar, yogurt, garlic and olive oil

Salad, *Salata*
Rus Salatası, mixed Russian salad with carrots, peas in mayonnaise
Çoban Salatası, mixed chopped salad of tomatoes, cucumbers, peppers, etc.
Karişik Salata, mixed salad
Patlican Salatası, cooked aubergines with yogurt
Yeşil Salata, green salad

Fish, *Balık*
Alabalık, trout
Barbunya, red mullet
Kefal, grey mullet
Lüfer, bluefish
Palamut, tunny

Meat, *Et*
Bonfile, fillet steak
Döner Kebab, slices of lamb roasted on a vertical spit
Köfte, croquettes of lamb in gravy
Pirzola, lamb chops
Sebzeli Rosbif, roast beef served with vegetables
Şis Kebab, charcoal-grilled chunks of lamb and tomatoes
Şeftali, minced meat and herbs in a sausage-type skin, grilled
Şis Köfte, grilled croquettes of lamb

Vegetables
Bezelye, peas
Biber, sharp green peppers
Havuç, carrots
Kabak, marrow or pumpkin
Lahana, cabbage
Taze Fasulye, French beans

Dessert, *Tatlı*
Baklava, layers of filo pastry filled with nuts and covered with syrup
Dondurma, ice cream

Fruit, *Mevya*
Erik, plums
Incir, figs
Kiraz, cherries

Kavun, yellow melon
Karpuz, water melon
Şeftali, peaches
Üzüm, grapes

Drinks
Ayran, yogurt diluted with water and chilled
Çay, tea, served black in a small glass with cubes of sugar
Kahve, Turkish coffee. Sugar is added during preparation so you should tell the waiter whether you want it *sade*, without sugar; *az şekerli*, with a little sugar; *çok şekerli*, very sweet
Maden Suyu, mineral water
Rakı, an aniseed-flavoured spirit on considerable potency resembling Greek *ouzo*

Water
In common with the whole island there is a serious shortage of water in North Cyprus. Visitors are recommended to use bottled water for drinking. This is cheap and available everywhere.

General information

Beaches
North Cyprus has some excellent beaches. Try those at the **Denizkızı** and **Mare Monte hotels** to the west of Girne and at **Karakum**, **Acapulco**, **Lara** and **Turtle Beach** to the east of the town. There is a fine stretch of sand at ancient **Salamis** and well kept beaches by the **Salamis Bay** and **Mimoza hotels**. The luxurious **Palm Beach hotel** at Gazimağusa (Famagusta) has a small, clean stretch of sand which is open to non residents. On the Karpas Peninsula are **Limanouri beach** and the huge dune fringed stretch of **Nangomi Bay**. There have been reports of sand flies on some of the more remote beaches. Take an insect repellant as well as suntan lotion!

British Residents' Society
The British Residents' Society was established in 1975 for British nationals who had come to live in North Cyprus. Its office, behind the post office in Girne, is open every Saturday morning between 10.00 and 12.00.

Diplomatic representation
For information about contacting foreign diplomatic representatives, see the chapter on Northern Nicosia.

Disabled travellers
There are few facilities specifically designed for disabled travellers. However, at Ercan Airport and at most hotels there are luggage ramps which can be used by travellers in wheelchairs. The castles on the Gothic Range and parts of some of the ancient sites are difficult to negotiate because of uneven surfaces or dense

undergrowth. Disabled travellers are advised to consult the tourist office before visiting them.

Electric current
The voltage is the same as in South Cyprus. Electricity, which comes from generating stations in the South, is sometimes interrupted for several hours. However, most hotels, restaurants and shops have portable generators which are switched on when the supply from the South is cut.

Emergencies
In emergencies call the following numbers:

Fire	199
Police	155
SOS.	112

Green Line
Be careful when approaching the Green Line which separates North and South Cyprus. The only official crossing place is at the Ledra Palace hotel in Nicosia. Note. Visitors to North Cyprus are **not** allowed to cross over into the South.
Military areas are signposted as follows:
Askeri Bölge: Girilmez, ie. Military area: No entry.

Medical services
Visitors should take out a holiday insurance before leaving home. The cost of medical treatment North Cyprus is lower than in the UK. Local medical practitioners deal with minor ailments. There are hospitals in Nicosia, ☎ 0392 2285441; Famagusta, ☎ 0392 3662876; Kyrenia, ☎ 0392 8152254 and Yesilyurt, ☎ 0392 7236351. In addition, there are several private clinics. Details of their charges for treatment and/or operations may be obtained before admission.

Mosques
Shoes must be removed before entering a mosque. Visitors wearing shorts, short dresses and short sleeves may be refused admission. Do not go in during prayer times or walk in front of someone who is praying. In general, behave in a quiet and respectful manner. Ask before taking photographs of the interior.

Museums and archaeological sites
From May to September museums are open between 09.00 and 13.30 and 16.00 and 18.30. From October to May the hours are 08.00 to 13.00 and 14.30 and 17.00. The ruins of Salamis are open from 08.00 to 19.00 in summer and until 17.00 in winter. At other sites the custodian's hut is not always manned. There is usually a small charge for entrance to museums and archaeological sites in North Cyprus. This may vary from time to time and from place to place. A special permit is usually required for photography in museums. Apply for this well in advance.

Opening hours

During the summer **shops** are usually open between 08.00 and 13.00 and 16.00 and 19.00. In winter the hours are 09.00 to 13.00 and 14.00 to 18.00.

Banks are open from Monday to Friday between 08.00 to 12.00 in summer and between 08.00 and 12.00 and 14.00 and 16.00 in winter.

Photography

As a rule Cypriots do not object to be photographed. However, it is courteous to ask their permission.This is important in the villages particularly if taking pictures of girls or women.

The use of cameras at military areas and some other places is forbidden. These are marked Fotograf Çekmek Yasaktır, ie, No Photography.

Postal and telephone services

On weekdays **post offices** are open from 08.00 to 13.00 and from 14.00 to 17.00. On Saturdays the hours are 09.00 to 12.00. They are closed on Sunday. Letters to North Cyprus should include 'Mersin 10, Turkey' in the address and **not** 'North Cyprus'. (Letters bearing the words 'North Cyprus' are likely to end up in the South.)

There are few public **telephone boxes** in North Cyprus. Call from your hotel or the local Telecommunication Office. The prefixes for local calls are: North Nicosia, (0)20, Girne (0)81, Gazimağusa (0)36.

Public holidays

1 January	New Year's Day
23 April	Children's Day
1 May	Labour Day
19 May	Youth and Sports Day
20 July	Peace and Freedom Day
1 August	TMT Day—foundation of Turkish Cypriot Resistance Day
30 August	Victory Day
29 October	Turkish Republic Day
15 November	Proclamation of the Turkish Republic of North Cyprus

In addition there are several religious holidays. These include the Birthday of the Prophet, which is celebrated on 23 October, and two holidays determind by the solar calendar whose dates vary from year to year: Kurban Bayramı (4 Days) and Şeker Bayramı (3 days).

Returning home

Independent travellers should contact their carrier at the following numbers: **Cyprus Turkish Airlines** ob 228 3901/ 3045 or **Turkish Airlines** on 227 1382/227 1061 to confirm their return flights. Group travellers should consult their courier or the representative of their tour company.

Shopping

Locally made pottery and handicrafts are amongst the best buys. Look for fine, handmade baskets in the market in Nicosia. Turkish Delight and fruit in season—especially, oranges, grapes, pomegranates, cherries and figs—are difficult to resist.

Sports

There are tennis courts at all the resorts and new players are always welcome. Hotels like the Denizkızı west of Girne have windsurfing and other watersports facilities during the holiday season. There is a seven hole golf course at Guzelyurt. Stables at Karaoğlanoğlu near Girne offer horse riding. Fishing may be enjoyed almost anywhere along the coast. Ramblers will enjoy leisurely walks along the slopes of the Kyrenia range.

Toilets

There are a few public toilets in North Cyprus. As a rule hotels do not object to non-residents using their washroom facilities. It would be tactful to buy a drink or a snack afterwards!

Tourist offices

Brochures, maps and general information may be obtained from the following local tourist offices:
Girne (Kyrenia), 30 Kordonboyu, ☎ 081 52145; **Gazimağusa (Famagusta)** 5, Fevzi Cakmak Bulvari, ☎ 036 62864; **Nicosia**, 95, Mehmet Akif Cad., ☎ 020 75051/2/3; **Ercan Airport**, Terminal Building, ☎ 023 14737.

Weights and measures

Although the metric system has been officially adopted, land is still measured in Ottoman *donums* and food is sometimes weighed in *okes*. An *oke* is equal to 1.268kg or 2.9lbs.

Introduction to the food and drink of Cyprus

by Sir David and Lady Hunt

At several excellent restaurants in Nicosia, Larnaca, Limassol, and Paphos, and also in the larger hotels, it is possible to enjoy all the standard dishes of the international cuisine. In smaller places you can usually find the British soldier's favourites, with plenty of chips. But presumably those who have travelled as far as the Eastern Mediterranean will want to add to their other experiences by sampling the local dishes, accompanied by the local wines. The following brief appreciation is intended as a guide to some of the less familiar specialities of the island.

The principal influences on Cyprus cookery come from mainland Greece, Asia Minor, and the Levant. The most typical dishes are rich because they are usually prepared with olive oil and contain plenty of vegetables cooked with the meat to improve the flavour. Many are prepared with tomato purée, a method called *yiahni*. There are many varieties of *pilaffs*, made with rice or *bourghouri* (boiled crushed wheat). It is usual to start with *mezedhes* (sing. *meze*) or Hors d'oeuvres; or you can make a whole meal of them, in which case they will be accompanied as time goes on by samples of whatever is cooking in the kitchen. They include olives, tomatoes, cucumbers, *houmous* (an Arab purée of chick-peas with sesame oil and cayenne), *taramosalata* (paté of smoked cod's roe), *melintzanosalata* (roasted pulp of aubergines flavoured with garlic and lemon), sardines, sausages, *lountza* (smoked pork), fried squid, octopus, *haloumi* (a sheep's milk cheese unique to Cyprus), *moungra* (pickled cauliflower), and *dolmadhakia* (vine leaves stuffed with minced lamb and rice). Another speciality, produced in the mountain villages and sometimes included in *mezedhes*, is *hiromeri*, leg of pork marinated for 40 days in red wine and sea salt, pressed under millstones to reduce it to one-sixth of its size, and smoked for a whole winter; it is very good with melon. Lastly *sheftalia* is the name for the ubiquitous pork, veal, or mutton sausage.

A **soup** speciality is *trahana*, made with crushed wheat and yoghourt. Another one, *avgolemono*, is made with chicken broth, rice, egg, and lemon juice. Although Cyprus is an island, **fish** is neither plentiful nor cheap. However, *xiphias* (swordfish) is grilled on charcoal; *barbouni* (red mullet) is prepared with wine vinegar, tomato purée, rosemary and garlic; octopus is cooked in wine; and whitebait (*maridha*)can sometimes be found.

Meat. Lamb is served in a number of ways, especially as *souvlakia* (also known as kebabs), marinated in lemon juice, and cooked on a spit over charcoal, with tomato, onion, and green pepper pieces between the meat cubes. Another method is *kleftiko*, chunks of lamb cooked in a sealed clay oven, scented with bay leaves and origanum. *Tava* is a lamb stew, with plenty of onions.

Pork dishes include *aphelia*, a stew prepared with plenty of red wine and ground coriander seeds; *kolokassi*, which is a kind of sweet potato, stewed with pork, and tomato purée; and *zalatina*, head brawn with Seville orange juice. The main beef dish is *stifado*, a stew of beef (or hare) cooked very slowly in a casserole with wine vinegar, onions and spices.

Dishes with dried vegetables include *louvia* (black-eyed beans) and dried broad beans cooked together with spinach or turnip leaf and dressed with olive oil and lemon; *moukendra*, a lentil dish made in the form of a pilaff, mixed with rice and fried onion rings. Salads are dressed with olive oil and lemon, and usually incorporate local herbs such as *glystirida* (or *glytisterida*) and *roka* (rocket plant). Fresh vegetables, beans, peas and broad beans are either boiled and dressed with oil and lemon, or are sometimes cooked in what is called the *yiahni* way, with plenty of oil, tomato purée and onions. *Okra* (or ladies' fingers) is also prepared in a similar way.

Sweets are mainly Middle Eastern in style. *Loukoumi* is what is called in Britain 'Turkish Delight'; *baklava* is rather like a millefeuille pastry with nuts, cinnamon, and syrup; *kadeifi* has a similar filling in a cover resembling "Shredded Wheat'; *loukoumades* are honey puffs; *galaktopoureko* is a strudel-pastry tart filled with semolina pudding.

Apart from *haloumi*, which is strongly recommended, the **cheeses** you are likely to be served in Cyprus will be internationally known wrapped or packaged varieties. You may also find some *graviera*, a version of gruyere, or the rather similar *kefalotiri*, or *feta*, a soft white goat's milk cheese.

Cyprus is famous for its **fruit**: melons, water melons, apples, cherries, peaches, apricots, plums, oranges and tangerines. More exotic are *nespole* or *mousmoula* or *mespila*, which are loquats, like a big rose-hip but tasting more like an apricot; pomegranates, whose juice is often drunk iced in summer; and prickly pears, the fruit of the Opuntia, whose local name is *papoutsosika*. You will also find in the coffee shops, and may be offered if you visit a Cypriot home, fruit preserved in syrup. For "Turkish coffee' and its varieties, see p 28.

The following list includes most of the more common foods found in Cyprus:

Soups, Soupes
Avgolemono, chicken broth with rice and a sauce of egg and lemon
Faki, lentil soup
Hortosoupa, vegetable soup

Patcha, made from sheep's brains and eyes
Trahana, made with crushed boiled wheat and yoghourt

Hors d'Oeuvre, mezedhes
Bourekia, pies filled with meat, cheese or brains
Haloumi, sheep's milk cheese
Hiromeri, slices of locally-cured ham
Houmous, an Arabic dish of chickpeas and oil

Kalamaria, squids (fried or boiled in their ink)
Karaoli, snails (often used in a pilaff)
Kaskavali, a type of local cheese
Koupepia or dolmadhes, vine-leaves stuffed with rice and minced meat

(turnip leaves or marrow flowers are sometimes used instead of vine leaves; in Lent the meat is omitted)
Koupes, minced meat enclosed in an oblong case made of bourghouri; see below
Loukanika, sausages
Lountza, smoked pork
Melintzanosalata, roasted pulp of aubergines

Oktapodi, octopus
Sheftalia, a type of sausage made of minced meat wrapped in peritonium skin and grilled
Talatouri, a salad of cucumber cubes mixed with strained yoghourt to which oil and mint have been added
Taramosalata, smoked cod's roe beaten up with bread, olive oil and lemon juice

Fish, psaria

Bakaliaos, cod
Barbouni, red mullet; if small (barbounakia) usually fried
Garidhes, prawns
Lithrinia, grey mullet
Maridha, whitebait

Melanouri, a local black-tailed fish
Mineri, tunny
Orfos, garfish
Pestrophes, trout
Synagrida, sea bass
Xphias, sword-fish

Main dishes

Aphelia, cubes of pork stewed in red wine with crushed coriander seed
Bourekia tou keima, small pies made with pastry and filled with minced meat
Bourghouri, boiled crushed wheat with meat (in North Africa known as couscous)
Dolmadhes, stuffed vine-leaves
Dolmadhes melintzanes, stuffed aubergines
Keftedes, meatballs, usually lamb and beef (or pork) mixed, often in a flattened oval shape
Kleftiko, lamb roasted in a sealed oven or sealed earthenware pot
Kolokassi, Cyprus sweet potatoes cooked with pork or chicken, chopped onions and tomato purée
Kreatocoloco, marrow stuffed with rice and minced meat
Kritharaki, a type of pasta resembling barley
Makaronia pastitsio, macaroni in the oven; layers of thick boiled macaroni, minced meat and bechamel sauce

Moussaka, layers of fried aubergine and fried sliced potatoes interspersed with minced meat and covered with a bechamel sauce
Parayemista, 'stuffed'; this applies to things such as stuffed aubergines, marrows, etc.
Perdhikes, partridges
Pilafi rizi, rice pilaff
Souvlakia, kebabs, lamb or pork, cooked on a spit and sometimes served in pitta bread together with chopped tomatoes and chopped onions
Stifadho, veal, hare or beef cooked with onions
Tavas, lamb cooked with tomatoes and onions in a sealed earthenware pot
Tyropitta, cheese pie
Yiouvetsi, lamb with kritharaki
Yiouvarlakia avgolemono, small meat balls made with rice and minced meat, served with a thick egg and lemon sauce
Zalatina, brawn

Vegetables, horta

Anginares, artichokes
Bamies, okra or ladies' fingers
Bizelia, peas
Coliandros, coriander
Fasolia, beans
Glystiridha, purslane
Kolokithakia, marrows
Koukia, broad beans
Kounoupidhi, cauliflower
Lahana, turnip leaves, boiled and
used as salad
Louvia, black-eyed beans
Manitaria, mushrooms
Maroulia, lettuce
Moungra, pickled cauliflower
Moukendra, lentils; cooked with a
rice pilaff and onions
Ospria, dried vegetables (beans,
lentils, broad beans, chick peas)
boiled and dressed with olive oil and
lemon
Pantzaria, beetroot
Patates, potatoes
Prassa, leeks
Portokolokasso, Jerusalem artichoke
Radhikia, wild chicory
Repania, radishes
Rokka, rocket (for salads)
Spanahi, spinach
Spanakopita, layers of mille-feuille
pastry filled with spinach, cheese and
chopped onions

Sweets, glika

Amygdalota, sweets made with
almond paste and sugar
Baklava, layers of mille-feuille pastry
filled with ground almonds and
walnuts in a rich syrup flavoured
with cinnamon
Bourekia tis anaris, small pies made
with pastry and filled with unsalted
cream cheese
Galaktopoureko, thin pastry filled
with semolina custard
Glyko, preserved fruit in syrup,
offered to guests who call at a private
house
Halvas, sesame cake
Kadeifi, like baklava but in a casing
resembling Shredded Wheat
Kolokotes, pastry and sweet marrow
Loukoumadhes, honey puffs
Pittes, pastry opened up thinly like a
pancake and fried; a thicker version is
called Kattimeria
Shiamishi, a pastry filled with
semolina custard and fried
Vasilopitta, the traditional New Year's
Eve cake

Fruit, fruta

Akhladia, pears
Dhamaskina, plums
Karpouzi, watermelon
Kerasia, cherries
Mandarina, tangerines
Mila, apples
Nespole (also mespila and mous-
moule),
loquats
Papoutsosika, prickly pears
Peponi, melon
Portokalia, oranges
Rodhakina, peaches
Rodhia, pomegranates
Sika, figs
Verikokka, apricots

Some Cyprus specialities

Eliopitta, bread made with oil and containing olives

Flaounes, a special bread with local cheese for Easter

Ressi, crushed wheat porridge, eaten at weddings

Skordialia, bread sauce made with lots of garlic

Soutzoukos, a sweet made of solidified grape-juice

For information about Cyprus cooking recipes see *Kopiaste*, by Amaranth Sita, and *Kali Orexi*, produced by the Cyprus Red Cross Society and sold locally.

Wine

The wines of Cyprus were praised in antiquity both by the author of the Song of Solomon and by the Greek poet Hesiod in the 8C BC. In Roman times the elder Pliny speaks highly of them, which is evidence that they were exported since Pliny never visited the island. They had a great reputation in medieval times at the courts of the kings of England and of France and elsewhere in Western Europe. 'In all the world are no greater or better drinkers than in Cyprus': so wrote von Suchen in the mid 14C; while in the early 18C John Heyman recorded that 'The wine of Cyprus is also famous in every part of the Levant, as well as Europe', even if there were objections to its tarry taste (which might imply that at least some retsina was drunk then). 'A great deal of this wine was sent to Venice and England', he continued, remarking on it being improved by sea travel, and, so he said, 'accordingly an epicure of an Englishman who lived here, used to send his Cyprus wine to England, whence it was sent back again to him at Cyprus'. When the Portuguese settlers of Madeira wanted the best vines with which to plant their new possessions they sent to Cyprus for them; and when at the end of the 19C phylloxera devastated the vineyards, it was from there that they were restocked.

One of the favourite wines of the Middle Ages was malmsey or malvoisie; both names are corruptions of Monemvasia, the port in the Peloponnese from which it was shipped, but it was produced also in Cyprus. The red malvoisie grape is still grown on the southern slopes of the Troodos. You can come closest to appreciating medieval taste in wine by drinking Cyprus's unique **Commandaria**. Its name is derived from the Grand Commandery of the Knights of St. John at Kolossi. It is made by traditional methods, which include fermentation in open jars, from grapes grown within a restricted area, with an addition of ten per cent of white grapes. Its merit lies in the blending process and above all in the aging, for it is only sold after maturing for a long time in cask and in bottle. Really old wines, which are now hard to come by, are brownish and resemble a fine Bual; the usual bottle, whose label may indicate a vintage of as much as 50 years past, is a deep rich red. It is sweet but with a subtle flavour more reminiscent of Madeira than of port.

The other wines of Cyprus conform more closely to the varieties usual in Western Europe. Almost the whole of the island's wine production is in the hands of four main concerns: ETKO, KEO, LOEL, and SODAP, of which the last is a cooperative marketing union. In all cases the grapes are produced by individual growers to the number of 10,000 families; the producers exercise strict quality control. All four have large and modern wineries, to which visits can be arranged. Modern methods of production have brought about great improvement. The four main producers and the government have also encouraged the introduction of grape varieties from Western Europe, especially from France. As a result quality is consistently maintained and is steadily rising.

Cyprus **sherry** has enjoyed a good reputation in Britain, not necessarily connected with the price advantage derived from Commonwealth preference. The best selling brand is ETKO's **Emva Cream**; the other three main concerns produce cream sherries also, of which SODAP's **Lysander** is worth mentioning. There is an EMVA **Pale Cream** in the modern style, rather like a white port. The best dry sherry is KEO's **Fino**, which is made in the traditional way in an open cask with the development of **flor**; it is fully equal to some Spanish finos. There are also in all four ranges very drinkable dry and medium sherries in the amontillado style.

Table wines continue to improve. Twenty-five years ago the whites were better than the reds, then the latter took the lead and now the whites, with the help of imported varieties of grapes and low-temperature fermentation, have perhaps regained first place. Quality control means that in both categories there are wines which are at least equal to the better wines of Italy and Spain.

Among the wines three well-established brands, all dry enough to be refreshing, and forceful enough to accompany spicy foods, are KEO **Hock**, **Arsinoe**, and **Aphrodite**. More recent productions are **Bella Pais**, light and slightly pétillant, **Fair Lady**, and **Thisbe**, a low-alcohol wine (10 per cent by volume) designed to meet the growing wine- bar market in Britain. LOEL has introduced **Palomino**, a rather drier wine, made from the Spanish grape of the same name, which is the basis of sherry, and proposes shortly to produce a Cyprus Riesling. ETKO's challenger for the whites in a Graves-type wine called **Nefeli**, a good, straightforward wine, dry but not acid, with a good back-taste. It competes well with the more exclusive, and expensive, white wine made by the Khrysorroyiatissa Monastery from the local Xynisteri grape and marketed under the name Ayios Amvrosios. There is an unpretentious sparking wine, **Duc de Nicosie**, made by the *méthode champenoise*, which is of good quality with a firm dry taste. There are also sweet and semi-sweet white wines, including some made from the Muscat grape.

All four concerns market a rosé wine; **Coeur de Lion** is considered a good example.

The red wines maintain a sound level. **Domaine d'Ahera**, KEO **Claret**, **Olympus Claret**, and **Afames** are solid, well-made wines with some sublety of taste. **Semeli** is a more recent production; full, fruity and dry, it should preferably be decanted a little time before drinking. An even newer wine is **Carignan Noir**, made from recently introduced grapes of that name. **Otello** is reminiscent of a good Rhône wine and improves greatly with bottle-age. The successful vintage of 1959 can still sometimes be obtained and is worth trying. The red wine of Khrysorryiatissa, made from local grapes grown on the north-facing slopes, is marketed under the name of **Ayios Elias** It is light, almost pink, in colour but has plenty of body. Perhaps the most interesting of the new generation of red wines is **Ino**, produced by ETKO from locally-grown Cabernet-Sauvignon grapes; the vines were planted in the 1970s. It has a long taste, with some tannin, and is a good example of the Cabernet-Sauvignon character, by which is meant equal to the Bulgarian and not far behind the better Australian.

The locally produced beer, made from imported malts, is excellent. Brandy is made in large quantities. The older and more expensive brands are very accept-able for drinking after dinner and the cheaper ones for making the popular local aperitif, brandy sour, where the sharp and perfumed flavour of the Cyprus lemons matches the special quality of the spirit. The Greek aperitif **ouzo** is also produced: this is an aniseed-flavoured spirit reminiscent of Pernod, and equally potent. The other Greek favourite, **retsina**, a white wine flavoured with pine resin, is hardly ever seen, though some is made. An orange-flavoured liqueur, **Filfar**, is drunk after dinner by those who like Grand Marnier.

This article first appeared in Blue Guide Cyprus, third edition.

Introduction to the monuments and early history of Cyprus

by Nicolas Coldstream

Prehistoric Cyprus to c 1600 BC

The earliest known inhabitants lived before 8000 BC in a cave near Cape Akrotiri, hunting and feeding off dwarf hippopotami soon to become extinct. The earliest Neolithic phase (eighth to seventh millennium BC) is best represented at *Khirokitia* on a hillock overlooking the Nicosia–Limassol highway, a farming village with closely-packed circular houses built of rubble, wood and mud-brick. Pottery as yet was unknown, but vessels and figurines were fashioned out of the local andesitic stone. At *Kalavassos (Tenta)* another Early Neolithic site, a fragmentary wall-painting of a human figure has been found. These Aceramic Neolithic sites were deserted during the sixth millennium BC

After a long break there followed a Late Neolithic phase (c 4500–3500 BC) for which the most illuminating settlements are *Ayios Epiktitos (Vrysi)* on the north coast near Kyrenia and, in the south, *Sotira (Teppes)* and *Kalavassos (Kokkinoyi)*. House-plans now tend to be square, and often partly underground. By this phase pottery had been well established, the most distinctive types being red jugs and bowls lightly scored with combed patterns. Both shapes have rounded bases recalling the gourd, that favourite vessel of the Cypriot villager from time immemorial.

The **Chalcolithic Period** (c 3500–2500/2300 BC) saw the first appearance of copper tools alongside the traditional stone implements. Houses, once again, are circular, with interior hearths and wattle-and-daub superstructure; and a new pottery ware was introduced, with bright red designs painted on a white ground. The chief Chalcolithic settlements are in the south and west: *Erimi* near Episkopi, and two recently excavated cites near Paphos, *Lemba (Lakkous)*, and *Kissonerga (Mosphilia)* where several round houses have been fully restored with flat roofs. From burials in the Paphos region come the remarkable Chalcolithic human figurines in picrolite, a local blue-green stone; the finest have a slender cruciform shape with backward-tilted head, recalling the Cycladic marble idols of the Aegean. An ample enlargement of this form in limestone, evidently representing a fertility goddess, has been found in the earliest known Cypriot sanctuary at *Lemba*, while *Kissonerga* has produced a clay model of a circular house containing figurines in stone and clay, some portraying women in childbirth.

For an island so rich in copper ores, the transition to a fully bronze-using culture came surprisingly late. To represent the **Early Bronze Age** (c 2500/2300–1900 BC), the settlements of *Sotira (Kaminoudhia)* and *Marki (Alonia)* have only recently come to light; this period is better known through the rich contents of family chamber-tombs. Two northern cemeteries are especially informative, *Philia (Vasiliko)* for the change from Chalcolithic, and *Bellapais (Vounous)* for the full sequence of its Red Polished pottery, a ware first evolved in the north and eventually accepted all over the island. Apart from some Anatolian influence at the outset, Red Polished ware developed along its own lines with a typically Cypriot exuberance of spirit, seen especially in the vast composite vessels, and in the modelled figures of animals and humans sometimes applied to the surface. More usually, decoration consists of carefully incised recti-linear patterns filled with white paste; on the plank-shaped female idols in the same fabric, these patterns suggest the dress of the day. Further vignettes of daily life appear in the scenes modelled on the vessels, and also in independent models; among the latter, the most elaborate shows a circular open-air shrine where 19 worshippers sacrifice bulls to a trinity of plank-like deities.

Cyprus enters the **Middle Bronze Age** (c 1900—1600 BC) without experi-encing any great change; but now there are more signs of regional diversity. At the southern site of *Episkopi (Phaneromeni)*, where rectangular houses and chamber tombs of this period may be seen, the contemporary pottery is still Red Polished, sometimes with a mottled surface, and sometimes bearing decoration in punctured dots. A copper-working hamlet of this period is known at *Ambelikou (Aletri)* in the Troödos foothills. Meanwhile, among the tomb offerings at *Lapithos* on the north coast, there arises a new ceramic tradition in White Painted ware, bearing geometric patterns on a pale matt ground. This tradition spreads to the centre and the east, each district evolving its own style. At *Alambra (Moutes)* near Dali, a settlement of large rectangular rooms, the Red Polished ware predominates over White Painted. The Karpas peninsula, mean-while, evolved its own individual Red-on-Black ware. By the end of this period the eastern Mesaoria plain, with its chief settlement at *Kalopsidha*, was attaining to greater importance within the island; thence, too, came the first mass exports of pottery to Syria and Palestine. At the same time the building of numerous forts, notably in the inland Dali region, suggests a degree of internal unrest which continued some way into the Late Bronze Age.

The Late Bronze Age: c 1600–1050 BC

Hitherto, Cypriot civilisation had a homespun character, showing little sign of foreign influence or interference. Now, at last, the island emerged from its long isolation. Commercial exchanges were intensified with Egypt (XVII–XVIII Dynasties) and the Levant, especially with the emporium of Ugarit on the north Syrian coast. It is widely, though not universally, believed that the copper-bearing land of Alashiya, often mentioned in Ugaritic, Hittite, and Egyptian documents, must be Cyprus. Apart from copper, Cypriot pottery now enjoyed a wide circulation overseas. The two leading wares, still handmade, were Base Ring and White Slip. Base Ring is thin-walled, and coated in a dark lustrous slip; small juglets in this ware, shaped like poppy-heads, found special favour in Egypt and may have contained opium. Typical of White Slip ware is the 'milk-bowl' of traditional half-gourd shape, now painted with light and delicate patterns.

Commercial enterprise encouraged the growth of large cities, mainly on the south and east coasts. In the south, at *Kalavassos (Ayios Dimitrios)*, *Maroni (Vournes)*—and, most recently, at *Alassa* in the Troodos foothills—foundations of public buildings (13C BC) have been excavated, constructed of huge ashlar blocks dressed in the finest Near Eastern traditions. The most extensively exca-vated site, however, is *Enkomi*, near Famagusta. Founded around 1600 BC and twice destroyed amid the recurrent unrest of the next two centuries, Enkomi was eventually to enjoy an age of untroubled prosperity from 1400 to 1250 BC. Copper, the chief source of wealth, was worked there and at *Kition*, founded in the 13C BC. It was during this tranquil period that Mycenaean Greek merchants first became frequent visitors, in search of copper. In return, among other goods, they traded painted pottery of surpassing quality, including many vessels bearing figured scenes. The sophisticated wheelmade technique of these Mycenaean imports had its effect on Cypriot potters; and indeed almost every other form of art—seal engraving, gold jewellery and other metalwork, work in ivory and faience—now displays a blend of Aegean and oriental elements. Literacy, too, may have come to Cyprus through her westward contacts: the Cypro-Minoan syllabic script, named after its supposed derivation from the Linear A system of Crete, was employed from the 15-11C. It still awaits decipherment.

From 1250 BC onwards, Cyprus became embroiled in the general collapse of Bronze Age civilisations in the eastern Mediterranean. Peaceful commerce was interrupted by piracy; among the Mycenaean visitors, the merchant was replaced by the soldier of fortune. Enkomi and Kition were hastily fortified, only to suffer wholesale destruction in c 1220 BC by attackers as yet unknown. Both sites were then rebuilt on a quite different plan.

The new city of Enkomi, largely that which the visitor sees today, by far eclipses the old in architectural sophistication. The rambling rubble edifices of the preceding period are succeeded by an orderly grid plan, the more important buildings being faced with huge ashlar masonry. Refugees came here from more troubled lands in the Levant and the Aegean, bringing with them various technical and artistic skills. Under their stimulus, the Cypriot bronze industry flourished as never before. Of outstanding interest and quality are the four-sided bronze stands bearing Aegeo-oriental figured scenes in openwork or relief, and the large statuette of the Horned God from one of the sanctuaries at Enkomi. Another Enkomi bronze, portraying an armed god standing upon an ingot, attests the divine patronage of the copper industry; similarly, at Kition, the smithies were immediately adjacent to a vast new open-air temple in the finest ashlar masonry, with a triple holy-of-holies in the Near Eastern tradition. Contemporaneous, and equally impressive, are the monumental remains of the oldest open-air temple within the sanctuary of Aphrodite at *Old* (or *Palea*) *Paphos*. Minor arts which flourished especially at this time are ivory carving in relief, and gold jewellery, sometimes with cloisonné inlays of enamel.

These splendours, however, were short-lived. In c 1190 BC the coastal cities were devastated by marauders known from Egyptian sources as the 'Peoples of the Sea'. Further disruption was caused by the steady incursion of Aegean peoples, escaping from the final collapse of Mycenaean civilisation.. Initial resistance to them is suggested by the fortified native settlements at *Idalion* and *Episkopi* (*Bamboula*). Eventually, after a huge new influx in the 11C, the Mycenaean element prevailed, and homogeneity was restored: a new wheelmade pottery type, Proto White Painted, is closely akin to Aegean Submycenaean, and was manufactured throughout the island. Henceforth Cyprus was to be a predominantly Greek speaking land. By the end of the Bronze Age the Aegean newcomers had established themselves at the sites of all the historical Greek Cypriot kingdoms: *Salamis* (replacing Enkomi), *Lapithos*, *Marion, Soli, Old Paphos, Kourion,* and *Tamassos*. The oldest Greek inscription from Cyprus (c 1000 BC), written in a syllabic script, is an Arcadian personal name engraved on a bronze spit from a tomb at *Old Paphos* (*Skales*).

The Cypriot kingdoms of the Iron Age: c 1050–300 BC

After the turmoil at the end of the Bronze Age, the next two centuries were comparatively uneventful. Written sources are silent, and the archaeological record is virtually confined to the family chamber-tombs. Their contents show that the Greeks of Cyprus soon lost touch with their homeland, though not with the Near East. The tomb offerings from Old Paphos are especially rich and varied at this time.

During the 9C Phoenicians from Tyre founded a colony at Kition, where they refurbished the grandest of the Bronze Age temples in honour of their fertility goddess Astarte. Meanwhile the indigenous Cypriots (Eteocypriots) had founded their main settlement at *Amathus*. The lively interplay of influences between Greeks, Phoenicians, and Eteocypriots accounts for much of the artistic vitality of the island at the dawn of its recorded history. Yet the very remoteness of the Cypriot Greeks from their Aegean kinsmen made for extreme conservatism in their ways: they were never to know any constitution other than despotic monarchy in the seven independent Greek states; and their archaic dialect of Greek, akin to Arcadian, continued to be written even as late as the 3C in a syllabic script (Classical Cypriot) inherited from Bronze Age tradition—a deliberate rejection of the more practical Phoenician alphabet adapted by the Aegean Greeks well before 700 BC.

The 8C, as in Greece, was a time of recovery and rapidly widening horizons. Contact with the Aegean was restored, and eastward trade flourished once again. The royal tombs of *Salamis* (c 800-600 BC) illustrate a brilliant phase of Cypriot civilisation, richly compounded of Greek, native, and eastern elements. It may have been pride in their Mycenaean ancestry that inclined the Salaminians to bury their princes in a manner recalling Homeric epic, sending chariots with sacrificed horse teams to accompany their dead masters. Nevertheless the finery from these tombs is almost wholly oriental: the horse trappings are of Assyrian type, while the tomb furniture was fitted with delicate ivory plaques of Phoenician workmanship. Elsewhere in Cyprus, another notable Cypro-Phoenician art-form of this time is the shallow metal bowl embossed inside with scenes of cult, warfare, or animal life.

From 708 until 663 BC the Cypriot kingdoms came under the Assyrian empire, but retained their local autonomy; Assyrian rule left hardly any trace on the island's material record except perhaps to encourage the spread of Phoenician artistic influence. From the 6C the most remarkable monuments are the royal chamber-tombs of *Tamassos*, careful copies in stone of domestic dwellings roofed with wooden rafters, and decorated in relief with volute capitals of 'Protoaeolic' type. A brief period of Egyptian rule (c 560–540 BC) encouraged Cypriot commerce in Egypt. Thereafter the Cypriots transferred their allegiance to the rising Persian empire, while still enjoying a large measure of independence; king *Evelthon* of Salamis, for example, was able at this time to mint in his own name the first coinage of Cyprus.

In 500 BC, however, relations with the Persian overlord suddenly deteriorated when the Cypriot Greeks joined the abortive Ionian revolt against the Great King. A poignant memorial to their valour can be seen in the Persian siege mound at Old Paphos, riddled with ingenious devices of the defenders to undermine it. After the failure of the revolt, and during the 5C, the islanders showed little enthusiasm for various Athenian attempts to detach them from the Persian empire; the Phoenicians of Kition, meanwhile, annexed Idalion with Persian support. The finest architectural monument of this period is the palace of *Vouni* (c 500–380 BC), a spacious building of predominantly oriental character.

Rivalries between the Cypriot states prevented any more general uprising against Persia, until king *Evagoras I* of Salamis (411–374 BC) succeeded briefly in ousting the Persians altogether, and uniting the island by force rather than by consent. Cyprus was finally freed from Persian domination around 330 BC through the victories of *Alexander the Great*, but after his death became a battleground between his successors *Antigonus* and *Ptolemy I* of Egypt; during their wars Kition, Lapithos, Marion, and Cerynia were destroyed, never to be resettled in antiquity. *Nicocles*, the last king of Salamis, committed suicide in 310 BC; a large tumulus just outside Enkomi village has been identified as the cenotaph built in his honour. Subsequently the island was annexed by Ptolemaic Egypt, and we hear no more of any Cypriot kingdoms.

Pottery. The Cypro-Geometric wares (c 1050–750 BC), named after their simple linear decoration, continued the tradition of the wheelmade Proto White Painted pottery made at the end of the Bronze Age. At first they bore a family resemblance to contemporary Greek pottery, but new impulses tended to come from the Levant rather than from the Aegean. The chief types at first were White Painted (with the ornament painted on a light ground) and Bichrome, where red was added as a second colour after the Levantine fashion. From the 10C BC onwards these were joined by Black-on-Red and Red Slip, two wares with Phoenician associations; ornament on Black-on-Red vessels consisted chiefly small circles in concentric sets. Figured decoration, never common, occured mainly near the beginning and end of this period; the Hubbard amphora (c 800 BC), showing an oriental scene of libation and ritual dancing, is a typical work of its time.

During the first Archaic phase (c 750–600 BC) Cypriot pottery reached its most creative and imaginative stage. Regional distinctions are now noticeable: circles still proliferated in the conservative western style, while the potters of eastern Cyprus introduced oriental rosettes, cables, and lotus flowers. The best and most ambitious work was now in Bichrome Ware, including the Free Field style where single but elaborately drawn birds or animals spread themselves expansively over the flanks of baggy jugs.

The same wares persist into later Archaic (c 600–475 BC) and Classical times (c 475–325 BC), showing a steady deterioration in quality and invention. Any new inspiration now came from Greece, seen especially in the finely modelled female heads attached to some large pouring vessels.

Sanctuaries and Sculpture. Most Cypriot temples were small and unpretentious rectangular buildings, without any of the architectural refinement associated with the Greek orders. Worship was conducted around altars in rustic open-air enclosures, which might often have been crowded with a veritable forest of statues representing the votaries rather than the deity. A vivid impression of such a sanctuary is conveyed by the thick concentration of figurines from *Ayia Irini* displayed in the Cyprus Museum, Nicosia.

From its beginnings in the 7C Cypriot sculpture often attained life size, and employed either limestone or terracotta. Both male and female figures are almost invariably draped; facial expression always held more interest for the Cypriot sculptor than body anatomy. The earliest Proto-Cypriot statues, of indigenous inspiration, have vivacious and over-large features, often verging on the farouche. During the 6C the milder Neo-Cypriot style borrowed freely from Egyptian and Archaic Greek sources; Egyptian sculpture was imported and imitated during the brief period of Egyptian domination. In the first phase of Persian rule (c 540–500 BC) there flourished a lively and distinguished Cypro-Archaic school owing much to Ionian sculpture of the eastern Aegean. But with the failure of the Ionian revolt this Greek connection lapsed, and stagnation set in. A Sub-Archaic tradition in limestone sculpture persisted throughout the Classical period, soon losing its vitality; meanwhile, local work in a Classical Greek style was virtually limited to a few grave reliefs, some large terracottas from Greek moulds, and the fine limestone head of a youth from *Arsos* (c 400 BC) which combines a Classical face with an Archaic hairstyle. At the end of the 4C the expressive terracotta heads from Nicocreon's cenotaph recall the manner of the Greek sculptor Lysippus.

Hellenistic and Roman Cyprus: c 300 BC–AD 330

When Cyprus became part of the large Hellenistic state of Egypt, the island's aristocracy was replaced by a Ptolemaic elite. Consequently, the material record lost its characteristically Cypriot flavour and became merely provincial. In inscriptions, the local syllabary finally gave way to the Greek alphabet; the local dialect was superseded by the common idiom of Hellenistic Greek; and the coins began to bear the heads of the ruling Ptolemies. The new city of *Paphos* (or *Nea Paphos*), which replaced the old (*Kouklia*) around 310 BC, became in the 2C BC the island's capital, and the seat of the Egyptian governor (*strategos*). Of its Hellenistic monuments little survives apart from the subterranean 'Tombs of the Kings', each with a rock-cut peristyle court in the Doric order.

With the decline of the Ptolemaic kingdom, Cyprus was first annexed by Rome in 58 BC. Although it twice reverted to Egypt during the civil wars of the Republic, Roman control of the island was finally consolidated with the establishment of the Empire. There followed a long and prosperous period of *pax romana* when Cyprus was administered through a proconsul as a senatorial province, with its capital still at New Paphos. One such governor, *Sergius Paulus*, was an early convert to Christianity when *St. Paul* visited the island in AD 45 in company with a citizen of Salamis, *St. Barnabas*.

One symptom of the general prosperity of these times was the construction of spacious public buildings, many of which replaced older structures after the earthquakes of 15 BC and AD 76. Thus, after the earlier upheaval, a fine colonnaded gymnasium was built at *Salamis*, with a bath complex attached to its eastern portico (the existing remains, however, belong chiefly to repairs in later antiquity). The theatre of Salamis formed part of the same building programme; other well-preserved Roman theatres, of later date, can be seen at *Soli* and *Kourion*, the latter being converted in the 3C AD for spectacles of hunters fighting wild animals. In the sanctuaries, much rebuilding took place after the second earthquake of AD 76. To this period belong the small temple of Apollo Hylates at Kourion (now partly restored) and the more grandiose colonnaded temple of Aphrodite on the acropolis of Amathus, both of which exmplify a temporary fashion for Nabataean capitals. In the sanctuary of Aphrodite at Paphos, new courtyard buildings were added; their juxtaposition with the Late Bronze Age shrine argues an astonishing continuity of worship. Roman domestic architecture on a lavish scale is preserved at New Paphos, where the 3C House of Dionysus with its 70-odd rooms is named after the chief subject of its exceptionally fine mosaics. There, too, are the sumptuous mosaics of the even larger 'Villa of Theseus', now identified as the Roman proconsul's palace. The 4C mosaics in the House of Aion, which include the portrayal of a beauty contest between Cassiopeia and the Nereids, are thought to reflect the concepts of Neoplatonist philosophy, and a late glorification of paganism.

Early Christian and Byzantine Cyprus: 330–1192

The 4C saw the triumph of Christianity and the gradual elimination of pagan worship; and with the final division of the Empire into two halves, Cyprus was allotted to the province of Oriens, ruled from Constantinople. Within the island, Salamis became the capital once again, now rebuilt and renamed *Constantia* after two terrible earthquakes which ravaged the whole island in 332 and 342.

Lying far away from the ceaseless wars on the Empire's frontiers, Cyprus enjoyed an Indian summer of peace and prosperity during the next two centuries. The Cypriot church, at first controlled from the see of Antioch, won its independence in 478 thanks to *Abp Anthemios'* timely discovery of St. Barnabas' tomb at Salamis. City life, meanwhile, continued on a luxurious scale. In the baths of Eustolios at Kourion, built around 400, a mosaic inscription could still refer to both Apollo and Christ as the city's protectors. Nevertheless the rapid advance of Christianity, and the growing power of the bishops, are attested by the numerous basilica churches erected throughout the island during the 5C-6C. Among the excavated remains, exceptionally fine is the so-called *Kampanopetra* basilica at Salamis, lavishly adorned with carved marble capitals and extensive floor mosaics; along its flanks are long corridors where, according to the Syrian rite, converted catechumens assembled for baptism. Other imposing basilica churches of this period have been excavated at *Kourion*, and at *Peyia* in the extreme west. A fine 6C wall mosaic showing the Virgin and Child between Archangels, survives in the apse of a basilica at *Kiti*, near Larnaca, incorporated in a later church. A similar apse mosaic, in the monastic church of *Kanakaria* at *Lythrangomi* in the Karpas, was recently destroyed, but parts of it are now housed in the Byzantine Museum in the Old City of Nicosia. The small churches at *Aphendrika* in the Karpas, now in ruins, date from the 7C, shortly before the Arab invasions. Outstanding among early Byzantine artefacts are the early 7C silver dishes from the treasure of the bishops of Lapithos (*Lambousa*), chased with scenes from the life of David; but these may well be metropolitan work from Constantinople.

Life on the island was severely disrupted soon after the advent of Islam. Already masters of Egypt and the Levant, the Arabs invaded Cyprus first in 647; Salamis-Constantia was sacked, and never recovered. Once again Cyprus found itself on a frontier, a bone of contention between two warring empires. Within the next three centuries the island changed hands at least eleven times, sometimes a no-man's land between the two powers, and sometimes even paying tribute simultaneously to Byzantine emperor and Umayyad caliph: according to the English pilgrim Willibald, who visited Paphos in 723, 'Cyprus lived between the Greeks and the Saracens'. During these troubled times many Cypriots were slaughtered, or captured and deported to Arab lands as slaves. A pointless attempt by *Justinian II* to resettle the survivors by the sea of Marmara in 692 was abandoned six years later, but not without provoking yet another Arab invasion of Cyprus—an invasion which gave rise to the only significant memorial of the Arabs on the island: the shrine of *Hala Sultan Tékké*, near the salt lake outside Larnaca, where a much later mosque commemorates the spot where the Umm Haram, a kinswoman of the Prophet Mohammed, fell off a mule and died.

Exhausted by war and pillage, and also afflicted by drought and plague, the ancient coastal cities withered away, as the survivors moved to more defensible sites. Thus refugees from Kourion transferred themselves inland to the new seat of their bishop, *Episkopi*. Paphos became the headquarters of the Arabs, while many Cypriots retired to the inland stronghold of *Ktima*.

Relief eventually came with the reviving fortunes of the Byzantine empire, and the Arabs were finally ousted from Cyprus in 963 by the emperor *Nicephorus Phocas*. Secure at last from any further Islamic attack, and largely by-passed by the Crusaders, Cyprus now became a peaceful backwater for the next two centuries under the firm rule of a Byzantine *katapan* or governor. As the island recovered some measure of its commercial prosperity, new towns grew up in the neighbourhoods of the old: *Ammochostos* (Famagusta) became the successor to Salamis, *Lemesos* (Limassol) to Amathus. A new capital, *Leucosia* (Nicosia) was founded, perhaps on the site of the elusive ancient city of Ledra. Apart from the original structures of *St. Hilarion's castle*, very little secular architecture survives from this period; its chief glory is to be seen in the churches of the 11C–12C and their frescoed decoration. Their plans are simple versions of the basilica with apse, sometimes with transepts added. From an architectural point of view the multi-domed village churches of *Peristerona* and *Yeroskipos* have a special attraction as examples of a local Cypriot style. Churches in the Troödos mountains, protected against snow and rain by wooden gabled roofs above their interior domes, also contain the finest and best-preserved of the fresco paintings. Lively works of provincial character can be seen in *Ayios Nikolaos* at *Kakopetria* (11C) and at *Asinou* (1105), while the frescoes at *Lagoudhera* (1192) display a finesse reflecting the metropolitan style of Constantinople.

As the Byzantine empire began to crumble in the later 12C, it was inevitable that Cyprus should eventually fall into the hands of the Crusaders, who had become fully aware of its strategic importance. After a brief spell of independence (1184–1191) under the unstable and unpopular tyrant *Isaac Comnenos*, the island was overrun by *Richard I* of England on his way to the Third Crusade, sold at first to the Knights Templar, and then presented in 1192 to *Guy de Lusignan* who established a dynasty with a long future. The castle of *Saranda Colonnes* (Forty Columns) at Paphos, destroyed in 1222, is an early monument of the Crusaders and the Lusignan kingdom.

The Lusignans in Cyprus: 1192–1489

Under Lusignan rule Cyprus became closely involved in the fortunes of the later Crusades. From 1197 onwards the king of Cyprus was also king of Jerusalem— a hollow title after the final loss of that city in 1244. Distinguished visitors to the island included the emperor Frederick II Hohenstaufen, and also Louis IX of France, whom the king of Cyprus joined in the disastrous Seventh Crusade against Egypt (1248–1250). When Acre, the last Crusader outpost in the Holy Land, eventually fell to the Mamelukes of Egypt in 1291, Cyprus provided a haven for the Christian refugees. In the 14C the island enjoyed a golden age as the last bastion of Christendom in the eastern Mediterranean, and the natural centre of seaborne commerce; Famagusta, in particular, gained a reputation for its luxurious living. Outwardly, the Lusignan kingdom reached the height of its power under the energetic king Peter I (1359–69), who won temporary footholds on the Anatolian coast at Corycus and at Antalya, and then mounted the final crusade against the Mamelukes which achieved the sack of Alexandria.

Within the island, however, all was far from well for the Greek Cypriots. They had become a subject population under alien rulers, from whom they were divided by ethnic background, language, and religion. Their island was appropriated, and awarded on a western feudal system to Latin nobles. A Latin arch bishopric was established at Nicosia, with suffragans at Famagusta, Limassol, and Paphos. According to the *Bulla Cypria* of Pope Alexander IV (1260) the Latin Archbishop became Metropolitan of both churches, but the Greek Orthodox Church kept its own cathedrals and retained some measure of independence.

Thanks to the Lusignans, Cyprus abounds in western medieval architecture although it is a curious irony of history that virtually all such monuments are situated in what is now the Turkish-occupied zone. For the Gothic cathedrals and churches, France appears to have been the chief source of inspiration throughout; but a distinction can be drawn between a somewhat provincial manner in the 13C, and the sophisticated rayonnant style of later French Gothic reproduced in the finest buildings of the 14C. To the former stage belongs the main body of *St. Sophia's* cathedral in Nicosia. Its west front, however, was completed in 1326 in the latter style, seen at its finest in the abbey at *Bellapais*, the Latin cathedral of *St. Nicolas* at Famagusta, and (mixed with Byzantine elements) the small Orthodox cathedral of *St. George* in the same city. Secular monuments of this age include the three castles of the Kyrenia mountains—*St. Hilarion, Buffavento*, and *Kantara*—in their final forms; the square keep at *Kolossi*, housing the Knights of St. John; and part of a manor-house at *Kouklia* (Old Paphos). A vaulted undercroft recently excavated in Nicosia may be part of the Lusignan royal palace.

After the ambitious adventures of Peter I, the decline of the Lusignans was swift. A riot at his successor's coronation led eventually to the seizure of Famagusta by the Genoese. Worse still, a devastating invasion of Mamelukes in 1426 was bought off only by a ruinous indemnity, an oath of allegiance, and an annual tribute to their sultan in Cairo. In the 1450s Queen *Helena Palaiologina*, herself a Byzantine princess, tried to alleviate the lot of the Greek Cypriots. Her illegitimate stepson, who became king *James I* (1458–74), ousted the Genoese from Famagusta with aid from the Venetians, who then astutely provided him with a Venetian queen, *Caterina Cornaro*. Inheriting the throne on his death, Caterina assigned all important posts to her countrymen, and in 1489 was persuaded to hand over the island to the Venetian Republic.

The Venetians in Cyprus: 1489–1571

For the Venetians, Cyprus was a forward base against a rapidly expanding Ottoman empire, and a source of revenue through trade and taxation. For example, the sugar industry, introduced by the Lusignans, flourished greatly under Venetian rule, but its profits went to Venice rather than to the Cypriots. Levantine commerce, however, declined sharply after the opening of more profitable trade routes across the Atlantic and around the Cape of Good Hope; thus Famagusta, once a flourishing emporium, became little more than a naval station. The new administrators, closely watched from Venice and relieved every two years, developed no interest in the island's welfare and soon alienated all sections of the population. The Lusignan nobles kept their estates but were excluded from political power. Although the Orthodox Church was allowed its independence (its 16C cathedral in Nicosia is the so-called *Bedestan*, a curious blend of Gothic, Byzantine, and Renaissance elements), the Greek Cypriot peasantry were impoverished by heavy taxation under a regime which became increasingly corrupt and ineffectual. The scene was set for the inevitable attack by the Turks.

To meet this menace, the Venetians constructed massive and handsome defence works. The castles of the Kyrenia mountains, rendered obsolete by the invention of artillery, were dismantled. An older fort guarding Kyrenia harbour was remodelled and enclosed within an immense stone-faced earthwork, to resist bombardment. Famagusta received a complete circuit; its rectangular citadel (romantically called 'Othello's tower' under the British Protectorate) was drastically redesigned. At Nicosia, only three years before the Turkish invasion, the peripheral districts were demolished to make way for a grandiose circular defence wall with eleven heart-shaped bastions.

All these precautions, however, were fruitless. When a vast Turkish armament landed at Larnaca in July 1570, the island waited in vain for a relieving force from the west, and resistance was confined to the fortified cities of Nicosia and Famagusta. The new defences could not withstand the combination of heavy bombardment and vast hordes of irregular attacking troops. Nicosia was stormed in September 1570; Famagusta, after a valiant resistance of ten months against overwhelming odds, capitulated to the Turks in August 1571.

Chronology

Pre Neolithic   c 8500 BC Akrotiri Cave

Neolithic
Khirokitia culture   c 7000/6800–6000 BC

Sotira culture   4600/4500–4000/3900 BC
                                           First handmade pottery made in Cyprus

Chalcolithic   4000/3900–2500 BC
Erimi culture   First metal objects in Cyprus

Transitional   2600/2500–2300 BC
Philia culture   First colonists from Anatolia?

Bronze Age
Early Bronze Age   I   2300–2075 BC
                    II   2075–2000 BC
                    III   2000–1900 BC
Middle Bronze Age   I   1900–1800 BC
                    II   1800–1725 BC
                    III   1725–1650 BC
Late Bronze Age   I   1650–1475 BC
                    II   475–1225 BC
                    III   1225–1050 BC
                                           Trade with the Near East,
                                           Egypt and the Greek world
                                           c 1100 BC Substantial Greek immigration

Iron Age   1050–750 BC
or Cypro-Geometric Age

                                           Phoenicians establish a colony at Kition mid-9C BC

Archaic Age   750–475 BC
                                           City Kingdoms flourish
                                           c 709–c 689 BC Cyprus ruled by Assyria
                                           570–545 BC Cyprus ruled by Egypt
                                           c 545–333 Cyprus ruled by Persia

Classical   475–325 BC
                                           411–373 BC Evagoras I attempts to
                                           throw off Persian yoke
                                           Birth of Zeno of Kition, founder of
                                           Stoic Philosophy
                                           333 BC Cypriot cities submit to
                                           Alexander the Great

Hellenistic Period

325–30 BC
City kingdoms abolished
294 BC Cyprus taken by Ptolemy I
58 BC Cyprus becomes part of Roman province of Cilicia
c 47–30 BC Cleopatra VII rules the island

Roman Period

30 BC –AD 395
AD 45 SS Paul and Barnabas visit Cyprus
AD 116 Revolt of the Jews in Cyprus
AD 117–137Construction of Salamis
AD 350 Constantius III rebuilds Salamis
AD 395 Cyprus becomes part of the Eastern Roman Empire

Byzantine Period

AD 395–1192
AD 478 Anthemios, Archbishop of autocephalous Church of Cyprus
AD 646 Death of Umm Haram at Larnaca
AD 646/8 Arab invasions begin
AD 958 Cyprus retaken by the Emperor Basil I
AD 1184–1191 Isaac Comnenus, self styled Emperor of Cyprus
AD 1191 Richard Coeur de Lion defeats Isaac Comnenus and sells Cyprus to the Knights Templar
AD 1192 Insurrection against Templars, Cyprus restored to Richard Coeur de Lion

Lusignan Period

AD 1192–1489
AD 1193 Richard sells Cyprus to Guy de Lusignan, former King of Jerusalem
AD 1194 Amaury de Lusignan, first king of Cyprus.
AD 1222 See of Kition abolished by Cardinal Pelagius
AD 1260 Pope Alexander IV issues the *Bulla Cypria*
AD 1300 Famagusta, fortress city and trading centre
AD 1362 Peter I seeks European aid for Crusade
AD 1367 Peter I recognised as king of Armenia
AD 1369 Peter I assassinated
AD1372 Fracas between Genoese and Venetians during the coronation of Peter II in Famagusta
AD 1373 Invasion of Cyprus by the Genoese
AD 1396 James I proclaimed king of Armenia
AD 1424 Mamelukes plunder and burn Limassol
AD 1426 Mamelukes defeat and capture King

Janus at the battle of Khirokitia
AD 1427 Janus ransomed, returns to Cyprus
AD 1459 Jacques de Lusignan, later James II,
attempts to dispossess his sister, Queen
Charlotte, of the throne with the assistance of
the Sultan of Egypt
AD 1460–1475 James II
AD 1472 James II marries Caterina Cornaro
AD 1473 Death of James III in suspicious
circumstances
AD 1474-78 Caterina Cornaro Queen of Cyprus
AD 1481 Leonardo da Vinci visits Cyprus
AD 1489 Caterina Cornaro cedes Cyprus to
Doge Agostino Barbarigo. Francesco Barbarigo,
first Lieutenant-Governor of Cyprus

Venetian Period

AD 1489–1570
AD 1505 Christopher Moro (? Shakespeare's
Othello), Lieutenant Governor of Cyprus
AD 1560 Archbishop Filippo II, last Latin
Primate of Cyprus
AD 1567 Refortification of Nicosia started under
Francesco Barbaro, Provveditore
AD 1570 Turkish invasion of Cyprus. Surrender
of Limassol. Nicosia captured.
AD 1571 Famagusta captured

Turkish Period

AD 1571–1878
AD 1572 Expulsion of Latin Hierarchy.
Restoration of Orthodox prelates
AD 1692 Plague. One third of inhabitants die
AD 1748 Cyprus declared an Ottoman colony
AD 1799 Revolt of Janissaries on the island
AD 1821 Execution of the archbishop, bishops
and 200 notables on suspicion of treason
AD 1876 General di Cesnola, American Consul,
finds treasure at Curium
AD 1876 Earliest known bilingual Phoenician
and Cypriote syllabic text found at Idalion

British Period

1878–1960
AD 1878 Cyprus ceded to Great Britain. Sir
Garnet Wolseley first High Commissioner
AD 1915 Cyprus offered to Greece on condition
that Greece entered the war on the Allies' side.
The offer was refused

Republic of Cyprus

Following a campaign to unite Cyprus with
Greece led by Archbishop Makarios, the island

was given its independence by Britain in 1960. After the overthrow of the President, Archbishop Makarios, and intercommunal strife, the Turkish army invaded Cyprus in 1974. There followed a *de facto* partition of the island and the establishment of the Turkish Republic of North Cyprus. A United Nations force mans the so called Green Line which separates North Cyprus from South Cyprus. So far all efforts to establish a rapprochement between the two communities have failed

Glossary

ACROPOLIS, fortified hilltop, citadel of a city

AGORA, public square or market place

AMAZONOMACHIA, combat between Greeks and Amazons

AMBO, pulpit in a Christian basilica

AMPHITHEATRE, elliptical or circular space surrounded by seats used by the Romans for gladiatorial contests

AMPHORA, two handled container for wine or water

ANALEMMA, supporting wall at the side of a theatre

APSE, semicircular recess in a wall, especially in a church

ARCHITRAVE, a lintel or main beam resting on columns; the lowest member of the entablature

ASHLAR, square cut stone and masonry made of these

ASKOS, pl. -oi, small flat vase with narrow sloping spout and arching handle

ATRIUM, court of a house open to the sky, but roofed at the sides, or entrance to a Byzantine church

AYIASMA, holy water

AYIOS, male saint, Ayia, female saint, plural Ayii

BASILICA, Roman public building with a central hall flanked by side halls, a church of this type

BEDESTEN, a covered market

BEMA, the area of a church in which the altar is located; the sanctuary. From the Greek bêma, step, platform

BOTHROS, pit for votive offerings and sacred objects discarded from a sanctuary

CAVEA, the auditorium of a theatre

CELLA, the great hall of a temple which housed the cult

CHRIST PANTOKRATOR, Christ, Ruler of all mankind

CIPPUS, Lat. pl. cippi, a post or marker esp. a gravestone

COLONNADE, a row of columns supporting an entablature

CORNICE, upper member of the entablature

CUNEUS, pl. -ei, wedge-shaped divisions in the cavea of a theatre

DEISIS, representation of Christ flanked by the Blessed Virgin and St John

DIACONIKON, compartment to the right of the bema used by the deacons: the sacristy

DIADOCHOS, pl.- oi, successor of Alexander the Great

DIAZOMA, horizontal passage in the cavea of the theatre

DORMITION, scene showing the death of the Blessed Virgin

DRAGOMAN, the Dragoman of the Serai, appointed by the Archbishop of Cyprus, was the official link between the government in Constantinople and the people of Cyprus

DROMOS, pl. -oi, passage leading to a tomb

EKKLISIA, a church

ENTABLATURE, stonework resting on a row of columns, including architrave, frieze and cornice

EPHEBOS, pl. -oi, ancient Greek. Youth of 18 or over usually training in the army

EXEDRA, semi-circular recess in a classical or Byzantine building

EXONARTHEX , a transverse vestibule preceding the facade in a Byzantine church

FIBULA, pl. -ai, a clasp, buckle or brooch

HIPPODROME, a place for horse or chariot races

HYDRA, a water jar

ICONOCLAST, religious fanatic opposed to religious images, a person who destroys them

ICONOSTASIS, a screen hung with icons separating the nave from the apse or the bema in an Orthodox church

KAKO-, bad, evil

KALO-, good

KATHOLIKON, nave

KATO-, lower

KHRYSO, golden

KONAK, an Ottoman town house

KYLIX, Gr. pl. kylikes, large wine cup with shallow bowl, two horizontal handles and a high stem above the foot

LEKYTHOS, pl. -oi, an oil bottle

LINOBAMBAKOI, literally 'flax-cottons'; Orthodox Christians who appeared to convert to Islam to avoid extra taxes

LOCULUS. Lat. pl. loculi, a small receptacle or a small place

MAENAD, a Bacchante. Literally a 'raver', from the Greek Μανιάς raving, frantic

MEGARON, principal hall of a palace or large house

MESCIT, a small mosque

METOPE, Doric—plain rectangular panel; Classical—sculptured relief

MIHRAB, niche in mosque indicating the position of Mecca

MIMBER, pulpit in mosque

NAOS, nave of church, cella of a temple

NARTHEX, narrow vestibule at the west end of a Christian church

NEOS, new

NECROPOLIS, Gr. pl. necropoleis, literally, City of the Dead, the name is derived from a suburb of Alexandria used as a burial place

ODEUM (Latin), ODEION (Greek), small building with semicircular seating used for concerts and meetings

ORCHESTRA, large circular space occupied by the actors and chorus in a Greek theatre

OUBLIETTE, a secret dungeon, accessed by a trapdoor, into which prisoners were thrown.

PALAESTRA, training area used by athletes

PALAIOS, or PALEO old

PAN, the god of shepherds and flocks. Usually depicted as half-man, half-animal

PANAYIA, the Blessed Virgin Mary

PANO, upper

PAPAS, a priest

PARODOS, Gr. pl. parodoi, space between the cavea and the stage of a theatre

PELTE, small light rimmed shield

PERISTYLE, A row or rows of columns surrounding a building or an open courtyard

PETRA, stone

PITHOS, large earthenware jar used for storing oil, water, grain etc

POTAMOS, a river or stream

PRODHROMOS, St. John the Baptist, literally the Forerunner

PROTHESIS, the compartment to the left of the bema,where the preparation of the eucharist takes place

RHYTON, one-handled cup shaped like an animal's head

RINCEAU, an ornamental leaf scroll, usually vine,

SATYR, a follower of Dionysus, usually depicted as half-animal, half-human, with tail, hooves and permanently erect phallus

SCAENAE FRONS, elaborately ornamented front of the scene building of a theatre

SILENUS, ugly, fat, elderly, drunken follower of Dionysus

SKYPHOS, a deep cup with two horizontal handles at the rim

STAVROS, the Cross

STIRRUP JAR, a closed pot for the

storage of wine or oil with a spout on the shoulder and a handle in a form reminiscent of a stirrup over the closed top

STOA, a portico or roofed colonnade

STRIGIL, a skin-scraper used after excerise

SYNTHRONON, a semicircle arrangement of seats in the apse for the clergy

TEKKE, a Dervish convent

TEMENOS, a sacred enclosure

THOLOS, a circular building, some-times underground beehive shaped tomb

THYRSUS, staff wreathed with vine leaves and ivy and surmounted with a pine cone, carried by Dionysus and his followers

TRIGLYPH, part of a Doric frieze bearing three vertical grooves; triglyphs alternated with the metopes

TUĞRA, signature of the sultan

VOMITORIUM, pl. -a, covered exit in a Roman theatre

Further reading

Albrecht. P.J., *North Cyprus, a Travel Book*. Havellia, London 1994

Bannerman. D and M., *Handbook of the Birds of Cyprus*. K. Rustem, Nicosia

Brownrigg. R., *Pauline Places*. Hodder & Stoughton, London 1989

Cobham. C.D., *Excerpta Cypria. Materials for a History of Cyprus*. Cambridge University Press 1908. Reprinted by Kemal Rustem, Nicosia 1969

Durrell. L., *Bitter Lemons*. Faber & Faber, London, 1957

Gunnis. Rupert, *Historic Cyprus*. Reprinted by Kemal Rustem, Nicosia, 1973

Hanworth. R., *The Heritage of North Cyprus*. Ministry of Communications Public Works & Tourism, Nicosia, 1989

Herodotus, *The History*. Translated by David Grene, University of Chicago Press, Chicago & London, 1987

Hunt. D. & Hunt. I. editors, *Caterina Cornaro*. Trigraph London 1989

Hunt. D. editor, *Footprints in Cyprus*. Trigraph London 1982

Karageorghis. V., *Cyprus, From the Stone Age to the Romans*. Thames & Hudson, London, 1982

Karageorghis. V., *The Cyprus Ancient Monuments*. C. Epiphaniou Publications, Nicosia, 1989

Karageorghis. V., *Cyprus Museum and Archaeological Sites of Cyprus*. Ekdotike Athenon S.A. Athens, 1991

Karageorghis. V., *The Ancient Civilization of Cyprus*. Barrie & Jenkins, London, 1970

Luke. Sir Harry., *Cyprus*. Harrap, London, with Kemal Rustem, Nicosia, 1973

Maier. F.G. & Karageorgis. V., *Paphos, History and Archaeology*. A. G. Leventis Foundation Nicosia, 1984

Michaelides. D., *Cypriot Mosaics*. Dept. of Antiquities, Cyprus 1992

North Cyprus Museum Friends, *North Cyprus, Mosaic of Cultures*. A Turizim Yayınları Ltd Şti., Istanbul

der Parthog. G., *Byzantine and Medieval Cyprus*. Interworld Publications, New Barnet, Herts., England. 1995

Polunin. Oleg and Huxley. Anthony, *Flowers of the Mediterranean*. Chatto & Windus, London, 1981

Rasmussen. T. and Spivey N., *Looking at Greek Vases*. Cambridge University Press 1991

Runciman. Sir Stephen, *History of the Crusades*. 3 vols. Cambridge University Press, 1951

Strabo, *The Geography*. Trs. H.L. Jones vols. 6 and 8 Loeb Edition

Sandars. N.K., *The Sea People Warriors of the Ancient Mediterranean*. Thames & Hudson, London 1978

Sullivan. R.D., *Near Eastern Royalty and Rome*. University of Toronto Press, Toronto Buffalo London, 1990

Tatton-Brown. V., *Ancient Cyprus*. British Museum Publications, London 1987

Thubron, Colin, *Journey into Cyprus*, Wm. Heinemann, London 1975; Penguin Books, 1986

Cambridge Ancient History, Vol. I Part 2B, Chapter XXVI (b)

Cambridge Ancient History, Vol. II Part 2A, Chapter XXII

THE GUIDE

Larnaca

Highlights
The Pierides Museum, Larnaca Fort and Medieval Museum, Cami Kebir, the Church of Ayios Lazaros, Ayia Feneromeni, Larnaca District Archaeological Museum, Kition

According to the Carmelite friar Nicole Huen, who visited Larnaca in 1487, there were no buildings apart from the church dedicated to St Lazarus and a house which served as a tavern. A century later the Dutch lawyer Iohann van Kootwyck found little change. There were, he reported, 'some small buildings, few and poor, of one storey only, and the ruined governor's palace which had been erected by the Venetians.

Today Larnaca is a brash, glossy tourist resort, with a population of c 62,000, a marina which can house 450 yachts and a busy commercial harbour. Many visitors to South Cyprus land at the international airport which has been built over saltflats c 5km to the south west of the town. Within Larnaca's boundaries are the important Pierides Collection of Cypriot Antiquities, an excellent archaeological museum and the site of ancient Kition. Larnaca is a good centre for visiting the south east part of the island.

■ Practical information

Tourist information
The main office in Plateia Vasileos Pavlou is **open** every day in the morning (except Sunday) and on Monday, Tuesday, Thursday and Friday afternoons. A subsidiary office at the airport provides a 24-hour service. The multilingual staff at both offices offer advice, answer queries and provide pamphlets and a very useful large scale map of the town.

Post office
The central post office is in Aviou Lazarou.

Accommodation
Larnaca has a wide range of accommodation from the 5-star **Golden Bay**, ☎ (04) 645444; the **Lordos Beach**, ☎ (04) 647444, the **Palm Beach**, ☎ (04) 646500; the **Princess Beach Sunotel**, ☎ (04) 645500, the **Sun Hall**, ☎ (04) 653341 and the **Sandy Beach**, ☎ (04) 646333 and all 4-star, to more modest

establishments. The **Sun Hall** in Leoforos Athinon, which has excellent sea views and a friendly and helpful staff, is recommended.

Restaurants
Leoforos Athinon is lined with restaurants and there are many more in the streets behind. Almost all offer some Cypriot dishes, but 'international cuisine' is taking over and, usually, there are chips with everything.

Transport
Buses 21 and 19 run from the airport to Leoforos Athinon at frequent intervals. Buses 19 and 6 will take you near the Tekke of Hala Sultan. Bus 6 continues to Kiti village. Services to Nicosia, Limassol and Aya Napa start from Leoforos Athinon. Buses usually operate from 06.00 to 17.00 from Monday to Friday and until lunchtime on Saturday. There is no service on Sunday.

Service taxis, which can carry several passengers, run between 06.00 and 18.00 during the week to Nicosia, Limassol and Paphos. Bookable by telephone, they pick passengers up from their hotels and take them to any address at the destination. Each passenger pays for his own seat. These taxis are often driven at terrifyingly fast speeds and are not very comfortable. Cars may be hired at the airport from a number of firms including **Hertz** and from companies in the town.

Church services
Greek Orthodox: Agios Lazaros. **Roman Catholic**: Santa Maria della Grazia. **Armenian**: St Stephanos. **Anglican**: St Helena. **Protestant**: The International Evangelical Church.

History
Early History. Tombs excavated near the church of Panayia Chrysopolitissa, Our Lady of the Golden City, on the north side of Larnaca, have produced pottery sherds which have been dated to the beginning of the 13C BC. Originally known as Kition or Citium, the Chittim of the Old Testament (Isaiah and Daniel), c 1220 the settlement was destroyed by the raiding Sea People, but rebuilt shortly after. The first wave of Achaean immigrants came c 1190. Kition revived in the 9C BC, when it came under Phoenician rule, and continued to prosper. Its harbour, which may have been enclosed, was used for the export of copper from the mines of Tamassos, c 40km to the north west. The town probably stood a short distance back from the sea. Kition's sympathies lay with the Persians during the Greek-Persian War, and in 450 BC it was besieged by Cimon, who had defeated the Persian fleet at the battle of the Eurymedon river c 466. (See *Blue Guide Turkey*.) He died during one of the skirmishes outside the walls. Look for his idealised portrait bust on the seafront.

Little is known about Kition during the Roman and Medieval periods. It appears to have been of comparatively little importance. In the 7C it was raided at various times by the Arabs.

Medieval Period. Under the Lusignans the town was called *Salina* or *Salines* because of the neighbouring salt lake. During the siege of Famagusta by the Genoese (1373 to 1374) many foreign traders moved here and it was known as *La Scala,* the landing stage, after its roadstead. Its present name, Larnaca, is probably derived from the Greek, λάρναξ a chest, cinerary urn or coffin, because of the number of sarcophagi found in the surrounding area. This name was not in general use until c 1600.

Ottoman Rule. During the period of Turkish rule Larnaca grew in importance as a port, and was long the main place of residence of a small English colony and, from 1683, of foreign consuls in the island. It would seem that some of these gentlemen spent little time on consular matters, preferring to occupy themselves with the search for ancient remains in the area around the town. The first reference to an English Consulate here dates from 1626.

J.-B. Tavernier, writing c 1650, refers to the population of the island as being 'all clad after the Italian manner, both men and women'. At carnival time masquerades were in vogue, but the practice was forbidden in 1681 because some young gentlemen had taken to visiting the bazaars in female attire.

John Heyman, the Professor of Oriental Languages at Leyden, who visited Larnaca during the first decade of the 18C, remarked that the English consul's house here was the best on the island, 'though the outside of it is only of clay, but nothing can be more neat, or elegantly ornamented than the inside. It has also the largest hall I saw in any part of the Levant; but, what is of much more importance, the English consul is highly respected all over the island, as jointly with his company he advances money to the inhabitants, for getting in their several harvests, in which otherwise they would be at a great loss'. This house was built by the consul and merchant Mr Treadway, who, it is said, was much in debt. He solved his pecuniary problems in an interesting way. One evening he invited all his creditors to a grand banquet. After they had assembled he begged to be excused for a few moments. Slipping quietly out of the house he made his way to the harbour and boarded a friend's ship in which he had stowed all his valuables under cover of darkness the previous night. The ship set sail and Mr Treadway was never seen again. His creditor-guests waited in vain. The promised dinner never reached the table.

In 1778 some 40 Maronite Christians lived here. As they had no priest of their own, their spiritual needs were met by Franciscans. In 1800 Lieutenant-Colonel William Martin Leake (1777 to 1860), the topographer of Greece, visited the town briefly. He remarked that the stone foundations of ancient walls and other remains of antiquity were being 'removed for building materials almost as soon as they were discovered'. In 1815, according to William Turner, diplomat and traveller, Larnaca contained about 1000 houses, and in the marina or port area there were about 700 more. Turner complained of being kept awake at nights by the croaking of frogs in the marshes, 'always excessively loud...with such incessant noise, that it required the exertion of all my great talents of sleeping to save me from being disturbed by them.' (*Exerpta Cypria*).

In 1841, with a population of 13,000, Larnaca was slightly larger than Nicosia. It has been estimated that in 1816 there were some 1000 Europeans here, 200 of whom were 'in transit'. By 1847 this number had dropped to 400, still a considerable figure when compared to the dozen or so at Nicosia and Limassol. As an entrepôt for business in the Levant the town prospered. A branch of the Ottoman Bank was established here in 1864. In the following year General Luigi Palma di Cesnola, who has been described as 'not so much an archaeologist as a systematic plunderer', was American—and Russian—consul at Larnaca. From here he undertook his depredations 'with the countenance and indulgence of the authorities and public officers', to quote his own exculpatory words; and, apparently, with financial backing to the tune of £1000 from John Ruskin.

The Arrival of the British. Britain acquired Cyprus from Turkey in 1878 as part of a defensive alliance between the two countries which would guarantee the Sultan's Asiatic possessions from Russian encroachment.

On 4 July 1878 Captain Harry Rawson on HMS *Minataur* arrived in Larnaca roads. On the 10th with Walter Baring, second secretary at the British Embassy at Constantinople, and Sami Paşa, representative of the Porte, he made his way to Nicosia to initiate negotiations for the transfer of Cyprus from Turkish to British rule. On the morning of the 12th Rawson with Vice-Admiral Lord John Hay and a detachment of 50 marines and 50 bluejackets entered Nicosia by the Famagusta Gate. The sultan's firman was presented to the Turkish governor, Bessim Paşa, who handed over the administration to Hay, as agreed. The Union Jack was hoisted and a crowd of curious onlookers applauded enthusiastically. On the 23rd Sir Garnett Wolseley landed at Larnaca with some 1500 troops. For the next six months they made Larnaca their HQ.

From the 1940s the port was gradually superseded in importance by Famagusta and Limassol; but since 1976 work has been in progress to extend its facilities.

Famous citizens. The city had two famous sons. Zeno of Citium (c 335 to 263 BC), whose family was probably of Phoenician origin, taught philosophy at Athens in the Stoa Poikile—hence the epithet 'stoic' which was applied to his teachings and those of Cleanthes and Chrysippus who together are regarded as the founders of the Stoic school. Zeno proposed in his *Politeia*, ie, 'Republic' that there should be a world state in which there would be no lawcourts, money, temples or gymnasia. Women would be held in common. For him virtue was the main purpose of life. Pleasure and pain were of no importance. Zeno committed suicide at the age of 98.

Apollonius of Citium (c 90 to 15 BC?) founded an important school of medicine in Alexandria, Egypt, and became the *archiatros*, ie, principal citizen, of that city.

The Pierides Museum

In the centre of Larnaca at 4 Zinonos Kitieos Street is the **Pierides Museum of Cypriot Antiquities**. It is housed in a two storey neocolonial style house built in 1840 which at various times has served as the consulate of Great Britain, the United States of America, Norway, Germany and Sweden. The Swedish coat of arms is still affixed above the main entrance. The Pierides family are descendants of Zantiot merchants and bankers who settled in Venice before coming to Cyprus in 1772. The collection was started in 1839 by by Demetrios Pierides (1811 to 1895) and continued by subsequent generations of the family. Objects are displayed in five rooms and in the corridor on the ground floor. Books in the small reference library may be consulted by visitors.

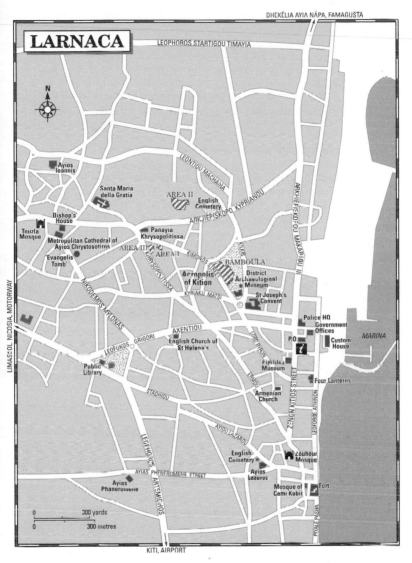

- **Open** from 15 June to 30 September between 09.00–13.00 and 16.00–19.00 and from 1 October–14 June between 09.00–13.00 and 15.00–18.00. There is a small admission charge. Postcards of some of the objects in the collection and booklets about it are on sale.

The **Entrance Hall** has a display of antique chests and carved woodwork.

Room 1 houses artefacts from the Chalcolithic Period to the Classical, Hellenistic and Roman periods.

Case 1: Chalcolithic Period (3900 to 2500/2300 BC). Terracotta of a nude male seated on a four-legged stool. Liquid poured into his skull could be drunk from his penis. From Souskiou (Paphos district) the largest Chalcolithic terracotta figure to be discovered so far in Cyprus. Steatite idols and a Red-on-White vase, also from Souskiou. Early Bronze Age (2500/2300 to 1900 BC). Vessels of Red Polished ware.

Case 2: Early Bronze Age (2500/2300 to 1900 BC). Pyxides of Red Polished ware from Margi and Kotsioitis (Nicosia district). Flat, oblong terracotta idol of Red Polished ware. This represents an infant in a cradle. Vases of Black Polished ware.

Case 3: Middle Bronze Age (1900 to 1650 BC). White Painted ware, vases with anthropomorphic characteristics. Ring-shaped jug. From Margi (Nicosia district) a large bowl of Red Polished ware decorated with scenes of daily life— the subjects include pregnant women, infants in cradles, animals.

Case 4: Late Bronze Age (1650 to 1050 BC). Vases of White Slip ware. Vases of Base Ring ware I-II. Mycenaean rhyton in the shape of a hog or hedgehog's head. From Kition a terracotta idol of Astarte with birdlike face, holding an infant.

Case 5: Geometric Period (1050 to 750 BC). Bichrome Wheelmade ware. Pyxis in the form of a rectangular sarcophagus with four legs and a flat lid.

Case 6: Archaic Period (750 to 475 BC). Terracotta votive figures. Terracotta figure of a goddess with uplifted arms. She wears a tiara, necklaces and pendants. Terracotta figurine of a warrior. In his right hand he held a spear (now missing), in his left he holds a shield. Terracotta model of a wine cart. A bird shaped askos.

An unnumbered case in this room contains Roman lamps (50 BC to AD 395), a terracotta figurine holding musical instruments (750 to 475 BC), limestone fragments from the Classical and Hellenistic periods (325 to 50 BC) and a feeding bottle from the Classical Period.

Room 2 has artefacts from the Archaic to the Classical Period.

Case 1: Archaic Period. Bichrome Wheelmade IV ware (700 to 600 BC). Bowls with feet, jugs from Marion with moulded female figures holding miniature jugs on their shoulders. Pitchers ornamented with large bulls' heads.

Case 2: Archaic Period. Jugs of Bichrome ware decorated in the 'free-field' style with birds, fish, animals, hunting scenes and sacred trees. Jugs with 'spaceman' ornamentation.

Case 3: Classical Period (475 to 325 BC). Terracotta moulded heads from Pomos (Paphos area)—evidence of Classical Greek sculpture influence. Terracotta figurines of comedy actors of the 4C and 5C BC.

On a stand: terracotta heads from Pomos. Limestone heads of various periods—Classical, Hellenistic and Roman. Small terracotta statuettes of females holding votive offerings (Archaic Period). Roman limestone portrait head of a youth (? Nero). Funerary terracotta of a seated man holding a bird (from Polis, Paphos district) and a funerary figure of a reclining bearded middle-aged man. Both from the Classical period.

Room 3. Medieval glazed pottery of brown and green sgraffito ware. This is decorated with various motifs—hunting scenes, birds, animals, knights and noble women. 'Marriage bowls' with couples in close embrace (AD 13C to 16C). Byzantine icons from the 16C to the 18C.

Room 4. A collection of 360 pieces of Roman glassware.

Room 5. This room houses examples of folk art, including wood carving, silverware, bronze utensils, embroidery and weaving, and traditional town and rural costumes.

Corridor. Maps of Cyprus from the Venetian period (1489 to 1571). Ottoman period weapons (1571 to 1878). Coats of arms of Cyprus, Armenia, and Jerusalem from the Lusignan period (1192 to 1489). Diplomatic certificates given to the Pierides family for consular services. A tombstone bears the following inscription: ΕΝΘΑΔΕ ΚΕΙ ΜΑΙ ΣΙΜΑΛΗ ΙΠΠΑΡΧΟΥ ΘΥΓΑΤΕΡ ΚΑΛΛΕΙ ΠΡΟΦΕΡΟΥΣΑ, 'Here I lie Simaly the good daughter of Hipparchos'.

The Larnaca Club across the road was once a *han*. Note the high doorway to admit laden camels.

Southern Sector

Larnaca's commercial harbour is a short distance to the north. The more interesting **Fishermen's Harbour and Yacht Marina** lie to the south. Leoforos Athinon, a pleasant palm-lined promenade, has a long line of open air restaurants. The rooms of the pleasant Sun Hall hotel overlook the promenade and the beach beyond. There are plans to improve the beach and its amenities, but the bathing here is not recommended. The best beaches in the Larnaca area are on the road to Ayia Napa (see below).

At the southern end of the promenade is **Larnaca Fort and Medieval Museum**.

■ **Open** every day except Sunday from 07.30 to 19.00 (summer); 07.30 to 17.00 (rest of the year); Thursday 07.30 to 18.00.

Built by the Turks in 1625, it served as a prison and barracks during the early period of British rule. There is a small courtyard agreeably shaded by trees. The only reminder of the fort's violent past is provided by a collection of antique ordnance. In an upstairs room there is a photographic exhibition of Byzantine churches. Cabinets contain sgraffito ware, Islamic pottery and Ottoman period kitchen utensils and ware. There is also a small collection of 18C and 19C swords, armour and muskets. Spend a few minutes on the sea wall for the splendid views it provides of the town and its environs.

Here, in what was formerly the Turkish Cypriot quarter of Larnaca there are two mosques. Enter the simple rectangular prayer hall of the late 16C **Cami Kebir** through an elegant portico and you will be encouraged by the custodian to climb to the top of the minaret. A fine view of the old Turkish houses, which cluster around the building, more than justifies the effort. This mosque was restored by a 19C governor of the island, Seyit Elhac Mehmet Ağa. The nearby **Zouhour Mosque** has lost its minaret. A part of the adjoining **bedesten**, which once provided shelter for travellers has, appropriately, been turned into a youth hostel. For the **Fishermen's Harbour** continue along Piyâle Paşa street.

A short distance to the north west of Cami Kebir is one of the most interesting structures in Larnaca. Partially hidden by unattractive gates and an untidy clutter of associated buildings is the church of **Ayios Lazaros**. There is a tradition in the Greek Orthodox Church that, after Jesus raised him from the dead,

Lazarus, the brother of Martha and Mary, came to Cyprus and was later consecrated bishop of Kition by Paul and Barnabas. During the Arab raids the place of
his burial was forgotten. Rediscovered in 890 his remains were sent to
Constantinople. Stories that they were subsequently taken to France probably
arise from confusion with an early bishop of Aix of the same name.

The original church is believed to date from the 9C. In 1571 Cyprus came
under Turkish rule and in 1589 the Turkish authorities sold the church to the
Orthodox. From then until 1758 it was shared by Orthodox and Latin
Christians. It was reconstructed in the 17C. Later a campanile, one of the few
permitted by the Turks before 1857, was added. Church bells were not permitted
by the Turks until 1857, as they believed that they could be used to summon
subject peoples to rise against their masters.

To the south of the tower is an open porch, from which steps descend into the
church. It has two aisles and a central nave covered by three domes which are
now boarded in. The roof is supported by four twin piers on which there are
several reused Byzantine capitals. In one of the piers a stair ascends to the elaborately decorated pulpit. Note particularly the icon of the Virgin and Child on
the north pier at the crossing, that of St George and the Dragon (1717), the
silver filigree icon of 1659 depicting the Raising of Lazarus, and another of the
same subject in which a spectator, overcome by the stench of corruption from
the corpse, is holding his nose. The saint's empty marble sarcophagus is reached
by steps which descend from the bema near the southern side of the apse. The
18C iconostasis was damaged by fire in 1970. The modern candelabras and
icons on the side walls detract somewhat from the church's impressive interior.

In an enclosure to the north-west of the church are the gravestones of the tiny
English Cemetery. Dating from c 1685 to 1850, they are mostly of members
of the Levant Company, which was incorporated in 1581, and of consuls and
their families. Among them are Captain Peter Dare, Commander of the ship
Scipio, died 1685; Ion Ken, 'of London, Merchant' (1672 to 1693) and William
Ken, Merchant of Cyprus, died 1707; Mary, the wife of Samuel Palmer, who died
in 1720, and her infant daughter; George Barton who died in 1739, consul prior
to 1730, and from 1738; Michael de Vezin, consul 1785 to 1792, and James
Lilburn, consul 1840 to 1843. There are also memorials to the missionary
Lorenzo Warriner Pease, 'Native of the United States of America' who died in
1839 and of William Balls, 'late seaman on board HBMS *Volage*' who died in
1849 and whose tomb was 'erected as a token of respect by his shipmates'.

A short distance to the west is **Ayia Faneromeni** which dates from 1907.
This was originally an ancient tomb which has suffered much from the trans-
formation. The church was believed to possess magical properties. Lovelorn
maidens prayed here for the safety and wellbeing of absent swains, while
sufferers from malaria, headaches and other illnesses walked three times around
the church and then placed some personal item like a lock of hair or a piece of
clothing on a grill near the south window. Near the church there are two rock
tombs. The inner tomb, covered by a large stone has been dated to c 80 BC.

Northern Sector and Kition

From the Tourist Office walk in a north westerly direction to Leoforos Grigori
Afxentiou and then turn right into Kimonos St. This leads to a small square, on
whose eastern side is the mid-19C convent and school of St Joseph and on the

north, in a small garden filled with an interesting clutter of tombs, architectural fragments, stone anchors and a circular mosaic, the Larnaca District Archaeological Museum.

Larnaca District Archaeological Museum

■ **Open** Monday to Friday from 07.30 to 17.00 and in summer 07.30 to 19.00.

The room to the left of the entrance is devoted to **sculpture**, mostly in lime-stone. This includes female votive torsos from Arsos—one with traces of colour—a crowned head, a bearded head from Pergamos, another, wreathed and bearded, from Larnaca (c 500 BC) and inscribed funerary stelae. In a wall-case there is a collection of terracotta figurines of females. Of various periods these include a Late Cypriot II mother and child from Larnaca. Many wear head-dresses and some show traces of paint. There are also several limestone stat-uettes and heads.

The room to the right contains the **ceramics**, mostly from Kition, from the Early Cypriot III period, and Livadhia, Middle Cypriot period. There are also 14C Mycenaean craters and vases, and from Kornos, Cypro-Classic. Note the finds from Khirokitia, Kalavassos (Tenta), including an Early Bronze Age bowl, Pyla, Athienou, and Maroni; the alabaster vases from Kition and an ivory figure of the Egyptian god Bes.

In a wall-case there are stone, clay, glass, faience, ivory, and bronze ornaments, jewellery, paste amulets, dating from the 7C to 6C BC, and seals of the 8C to 7C BC, together with Late-Cypriot cylinder-seals, a Middle Cypriot limestone seal; Cypriot type picrolite scarabs, and Egyptian style faience scarabs. Another case has Roman glass, 6C to 3C BC alabaster bowls, and clay lamps of various periods. Note the silver staters of the Cypriot Kingdoms, and coins from the mint at Kition and elsewhere which were found in the area, also examples of 'Late Cypriot Base Ring' ware; bronze tools, weapons, metalwork, and mirrors from the second millennium to the 4C BC. Finally, there are Neolithic I stone vases, Neolithic II pottery, stone tools, conical and engraved stones and stone idols from Khirokitia.

In the end room there are objects from various periods found at Bamboula, the necropolis of Kition, together with scarabs, a clay chariot and equestrian figures from the necropolis of Ayios Georghios and artefacts from a number of other sites. There are coin hoards from Kition and Larnaca and displays of jewellery. At the far end of the room there are tombs from Ayios Prodromos. Note the carved heads on two of the lids.

If you wish to see the what remains of the **acropolis** of Kition, continue along Kimonos St. The hill, largely levelled by the British Army in 1879, is being exca-vated. In addition to the fortified area there was probably a temple here.

Area II of Kition

To reach the so-called Area II of Kition take Kilkis St to the right of the museum and then Leontiou Machaira St. The entrance to the site is almost concealed by new houses. For an overall view of the excavated area go to the raised wooden gangway at the north west side near the custodian's lodge.

■ The site is **open** Monday to Friday from 07.30 to 14.30 (Thursday 07.30 to 18.00). Closed in the afternoons in July and August.

The oldest remains found at Kition are from an Aegean colony of the Mycenaean Age (13C BC). Kittim, the name given to the place in the Bible, was also applied to the whole island of Cyprus. Balak is told, in the prophecy of Balaan, that 'ships shall come from the coast of Kittim, and they shall afflict Ashur, and shall afflict Eber'. Partially destroyed by an earthquake c 1075, Kition was rebuilt but later abandoned. Colonised by Phoenician traders in the 9C—a dedication to 'Baal of Lebanon' has been found here—it remained under their control until 312 BC. A monument to Sargon II indicates that it was the administrative centre of Cyprus during the period of Assyrian rule (708 to c 663 BC). During the revolts of the Greek Cypriots in the 5C and 4C BC, Kition took an active part on the side of Persia. The city retained a measure of importance, although devastated by earthquakes, until the Middle Ages when its habour silted up. Then the remaining inhabitants moved to Larnaca.

Like many ancient sites Kition is a confused area of low walls partially, indeed in some places completely, covered by vegetation. To the north of the main street are the remains of two temples, **Temple 2** to the right and **Temple 1** to the left of the gangway. Temple 1, the principal temple, measures 35m by 22m. It was approached by a monumental entrance which was sited to the north west of **Temenos B**. Its south, west and east walls were constructed of ashlar with a rubble infill. On the outer side of the south wall there are crude graffiti of ships. To the east of the temenos are the remains of two smaller temples, 4 and 5, which were excavated in 1974/75. Part of the foundation of Temple 4 is made up of reused anchor stones.

To the west, in Plateia Mitropoleos, are the **Metropolitan Cathedral of Chrysosotiros**, largely rebuilt in 1843, and the **Residence** of the Orthodox Bishop of Kition. Note the gargoyles, the ornate late 18C cathedra, the pulpit high on the north wall, the early 18C tortoise-shell and ivory icon stand and the carved iconostatis.

A short distance to the north west is the 17C church of **Ayios Ioannis**. Heavily restored in 1850, this has an iconostasis of c 1700 with repainted icons, a Venetian black and white marble doorway built into a room by the narthex, an exterior pulpit and painted wooden balcony.

To the south east in Terrasantas is the large domed Catholic church of **Santa Maria della Grazia**, also known as **Terra Santa**. This was restored in 1843.

Area I of the Kition excavations, which lies to the right of Kimonos St., is of little interest to the non-specialist visitor. Excavations here in 1962/63 produced a wealth of objects, including Mycenaean IIIB pottery, alabaster vessels, faience ornaments and scarabs from Egypt, carved ivories, gold jewellery, and a fine enamelled 13C BC rhyton with hunting scenes. These were found in chamber tombs in the courtyards of houses of the Late Cypriot II period, similar to those of Enkomi and Ugarit in Syria. A complex of copper workshops was found here later.

Tombs of the same and slightly later periods, and what appears to have been a Hellenistic bathing establishment, have been found at **Area III** of Kition which is located in nearby Chrysopolitissis St.

Apart from the **aqueduct**, which is described below, the only other monu-

tions. It had been visited in 1745 by the British Consul at Aleppo, Alexander Drummond. He considered the church to have been built in a 'mean manner' and judged the painting 'so monstrous, that it would even disgrace a paltry alehouse in' his country. In 1787 Dr John Sibthorp, the botanist and author of *Flora Graeca*, tried to break into the deserted monastery. It was eventually opened to him and he passed the night on a straw mattress below the altar!

Note. As the community follows the Mount Athos rule, only devout males, properly dressed, are admitted to the monastery. Cameras and video-cameras are forbidden.

Before entering the monastery precincts note the fine view of the eastern foothills of the Troodos mountains. Take the stairs to a landing and continue by way of a small open space to the church. A wooden cross dating from 1476, which may represent that of the Good Thief brought by St Helena, stands to the right-hand side of the iconostasis. Carved with tiny representations of the life of Christ, this was encased in silver in 1702. A **fragment** believed to be from the True Cross, protected by a 17C gold frame, is set into the larger cross.

A corridor to the left, passing rather spartan guest cells where male visitors may stay over night, leads to a platform behind the apse which commands panoramic **views** of the mountains surrounding the monastery. On the wall of this corridor there is an **inscribed prayer** by an 11C monk.

Some of the monks are occupied with the production of honey and cheese. It is said that the members of the community were the first in Cyprus to cultivate the sultana grape. Others paint icons which are sold to visitors. Only a proportion of the community resides here at any one time. They take it in turns to stay on the summit where they have the companionship of sleek, well-fed cats originally brought here to control the local population of vipers (cf. St Nicholas of the Cats on the Akrotiri Peninsula).

The nearby monastery of the **Panayia Galaktotrophousa** was founded in 1947 and completed in 1963 by dissident monks from Stavrovouni who prefer to follow the old calendar. Access is not easy.

At **Delikipo** there is a tiny church of 1723 dedicated to the **Transfiguration of Christ**, the Metamorphosis. This incorporates some fragments from an older building. There are 18C icons and a 16C alms plate.

Kornos is famous for its coarse clay anthropomorphic pottery. The larger storage jars are built up by hand not thrown on a wheel.

The **Monastery of Ayia Thekla**, dating from 1471, is said to have been built on the site of a 4C church built by St Helena. It has a silver iconostasis and many wax ex voto figures.

The 18C church of **Panayia Khrysogalatousa** has a painted iconostasis of 1715 and an icon of the same date. Three ancient shrines have been found near the village of **Mathiati**. A head of Dionysos, now in the Cyprus Museum Nicosia, was found in one of them.

Excavations at an area to the south west of **Alambra** have uncovered a Middle Bronze Age settlement. One of the flat roofed houses had two rectangular rooms arranged in an L-shape. The walls were of mudbrick on a foundation of rubble. Animals were kept in a central enclosure. In the late 12C church of **Ayii Apostoli** just outside of **Perakhorio** there are the remains of contemporary frescoes. Note the fine frieze of angels. In the drumless dome there is a damaged representation of the Pantokrator, in the semi dome a painting of the Blessed Virgin Mary with SS Peter and Paul and, below, the Fathers of the Church. The frescoes on the south wall are of a later date.

At **Kochati** near **Ayia Varvara** there is a huge medieval cistern. In this area some of the villages are inhabited by Maronite Christians.

Klavdhia's name is probably derived from the Latin 'Claudia'. A Late Bronze Age site was excavated here in 1899 by an expedition from the British Museum, where the finds now are exhibited. Klavdhia's mosque was once a Byzantine church. The village was the birthplace of Haji Bakis, Paşa of Cyprus from 1775 to 1783.

A rough road from Klavdhia towards Pyrga, passes the remains of a former Latin monastery. Possibly a 15C Cistercian foundation, it is now known as **Stazousa**. The nave has a good ribbed vault. A fine doorway on the west side provided access to the monastic complex.

West of Larnaca

Highlights
The Salt Lake, Hala Sultan Tekke, Dhromolaxia, Kiti and Panayia Angeloktistos, Perivolia, Mazotos and Kophinou

Just outside Larnaca skirt the south east side of the **Salt Lake** which has an area of c 6 km². On the far bank of the lake the dome and minaret of the **Hala Sultan Tekke** are surrounded by a verdant grove of cypress and palm trees.

The **Lake**, which is 3m below sea level, has been a source of commercial salt from ancient times. Collection, which begins in August when the water has evaporated, is largely done by workers from Aradhippou. It has been a government monopoly for centuries, although there is some evidence that an Englishman named Pervis was farming the revenue of the Salines in 1603. The salt, once a source of great revenue to the island—it was said to be worth £10,000 a year and in the 16C was exported to Venice—is now largely consumed locally. According to tradition, the district was covered by vineyards until St Lazarus asked a local woman for some of the grapes she was carrying. Mockingly she refused him, saying that more salt than wine was likely to be got from that soil. At which the saint retorted, 'Then let it be so; from henceforth the soil shall produce salt, not the juice of the grape'.

With Akrotiri Lake near Limassol it is an important resting place and winter habitat for migrating birds, especially flamingos, *Phoenicopterus ruber antiquorum*, flocks of which may be seen here between October and March.

Larnaca's **International Airport**, a landing-field since 1939, was entirely reconstructed in 1975 and in late 1976 its runway was extended to accommodate jet aircraft. As Nicosia airport was closed in 1974 and subsequently occupied by UNFICYP, Larnaca and Paphos airports share the entire air traffic of the Republic.

Hala Sultan Tekke

A right-hand turning immediately beyond the bridge across the Salt Lake leads to the Hala Sultan Tekke, sometimes known as the **Tekke of Umm Haram**. The Lady Umm Haram was a relative of the Prophet Mohammed. While accompanying her husband on an Arab raid on Cyprus in 649, she fell from her mule here and, according to the chronicle, 'broke her pellucid neck and yielded up her victorious soul, and in that fragrant spot was at once buried'. The *tekke* was established in 1767. Regarded as one of the most important shrines in the Islamic world and, clearly visible from the sea, it was saluted by Turkish ships which dipped their flags as a mark of respect. The present buildings date from a complete reconstruction in 1816 by the Governor of Cyprus, Seyit Mohammed Emin.

■ Open daily from 07.30 to 17.00 (summer 07.30 to 19.30).

Surrounded by trees, the octagonal **mosque** with its restored minaret is a haven of calm and peace. The *şadirvan*, where worshippers perform their ablutions before praying, is in the garden. Visitors should leave their shoes at the entrance to the mosque. Eight columns support the dome of the prayer hall. The finely carved *mihrab*, which indicates the direction of Mecca, and the *mimber* or pulpit are votive offerings. Entrance to the inner domed sanctuary of 1760 is through a medieval doorway. The tomb of Umm Haram is a trilithon—two upright stones, almost 5m high, with the third stone resting on top of them. All are covered in green draperies. The stones were probably a cromlech of great antiquity. According to a pious legend they were transported from Palestine by angels. The shrine, which ranks in importance after Mecca and Medina, is much visited by Moslems particularly at the festivals of *Şeker Bayramı* and *Kurban Bayramı*.

In the cloister is the tomb of King Hussein of the Hedjaz's second wife, a Turkish lady who died in Cyprus in 1929. A white marble slab outside the entrance to the *tekke* has a finely carved inscription referring to Baldassare Trivizani, the Venetian Lieutenant-Governor of Cyprus from 1489 to 1491.

About 200m northwest of the *tekke* excavations have revealed the site of a **Bronze Age town**. Probably fortified, but destroyed c 1175 BC, it was temporarily re-occupied in the 4C BC. Finds include Mycenaean IIIA and B and Late Minoan IIIB pottery, ivory artefacts and bronze weapons, tools and utensils, and a lotus-shaped faience sceptre head decorated with the cartouche of the 18th dynasty Pharaoh Horemheb. The cartouche of Seti I (end of 14C BC) had been discovered previously at the *tekke*. In 1978 a hoard of 24 gold objects—beads, earrings and pendants—bronze, agate, carnelian, picrolite, and faience, was found at this site. Probably dating from Late Cypriot II, they were together with an alabaster bowl from Egypt and several rhyta of fine quality. In 1979 a tomb excavated here contained a magnificent bronze trident, weapons, and jewellery. The presence of so many Egyptian artefacts suggests the existence of extensive trading contacts with that country. The Salt Lake, which was probably open to the sea in ancient times, would have provided a safe anchorage for shipping.

About 2km due west of the turning to the *tekke* is the village of **Dhromlaxia** where a Bronze Age site was first excavated in 1898. The village was called Vromolaxia as late as 1865. As this means 'stinking gulch', it has been suggested that the famous purple dye of the Phoenicians made from the murex mollusc, which has a highly unpleasant smell, may also have been produced here. In 1425 the village was burnt by the Arabs. There are marble Corinthian capitals in the churchyard and another supports the font in the late 18C church. In the women's gallery there is a damaged icon of St John the Baptist which has been dated to 1794.

Material from the old church of **Meneou** (2km) was used in the construction of the Tekke of Umm Haram. There is an 18C aqueduct.

Kiti

A further 2km will bring you to Kiti whose name recalls the ancient city of Kition. There is a tradition that it was founded by settlers from there. During the Middle Ages it was known as **Le Quid**. Peter I built a fortified palace here in 1367. Charles de Lusignan, a later owner, had it taken from him by the usurper, James II, because of his loyalty to Queen Carlotta. In 1425 Kiti was sacked by the Mamelukes. The Venetians sold it to a wealthy Cypriote family, the Podocatoros. They held it until 1570 when the last Podocatoro was killed at the siege of Nicosia. The village bridge is a reminder of the period of Venetian rule. Today Kiti is an important market gardening centre.

A few paces to the north of the village centre is **Panayia Angeloktistos**, ie, the Church built by the Angels, which Gunnis described as being the finest village church in Cyprus. Constructed c 1000 on 5C foundations, it was rebuilt in the 12C and restored in the 16C. The central nave and the transepts of the cruciform building are unusually high and the crossing is crowned by a lantern dome. Entrance to the church is through the 13C Latin chapel which once belonged to a powerful medieval family, the Gibelets. It now serves as the narthex. On the outside wall of the chapel are three coats of arms—a plain cross, the royal quarterings of Jerusalem and Cyprus, and three lions' heads which is probably the coat of arms of the Gibelets. The gravestone bearing the effigy of a lady is that of Lady Simone, wife of Sir Regnier de Gibelet and daughter of Sir William Guers, who died on 5 November 1302.

The icons and iconostasis have been much repainted and are of little interest

Panayia Angeloktistos

except for the large mid 17C icon of the Archangel Michael to the right of the entrance.

Most visitors come to Kiti to see the wonderful **Byzantine mosaic** in the central apse of the church. Dating probably from the 6C AD, it is one of very few mosaics to survive the destruction wrought by the fanatics of the Iconoclastic Movement in the late 8C. The Blessed Virgin stands on a footstool and supports the Christ Child on her left arm. The sacred figures are flanked by the Archangels Gabriel and Michael (figure damaged) who hold wands of office and who offer the Christ Child the orbs of spiritual power. The archangels' wings are ornamented with peacock eyes. Note the elaborate patterned border of stags, fountains, parrots and ducks. There is some controversy about the age of the mosaic, dates from the 5C and the 9C have been proposed. The consensus favours the 6C, it being argued that the central apse was part of an earlier church which was largely destroyed in the 7C by Arab raiders. The balance of the composition and colouring of the mosaic equals work of this period found in Ravenna. The only other mosaics of this kind in Cyprus were in the monastery church of Kanakaria, near Lythrangomi, in the Karpas peninsula.

To the south of Kiti is the village of **Perivolia** which has a supermarket, banks and restaurants. Beyond, to the southeast, is **Cape Kiti**, with its mid-19C lighthouse. Nearby is a 16C, restored, **Venetian watchtower**. Note the lion of St Mark over the door lintel. A 9C BC Phoenician temple was found here at the site of ancient **Dades** in 1969. Underwater exploration of the area has brought to light a Byzantine shipwreck south of the cape and three Bronze Age stone anchors.

At **Kivisil** there are the ruins of a small Byzantine style church.

During the Midddle Ages **Mazotos**, 9km to the southwest, was the capital of one of the four Venetian provinces which had a Cypriot Commissioner. To the south, on the Roman road which circled the island, there are the remains of a Roman settlement known as **Laconicos** or **Alamina**. Two chapels dedicated to the **Panayia** stand on the ruins of the acropolis. According to Gunnis, it was off the coast here or at unidentified **Ceramaea** that in the mid-8C AD the fleet of Caliph Yezid III was destroyed by Constantine Kopronymos. Three *dromods* were allowed to escape so that they could carry news of the defeat back to Egypt.

The village of **Alaminos**, 4km to the west, was owned by Philippe d'Ibelin, seneschal of Cyprus, c 1300. In 1464 it was given by James II to Giovanni Loredano. Note the small 15C **tower** in the former Turkish part of the village. The long narrow recess on the west side, which extends from the door sill to the top of the tower, probably housed the drawbridge. In the dome of **Ayios Mamas** there is a fine representation of the **Pantokrator** with a frieze of angels beneath it. Most of the frescoes, which once ornamented the interior of the church, have been whitewashed over.

Kophinou, now inhabited by Greek Cypriots, is an ancient village. It was formerly a Turkish Cypriot enclave. The crumbling houses near the disused mosque are a reminder of the gratuitous attack by Grivas on the Turkish inhabitants in November 1967.

Limassol

Highlights
Limassol Castle, Folk Art Museum, Limassol District Archaeological Museum

Surpassed in size only by Nicosia, Limassol (135,000 inhabitants) has become, since the Turkish occupation of Famagusta in 1974, the busiest port on the island. During the last three decades it has tripled in size largely because of the influx of Greek Cypriot refugees. It is an active, working town centred on its harbour and apart from the castle and its museums has, at first sight, few obvious attractions for holidaymakers. However, on the northern outskirts there are pretty little hill villages, like Monagri, to visit and explore. Monagri, surrounded by vineyards and the home of artists and writers, is also the place where the excellent Menargos wines are produced. Visitors are made very welcome by the vineyard owners and may sample and buy some of their products. For those interested in Cyprus' past there are the ruins of ancient Amathus 10km to the east and of Kourion 13km to the west. A stroll through the old town with its market hall and myriad small shops and local restaurants will amuse flâneurs of all ages. Limassol has a Carnival in the spring, an Arts Festival in July and a Wine Festival in September. Finally, its inhabitants have a well-merited reputation for friendliness and hospitality.

A wide variety of products—including fruit and vegetables from the hinterland—is exported from Limassol. Industries include carob grinding and wine and spirit production. It is the nearest town to the British base at Akrotiri so, not surprisingly, off duty soldiers seek their amusements here. Modern Limassol has grown well beyond Makarios III Av. which was intended to take traffic away from the town centre. As a consequence it has been necessary to construct a second by-pass farther north.

■ Practical information

Tourist office
There are tourist offices near the castle and old harbour and at the ferry terminal in the new harbour. **Open** every day in the morning (except Sunday) and on Monday, Tuesday, Thursday and Friday afternoons.

Accommodation
Most of the hotels catering for mass tourism are concentrated on the east side of the town near ancient Amathus. Amongst these are **Amathus Beach**, ☎ (05) 321152. fax: (05) 327494, **Four Seasons**, ☎ (05) 310222. fax: (05) 310887). **Hawaii Beach**, ☎ (05) 311333. fax: (05) 311888, **Le Meridien Limassol**, ☎ (05) 634000. fax: (05) 634222, **Limassol Sheraton**, ☎ (05) 321100. fax: (05) 324394 and **Poseidonia Beach Hotel**, ☎ (05) 321000. fax: (05) 327040. All have 5 stars. Limassol **has** eight 4-star and 11 3-star hotels. Good reports have been received of the **Churchill Limassol**, ☎ (05) 324444. fax: (05) 323494

which is near the town centre, and the **Curium Palace**, ☎ (05) 363121, fax: (05) 359293, which is close to the Archaeological Museum. Both have 4 stars.

Recommended is the friendly, well-run 3-star **Arsinoe**, ☎ (05) 321444, fax: (05) 329908 near Amathus. In addition to the hotels there are many guest houses and apartment hotels. A full list of these may be obtained from the Tourist Offices. Try the **Helias Guest House**, ☎ (05) 363841 in the town centre near the Municipal Market.

Restaurants
There is a wide variety of restaurants in Limassol offering Cypriot and International cuisine. Recommended are the restaurant **L'Onda Beach Hotel**, ☎ (05) 321821 and fish restaurants near the old harbour like **Glaros**, ☎ (05) 357046.

Post office
There are three post offices in Limassol. The one used most frequently by visitors is near the town hall and the municipal market.

Transport
Long distance buses. Bus services to Nicosia and Paphos are provided by two companies: **Costas**, 9b Thessalonikis St. and **Kemek** from the corner of Enoseos and Eirinis streets; to Larnaca by **Kallenos Bus Co.**, from the corner of Spyrou Araouzou and Hadjipavlou streets.

Local buses. The most useful local bus is the no 30 which links the new harbour area at the west end of the town with Amathus at the east. The Episkopi bus from Limassol castle will take you to Kourion. Buses for Kolossi castle leave from the bus stop near the municipal market.

Shared taxis. For Nicosia and Paphos—**Kypros** from 49 Spyrou Araouzou St.; **Karydas** and **Kyriakos** from 21 Thessalonikis St. For Larnaca—**Makris** from 166 Hellas St. or **Acropolis** from the Kypros office.

Car Hire. Firms including Europcar and Eurodollar provide car hire services. A full list is obtainable from the Tourist Offices.

Boat trips to Egypt and Israel. Two day whirlwind cruises to Egypt and Israel are offered by Louis Cruise Lines and Ambassador Cruises. The emphasis is on boisterous diversions—night clubs and casinos—rather than museums. Bookings may be made with travel agencies or at hotels.

Religious services
Orthodox: Several churches including the Katholiki, near the Bishopric, Ayia Napa in Ayiou Andreou St., and Ayios Antonios near the sea front. **Roman Catholic**: Ayia Ekaterini near the junction of Jerousalim St. and the sea front. **Anglican**: St Barnabas at 177 Archiepiskopou Leontiou I St. **Armenian**: St George in Vasili Michailidi St.

History
The origins of Limassol are obscure. Ancient tombs have been found in the area and a cemetery of c 1600 BC discovered at **Ayia Phyla**, now a suburb. However, it was a place of little importance until nearby **Amathus** and **Kourion** began to decline as the result of a series of disastrous earthquakes in the 4C AD.

It was the see of the late 6C Bishop Leontios, later St Leontios, who wrote a *Life of St John the Almoner*. Born in Amathus, St John became patriarch of Alexandria in Egypt. Because of his efforts to redress social evils by alms-giving he acquired his sobriquet. It is said that one of his first acts as bishop was to distribute 80,000 gold pieces to monasteries and hospitals. He was the patron saint of the Knights Hospitaller.

After defeating the tyrannical, self-styled Emperor of Cyprus, Isaac Comnenus, Richard Coeur de Lion married Berengaria of Navarre on 12 May 1191 perhaps, as a local tradition would have us believe, in the fort of Limassol. Later on the same day she was crowned Queen of England by John, Bishop of Evreux. Alas, Berengaria was soon neglected by her new husband, as it appears Richard preferred to spend his days—and nights—with his comrades in arms.

The Emperor Frederick II Hohenstaufen landed here in 1228 en route to Acre and was met by a delegation of Cypriot nobles. He paused long enough on his return journey the following year to see his ward, Henry I of Cyprus, married to a daughter of the Marquis of Montferrat.

During the reign of the Lusignans the Orthodox Church lost most of its possessions and came under the control of the Catholic Church. This process culminated in 1260 with the issue of the **Bulla Cypria** of Pope Alexander IV which made the Catholic archbishop the supreme ecclesiastical ruler on the island. His authority extended over both Catholics and Orthodox. It was during this period that the Orthodox bishop of Limassol was banished to Lefkara in 1222.

After the fall of Acre to the Saracens in 1291 Limassol came under the protection of the Knights Templar and Knights Hospitaller, both military religious orders. It was then a partially walled town. Under Lusignan rule and protected by the the Knights, it flourished. Its vineyards were cultivated by the Knights Hospitaller. The order's headquarters in Cyprus at Kolossi Castle, the *Grande Commanderie*, gave its name to the island's most famous wine, **Commandaria**. (See the section on wine on page 36.)

The Hospitallers, known variously as the Knights of St John of Jerusalem, the Knights of Rhodes or the Knights of Malta, originated in a hospital in Jerusalem dedicated to their patron saint, John the Almoner. There they cared for sick and needy pilgrims. In 1113 they received papal approval as an order of canons regular. After the fall of Jerusalem to the Saracens in 1187, they moved their headquarters to Acre. There they continued to nurse the sick, to guard the roads, and to fight. Like the Knights Templar, the Hospitallers grew rich and powerful. After the capture of Acre in 1291, they moved first to Cyprus and in 1310 to Rhodes, which they defended successfully in 1480 against an attack by the Ottomans, but were obliged to surrender in 1522 to Süleyman the Magnificent. Given Malta in 1530 by the Emperor Charles V, they held it against later Turkish assaults. Following the defeat of the Turks at the battle of Lepanto in 1571, the order devoted itself to hospital work and continued to rule Malta until Napoleon I ousted it in 1798.

It was from Limassol that in 1306 the last Grand Master of the Templars, Jacques de Molay, made his fateful journey to Paris. The Knights Templar, sometimes known as the Poor Knights of Christ or the Knights of the

Temple of Solomon were members of a religious order established in 1118 by nine French knights to protect pilgrims to the Holy Land. They soon acquired a reputation for prowess and daring. Accumulating great wealth in the course of time, they became the subject of much envy and were persecuted in the early 14C by Philip IV of France. Jacques de Molay and other leading members of the Order were falsely accused of idolatry, unbelief and foul practices and were burned at the stake as relapsed heretics in 1314.

After the departure of the Knights from Cyprus, Limassol was devastated by the Genoese in 1373 and ravaged by the Saracens in 1426. During the early decades of the 15C it was repeatedly sacked by Egyptian sea raiders and in 1539 it was despoiled by the Turks.

It also suffered earthquake damage. Felix Faber, a Dominican friar from Ulm, who visited Cyprus in 1480 remarked that only 'one wretched church remains standing, without bells ... A few Latin clergy still live there'. In 1553 a certain John Locke observed that the 'towne is ruinated and nothing in it worth writing [about], save onely in mids of the towne there hath been a fortresse, which is now decayed, and the walls part overthrowen'. He also noticed a great number of locusts. Thirty-six years later another traveller, the Seigneur de Villamont of the Duchy of Brittany, described its poor single-storey houses as being 'built chiefly of earth covered with rushes', all the previous habitations having been destroyed in the serious earthquake of 1584. The doors of these houses were so low that one had to stoop to go in. This was done deliberately 'so that Turks on horseback or an angry crowd may not enter'.

During the period of Ottoman rule the castle was garrisoned. As the economy of Larnaca grew, that of Limassol tended to decline. In 1815 that peripatetic diplomat, William Turner described it as 'a miserable town, consisting of 150 mud houses, of which 100 are Greeks, and 50 Turks; yet of the fifty shiploads of wine which Cyprus exports annually, twenty are on an average despatched from Limassol'. In the late 19C matters improved. Wine and carob exports grew considerably. A new pier was completed in 1881. In recent years a modern port and ship-repair yards have been constructed in the southwest part of the town.

Limassol Castle

Near the west end of the rather unattractive **Promenade** is Limassol Castle. Set in a small garden, it is now the **Medieval Museum** and houses a representative collection of objects relating to the history of the town.

■ Open Monday to Friday 07.30 to 17.00; Saturday 09.00 to 17.00; Sunday 10.00 to 13.00.

The present building, which replaced the fort built by the Templars, dates from the 13C with some 14C alterations. The surrounding wall is 16C. The original structure had two floors connected by a spiral staircase. In the late 14C the interior was rebuilt. The keep was turned into the lofty hall seen today and a cellar was added. The central pillar supporting the vault of the Great Hall collapsed and part of the castle was demolished in 1525. After 1570 it became a Turkish

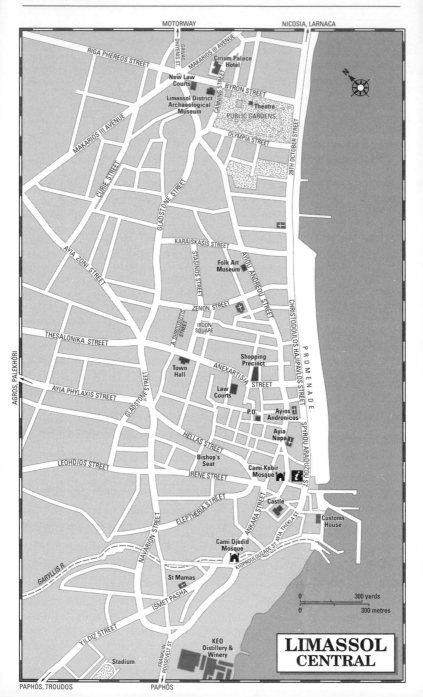

MOTORWAY

NICOSIA, LARNACA

RIGA PHEREOS STREET

MAKARIOS III AVENUE

Cirium Palace Hotel

New Law Courts

BYRON STREET

CANNING STREET

Theatre

Limassol District Archaeological Museum

PUBLIC GARDENS

OLYMPIA STREET

MAKARIOS III AVENUE

CURIE STREET

GLADSTONE STREET

28TH OCTOBER STREET

AYIA ZONI STREET

KARAISKASIS STREET

STASINOS STREET

Folk Art Museum

AVTOU ANDREOU STREET

ZENON STREET

A. DIMITRIOTIS STREET

IRODN SQUARE

THESALONIKA STREET

CHRISTODOULOS HAJIPAVLOS STREET

P R O M E N A D E

Shopping Precinct

Town Hall

ANEXARTISIA STREET

AYIA PHYLAXIS STREET

Law Courts

GLADSTONE STREET

P.O.

Ayios Andronicos

LEOHDIOS STREET

Ayia Napa

SPYROU ARAOUZOU ST.

HELLAS STREET

Bishop's Seat

IRENE STREET

Cami Kebir Mosque

i

ELEFTHERIA STREET

NAVARION STREET

Castle

ANKARA STREET

Customs House

Cami Djedid Mosque

KIOPROULOUZADE ST. AYIA THEKLA ST.

GARYLLIS R.

St Mamas

ISMET PASHA

AGROS PALEKHORI

YILDIZ STREET

KEO Distillery & Winery

0   300 yards

0   300 metres

Stadium

FRANKLIN ROOSEVELT ST.

PAPHOS, TROUDOS

PAPHOS

LIMASSOL CENTRAL

redoubt and a number of buildings were constructed on the roof. It served as a prison from c 1800 and continued to be used for that purpose by the British until 1910. In 1950 a considerable amount of restoration took place. This revealed a male skeleton 1.8m tall, the remains, perhaps, of a soldier who died fighting the Genoese in the 14C. A macabre collection of bones, every one of which was broken, is thought to have belonged to a traitor who opened the gates of the fortress to the Mamelukes in 1425/26.

There are fine views of the town and harbour from the roof of the castle. Begin your visit to the museum in the garden where there is an olive oil press in working order.

Great Hall. A fine collection of 14C tombstones and carvings.

Ground Floor. Lusignan and Venetian tombstones recovered from an Augustinian friary which was converted into a mosque after the Ottoman conquest. Note the finely carved representations of the deceased.

First Floor. Armour and stone carvings from various early Christian churches. In the display cases oil lamps and coins. In the cells there are collections of fine Ottoman pottery, gold, silver and bronze objects for religious and domestic use.

A short distance to the northeast of the castle and near the market is the **Cami Kebir** which is still used by Limassol's Moslem community. The original mosque, built in the 16C, was destroyed by a flood in 1894. The present building displays a rather unhappy mixture of architectrual styles.

Another mosque, now closed, stands at the west end of Ankara St. in what was once the Turkish quarter of the town. This overlooked the usually dry bed of the **Garyllis River**.

To the east of Cami Kebir is **Ayia Napa**. A rather ugly building, completed in 1903, this replaced a simple church of 1738 whose walls were covered with murals. A number of icons from the older building may be seen in the apse. Only one is dated, that of Christ in Glory. This was painted by the priest Joannikou in 1740. The interior of the modern church is garish in the extreme.

In the churchyard is buried, Esther Harriet, the infant daughter of an English eccentric, the Reverend Joseph Wolff, who visited Cyprus in 1828. The Rev. Wolff, the son of a rabbi, was born in Germany. Becoming a Roman Catholic while a student at Weimar, he later embraced Protestantism and became a missionary in the Near East. His extraordinary behaviour endeared him to the local people. During his travels in Uzbekistan in west central Asia he entered the city of Bokhara in surplice and mortar board reading an Anglican service. He was treated with the kindness and respect traditionally shown by Moslems to the mad.

Ayios Andronicos, built in 1870 in the Byzantine style, is just off the seafront to the east. In the chapel of St Mamas there is a late 17C carved, gilded iconostasis.

Continue along Ayiou Andreou to the **Folk Art Museum** which is housed in a fine town house.

■ Open Monday to Friday from 08.30 to 13.30 and on Monday, Tuesday, Wednesday and Friday from 15.00 to 17.30; June to September 16.00 to 18.30.

In the hall there are four beautifully carved chests. These *kasella* or *sentouki* were usually made of walnut or cypress and contained the household linen which a bride took to her new home. Note the plates from Iznik in Turkey in the ticket office. **Rooms 2** and **5** are devoted to weaving. In **Rooms 3** and **4** there are examples of traditional village costumes and, in **Room 4**, terracottas. **Room 8** is fitted out as a village kitchen. Among the household implements is a seal which impressed the sign of the cross on homebaked bread.

To the east, just off the seafront, is the Roman Catholic church of **Ayia Ekaterini**. In this church Mass is celebrated on Sunday in English, in Arabic and in Greek for Uniat Catholics. The Uniat Catholic Church is in communion with the Roman Catholic Church but retains its own languages, rites, and codes of canon law. Note the quartered Red Cross, the heraldic emblem of the Catholic Patriarch of Jerusalem, in the colonnade. There are some good modern frescoes of saints of the Eastern and Western Churches in the apse.

Limassol District Archaeological Museum

Behind the **Municipal Gardens** is the Limassol District Archaeological Museum.

■ Open Monday to Friday from 07.30 to 17.00; Saturday 09.00 to 17.00; Sunday 10.00 to 13.00.

In the garden there is a **Roman mosaic** of Venus and Cupid bathing, and a rather haphazard collecton of architectural fragments and statuary. Curiously, there is also a **sundial** which once belonged to Lord Kitchener. The following is a brief description of the principal objects in the museum. Note: from time to time objects may be moved to new locations in the building.

Room 1. Finds from a cave at Akrotiri which date from c 8500 BC. These provide the earliest evidence of the presence of man in Cyprus. Axeheads and various implements from the Neolithic and Chalcolithic I periods. Shards and tools from Sotira and Erimi. Neolithic II and Chalcolithic idols and querns. Bronze Age ceramics, including a fine rectangular bowl. Late Cypriot and Mycenaean pottery. Cypro-Geometric ware. Cypro-Archaic ware. Imported jugs decorated with figures. Hellenistic and Graeco-Roman ware. A range of pottery from 3000 BC to the 13C AD from the Limassol area. 12C BC to 4C AD pottery from Amathus, and from Kourion dating from 2300 BC to 4C AD. Six amphorae of 2300 BC and three dinoi, ie, drinking cups.

Room 2. Statuettes, lamps and glassware. Terracotta figurines with ear perforations. Model chariots. Cylinder-seals. Jewellery dating from the 17C BC to the 4C AD. Shell necklaces, ivories, and objects of steatite. Glass, alabaster objects, lamps, and limestone statuettes. Note the representation of a poppy on a pottery ring. Two cases display coins found in the district. These include a bronze coin of the Emperor Caracalla, AD 198 to 217, which shows the Temple of Aphrodite at Palea Paphos and gold solidi of the Emperor Heraclius, AD 610 to 641, and of his son and co-emperor Heraclius Constantine, AD 613 to 41. Other objects include razors and fibulae, a bronze bull, bronze mirrors, a strigil and a collection of amulets.

Room 3. Two 6C BC capitals from Amathus. A Hellenistic capital with the head of the Egyptian goddess Hathor, the divine mother. Statues of the grotesque Egyptian god Bes and of Artemis-Hekate. The lower part of a statue of a cross-legged figure found at Amathus. A 4C AD bearded head from Phasoula. Funerary stelae, including the 2C BC stele, decorated with two rosettes, of Theotime, daughter of Apollonios. Two cippi. A round marble table from Kourion on a limestone base from Amathus. A 4C AD headless statue of Zeus holding an eagle. Terracotta busts, including sphinxes supporting cups. A bull-masked figure. Sarcophagi. Delicate Tanagra-type figurines. Roman and Phoenician glass.

East of Limassol ~ Amathus and beyond

Highlights
Amathus, Panayia Iamatiki, Monastery of Ayios Yeoryios Alamano

Amathus
The site of the ancient city of Amathus is c 11km east of Limassol on the north side of the coastal road

■ Open daily from 07.30 to 17.00 (07.30 to 19.30 in summer).

Although little remains to be seen, the place was important and merits a visit. Amathus, which was occupied from c 1000 BC to the 12C AD, played a not unimportant part in the history of Cyprus. Spoliation of the city began during the period of Venetian rule when the last bishop pulled down the church of St Tykhonas and sold the stones to the Franks. This unfortunate precedent was repeated later. Much of the fine building stone was removed in the 19C and taken to Larnaca and the site was systematically robbed of its archaeological treasures by Cesnola and others. The cemetery was excavated by a British Museum expedition in 1893 and 1894. Excavations of the agora and the acropolis continue.

History
According to legend Amathus was founded by Cinyras, the son of Apollo and Paphos, who came to Cyprus from Asia, possibly from Byblos. He was said to have brought the cult of Aphrodite to the island. At Amathus Aphrodite was worshipped as Kypria, the goddess of Cyprus. Cinyras was a cunning man. He promised Agamemnon that he would send 50 ships to Troy, but he fitted just one—and 49 miniature terracotta boats—which were launched at the same time. Adonis was the product of the incestuous union of Cinyras and his daughter Zmyrna. As a punishment she was transformed into the myrrh tree.

Buses return to Limassol at 11.50, 14.50 and 15.50. Single tickets cost 60 Cents. Please check the current position, as departure times—in both directions—and fares may change. From the entrance to the site, the buses continue to Kourion beach, where there are several tavernas.

History

Although this part of the island has been inhabited since the middle of the fifth millennium BC—there is a Neolithic site at **Sotira**, 6km to the north, a Chalcolithic I site at **Erimi**, 3km to the northeast, and a Middle Bronze Age site at nearby **Phaneromeni**—the first settlement here probably dates from about the mid-second millennium BC. According to Herodotus, Argive colonists established Kourion and named it after Koureus, the son of Cinyras, traditionally the first king to reign in Cyprus (see Amathus). Evidence has been found of an Achaean settlement on the slopes of the Bamboula ridge. It would seem that the Achaeans came here in the 13C BC and that they were followed by a second wave after the Dorian invasion of Greece in the 12C BC.

The city played an important part in the rebellion of Onesilus against the Persians in 498 BC, but by changing sides at a crucial moment Stasanor, king of Kourion, helped the Persians to take Salamis and thus gain control of the island. Later, Pasicrates, the last King of Kourion, supported Alexander the Great with his fleet at the siege of Tyre in 332 BC.

Kourion retained its prosperity under the Ptolemys and the Romans. The geographer Strabo wrote in the last century BC, '...it is the starting-point of the western course aiming at Rhodes; very near it is a promontary from which they hurl those who have touched the altar of Apollo.'

It would appear that Kourion had early contact with Christianity. The 5C apocryphal Acts of Barnabas relates that the Apostle and his companion, Mark, were not allowed to enter the city. They were shocked to see a group of naked men and women assembled for a race. Later many of the citizens became Christians and one of its bishops, Philoneides, was martyred under Diocletian (285 to 305). Despite the fact that the city had suffered badly from earthquakes in the second half of the 4C AD, a basilica was erected at the beginning of the 5C. At the Council of Ephesus in AD 431 Bishop Zeno of Kourion obtained a favourable decision on the claim of the Church of Cyprus to be independent. Like its neighbours, Kourion suffered badly from the attacks of Arab pirates in the mid-7C and the bishop was obliged to move. His new place of residence began to be called Episkopi as a consequence. Kourion declined into insignificance and its see was suppressed by the Latins in 1222.

In 1876 Kourion was explored by General Luigi Palma di Cesnola. He claimed to have discovered near the theatre the superb hoard of gold and silver jewellery of various dates known as the Curium Treasure which was later sold to the Metropolitan Museum of New York. Cesnola's claim caused endless controversy. It has been argued that the treasure was the result of his ransacking various tombs throughout the island during the previous decade and that the area said to have been dug over by him had in fact been undisturbed.

Systematic excavation of the site began in 1933 with the work of George

McFadden and was continued by Dr B.H. Hill on behalf of the University of Pennsylvania Museum. After the war work was restarted by the Cypriot Department of Antiquities and various American institutions.

Entrance to the site is by the place where the **Paphos Gate** probably stood. Immediately to the left of the road is the **House of the Achilles Mosaic**. This had an open courtyard with a portico at the north end and rooms on either side. It has been suggested that it was used for the entertainment of distinguished visitors. It has been dated to the 4C AD. The mosaic, which gives the house its name, formed part of the pavement of the colonnaded portico. Achilles was told that, if he did not go to Troy, he would have a long, but inglorious, life. So, disguised as a maiden, he went to live in the court of king Lycomedes of Scyros. Odysseus, told by the soothsayer Calchas, that Troy could not be captured without the help of the hero, went in search of him. The mosaic shows the moment when Achilles inadvertently reveals his identity to Odysseus by choosing some weapons from a pedlar's pack made up mainly of embroidery implements. A smaller mosaic in an adjoining room shows the **Rape of Ganymede** Zeus conceived a violent infatuation for Ganymede and the mosaic shows the king of the gods, disguised as an eagle, carrying the handsome youth away to Olympos.

There is a section of the Roman aqueduct, one of two which supplied the city with water, by the side of the building.

Across the road from the Custodian's Office there are some new excavations. These have revealed part of a large **Hellenistic building** and to the south west a **stoa** measuring 65m by 4.5m. Believed to date from the beginning of the 3C AD, it probably formed part of the Roman forum. An Early Christian structure was built over it in the early part of the 5C AD. Part of a 1C AD **nymphaeum** was also laid bare.

The **House of Gladiators** gets its name from a mosaic in the peristyle court-

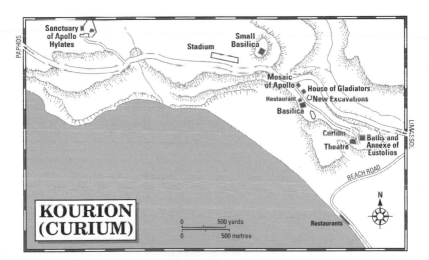

yard which has two panels showing gladiators. In the northern mosaic Hellenikos and Margaritis are depicted taking part in a practice bout with blunt weapons. In the central, damaged panel a gladiator, named Lytras, is shown moving menacingly towards another armed figure. Standing between them is a richly garbed, unarmed man, named Darius, who appears to be trying to restrain Lytras. There was probably a third panel which was lost when the house collapsed.

Just beyond the Tourist Pavilion are the ruins of an **Early Christian cathedral**, 70m long by 40m wide, which was probably erected in the 5C. On the north side there was a 6C **baptistery**. On the west there was a large courtyard with a hexagonal water tank in the centre. Flanking this was the **diakonikon** where worshippers left their offerings. To the north of the diakonikon was the bishop's residence. A wide **narthex** led to the central nave of the cathedral, which was reserved for baptised Christians, and to the side aisles where the catachumens worshipped. Four columns in the chancel supported a baldachino over the altar. The roof of the nave and the aisles were supported by two rows of 12 granite columns with marble bases and capitals. There was a single apse. Traces of the mosaic pavement remain.

The atrium of the baptistery, which is in a better state of preservation than the cathedral, was surrounded by marble colonnades. Only one column survives. The remains of several smaller columns seem to indicate the existence of an upper colonnade. In the centre of the atrium there was an octagonal fountain. The baptistery had a narthex, a nave and two side aisles. The **baptismal font** was in a recess on the south side. In a room on the west side of the font the catachumens undressed before being baptised by immersion.

Some evidence of an earlier structure on the site suggests that the cathedral may have been constructed from the ruins of a large pagan building which was destroyed, possibly by the earthquakes of 332 and 342.

The 2C AD **Roman theatre** of Kourion occupies a splendid position on the high ground at the southern end of the site. It replaced a smaller, 2C BC Greek theatre which had a circular orchestra and whose cavea was greater than 180 degrees. The present structure was excavated in 1949 to 1950 and partly restored in the following years. The cavea, which has a seating capacity of 3500, is divided into five cunei. There is a single diazoma two-thirds of the way up. At the top of the cavea there was a roofed colonnade. Only fragments of the elaborate skene remain. Access to the theatre was by stepped passages from the street at the back and by two vomitoria. Subsidence made it necessary to construct several buttresses at the east side of the analemma. When contests between men and wild animals became popular in the early 3C AD, some of the seats near the orchestra were removed and a metal grill erected to protect spectators. Later in that century the contests ceased and plays were again presented. The theatre was abandoned in the 4C and subsequently served as a useful source of cut stone.

Public performances of music and drama are given in Kourion theatre during the summer months. Details of these presentations are available from Tourist Offices.

At a slightly higher level are the **Baths and Annexe of Eustolios**. This palatial structure was originally built c 360 AD in the reign of Valens as a private villa. However, sometime in the early years of the 5C AD during the reign of

Theodosius II and after the destruction of the theatre and when Christianity had become firmly established in the city, it appears to have become a club or a public place of rest and recreation. Its mosaic floors were not laid until then.

Entrance to the complex was by way of a **vestibule** on the west side. This has a welcoming message on a floor mosaic (now damaged), 'Enter ... and good luck to the house'. Beyond was a rectangular garden courtyard which had a pool and fountain. On three sides of the courtyard there were porticoes with mosaic floors. An inscription here states that Eustolios built the baths and 'this cool refuge sheltered from the winds', a reference to Apollo, the former genius loci of Kourion. Another inscription, written in Homeric verse, is Christian in content, ' In place of big walls and solid iron, bright bronze and even adamant, this house has girt itself with the much venerated symbols of Christ'.

Steps lead up to the **baths**. In the long narrow centre room there is a floor mosaic with four colourful panels. One shows a partridge, another a bust of **Ktisis**, a female figure who personifies Construction or Foundation. She holds an object which may be a standard cubit measure in her right hand. This is c 29.3cm long and some commentators have pointed out that this is almost the length of the late standard Roman foot. To the east and north were the **frigidaria**, each with a shallow foot-bath. To the west were the **tepidarium** and the **caldarium**. Note the built-in basins in the latter. Here too were the chambers which served the heating system.

To the north of the baths there is a large water-storage tank.

The 2C AD **stadium**, partially uncovered between 1939 and 1947 by archaeologists from Pennsylvania University Museum, is c 1km to the west. There were three entrances, one on each of the long sides and one at the centre of the rounded end. The stadium had a capacity of c 6000. A small part of the seating has been reconstructed. The stadium ceased to be used at the beginning of the 5C AD.

A small late 5C **basilica**, c 200m to the east of the stadium, has been excavated by the Department of Antiquities. This had an atrium with four porticoes, a narthex, a nave and three aisles. During the Middle Ages a kiln to make lime from the marble ornamentation of the church was built in the centre of the atrium.

A sign-posted track leads from the main road to the **Sanctuary of Apollo Hylates**, Apollo of the Forest. 'Hylates' may be derived from υλη, forest or woodland, and the site is still surrounded by attractive woods which in ancient times formed a deer forest. However, the name may also originate from a fusion between Apollo and the Cypriot Hylates, the god of the woods. The existing buildings,

The partially restored Sanctuary of Apollo Hylates

which date from c 100 AD, were destroyed by earthquakes, probably in the mid 4C. The walls of some structures, which had replaced those demolished by an earthquake of AD 76 to 77, were found lying flat on the ground and have been re-erected. Artefacts from the site show that the cult of Apollo had been celebrated here from as early as the 8C BC and that it continued until the 4C AD. The site was excavated by the Pennsylvania University Museum between 1934 and 1954.

There were two entrances to the Sanctuary, the Paphos Gate on the west and the Kourion Gate on the east. Take the path from the Guardian's lodge, by the site of the **Paphos Gate**, to a paved area. Steps, partly restored, on the left lead to the poorly-preserved **northwest building**. This consisted of two long chambers with a central area separated from raised platforms by a line of Doric columns. These may have been used to accommodate visitors or to display votive offerings made to the god.

To the south, across the paved area, behind a partly preserved Doric portico which extended to the Kourion Gate, are five large rooms separated from each other by corridors. In each room a raised platform on three sides is divided from the central paved area by Doric colonnades. The middle room has been partly restored. Similarities in the design of this **south building** with that to the northwest suggest that it may have been used for the same purpose. According to an inscription over the door to one of the rooms, two of them were erected in AD 101 by Trajan.

Opposite the Doric portico and not far from the Kourion Gate there was a **bothros** or **votive pit** into which offerings to the god were reverently placed from time to time so as to make room for later ex votos. Many fine terracotta figurines, including some of horsemen, and pottery from the 5C BC were discovered here by the excavators. Two terracotta figurines found in the sanctuary are now in the British Museum. Dating from c 650 to 600 BC they are of two priests putting on ritual bulls' masks before taking part in a religious ceremony.

The small early 1C AD **Temple of Apollo** was approached by a paved sacred street which ran in a north/south direction. Destroyed by the earthquake of AD 364 to 365, it has been partly restored with the help of the Leventis Foundation. It had a podium and tetrastyle façade of four columns with Nabataean, ie, simplified Corinthian capitals. A broad flight of steps led up to the **cella** which housed the altar mentioned by Strabo. According to him those who dared to touch it were flung over the cliffs of Kourion. This temple replaced a Late Classical or Hellenistic rectangular sanctuary. The base of the existing structure belongs to the earlier building.

A short distance to the south of the temple is the **Archaic Altar Precinct**. Votive offerings, which antedate those found in the bothros, were discovered here. They include a fragment of a 6C to 5C BC bronze belt with repoussé decoration showing two lions devouring a griffin, miniature gold and silver figurines of bulls and a quantity of pottery. All date from the 8C to the early 5C BC.

The buildings south of the Archaic Altar Precinct may have accommodated the officiating priests and housed the treasury. Note the barred windows (a reconstruction) on the putative treasury building.

To the southwest of the temple are the remains of a curious structure which the archaeologists have called the **Circular Monument** and which is the only one of its kind found in Cyprus. Dated to the 6C BC this is a circular walkway covered with a pebble and mortar floor. In the centre seven pits have been cut into the rock. The walkway may have been used for processions or for ritual dances held in honour of Apollo Hylates around a grove of sacred trees rooted in the pits. During the Roman period a monumental entrance through the temenos wall was added on the northwest side and a simpler entrance made from the sacred street.

The **palaestra**, sited to the north of the Kourion Gate, has been tentatively dated to the Augustan period. In the north east corner there are the fragments of a large stone water jar used by the athletes. The adjoining Trajanic **baths** had, in addition to the usual arrangement of frigidarium, tepidarium and caldarium, two dressing rooms and an office for the bath attendant. Both the palaestra and the baths lay outside the precincts of the Sanctuary proper.

The Episkopi Cantonment, part of the **Western British Sovereign Base Area**, contains its HQ, housing for the personnel and various recreation facilities including polo and soccer fields, a stadium, beach, golf course and yacht club.

The village of **Evdhimou** was once walled and the centre of Lusignan and Venetian provinces. According to the 18C traveller Mariti it was one of the four cities built for Arsinoë by her brother Ptolemy Philadelphus. This seems unlikely. Until 1974 it was almost entirely a Turkish Cypriot village and built into the walls of its principal mosque are stones from an ancient church. The Mamelukes landed with over 3000 troops on the coast here in 1426.

At **Anoyira**, 3km northwest of Evdhimou, there is the site of a Chalcolithic II cemetery. On the right of the approach road to the village there are several ancient churches. These include the deserted late Byzantine monastery of **Timios Stavros** in which there are some interesting tombs. Opposite the church are the foundations of a small **Roman temple**. Farther on is the late 18C church of **Arkhangelos Michael** which has a women's gallery and an unusual sundial on the south wall. This probably came from an earlier building.

North of the main road are three villages **Ayios Thomas**, **Plataniskia** and **Alekhtora** which were abandoned by their Turkish Cypriot communities and are now occupied by Greek Cypriots. Alekhtora must have been of some importance in medieval times to judge by the number of ruins in the vicinity. The best preserved is **Ayios Kassianos**, c 2km to the northeast, where a 4C German saint of that name is said to be buried.

South of the main road, on the way to Pissouri, is Ayios Yeoryios which once had some interesting murals. Alas, they have been destroyed by smoke from the fires which shepherds lit in the interior.

On the way to Pissouri Bay, which is being developed as a resort, is **Ayios Mavrikios** set among vineyards. This was probably a Latin chapel dedicated to St Maurice. **Pissouri village**, from its lofty vantage on a cliff 245m high, commands extensive views.

East of Paphos

Highlights
Geroskipou Museum of Folk Art, Palaepaphos and Petra tou Romiou

Geroskipou

Geroskipou, a corruption of ιεροσκεπος, the Sacred Garden (of Aphrodite), is believed to have been a stopping place on the processional route from Nea Paphos to the sanctuary of the goddess at Palaepaphos. According to Gunnis there were the remains of a small Roman temple—a scatter of marble capitals and Corinthian columns—near the church. The town dates mainly from the Byzantine era.

There is a disputed tradition that the vineyards of Engadi, which are mentioned in the Bible, were located here. (A district north of Paphos also claims that honour.) Ludolf, a priest from Suchen in Westphalia, who visited Cyprus between 1336 and 1341, located them rather vaguely 'in the province of Paphos'. In the account of his travels, *De Terra Sancta et itinere Ihierosol*, he wrote: 'In this vineyard grow vines and clusters of many kinds, some of which produce grapes of the bigness of plums, others small grapes like peas … It belonged to the Templars, and more than a hundred Saracen captives were daily therein… And so we read of it in the Song of Songs "my beloved is unto me as a cluster (of Cyprus) in the vineyard of Engadi".'

Now almost a suburb of Paphos, Geroskipou has a few pleasant tavernas, a number of bars and a profusion of tourist shops. It is famous for its *Loukoumi*, ie, Turkish Delight.

After raising the siege of Acre, Royal Navy Commodore Sir William Sidney Smith came to Cyprus in 1799. At Geroskipou he met a youth from Cephalonia, one Andreas Zimbulaki. Struck by the boy's intelligence he appointed him British Vice-Consul. To show his appreciation, Zimbulaki adopted his patron's name and thereafter called himself Haji Smith.

The five domed Byzantine church of **Ayia Paraskevi** dates from the middle of the 9C. A vaulted building with three domes over the nave and one over each side aisle, its somewhat unusual design is found in only one other place in Cyprus, at Peristerona to the west of Nicosia. The quatrefoil structure to the south of the apse may have been a baptistery or a chantry chapel. The presence, until recently, of a medieval tomb suggests the latter. Nearby is a cave from which a spring, perhaps connected with the worship of Aphrodite, once gushed forth.

On the central dome of the church there is a late 15C representation of the Blessed Virgin *orans*, with the Christ Child. A fine 15/16C processional icon with the B.V.M. on the obverse and a depiction of the Crucifixion on the reverse was found hidden in a field near the church.

The **Museum of Folk Art**, in the house once occupied by Haji Smith, is **open** Moday to Friday from 07.30 to 14.30 and on Thursday 07.30 to 18.00 (not July, August). This doubled as the British Consulate from 1799 to 1864. On the ground floor there is a collection of domestic and farming implements. These include looms, bread boards—planks with saucer shaped depressions—cotton crushers, sieves of silk, a spinning-wheel, threshing boards and a pair of eel catching tongs. The upper floor has a colourful display of Cypriot costumes: silk shirts, waistcoats—*ghilekko* and *zimbouni*—pantaloons, etc, also a painted bride's chest or *sandouki*. There are collections of decorative pottery and carved gourds, one depicting an elephant, another the bombing of a warship in 1940, a Cypriot lute made from a pumpkin gourd and a painted clock which once belonged to Michael de Vezin, British Consul at Larnaca who died in 1792.

Akhelia's name is probably derived from the medieval French L'Eschelle, meaning port, cf the use of the Italian 'La Scala' for Larnaca. It was a centre of the sugar industry of the Commandery of the Knights of Rhodes in the Middle Ages. The 16C basilica of **Ayios Yeoryios** was restored in 1742 to 1743 when the narthex was destroyed, probably by an earthquake. Most of the church's magnificent woodwork was sold at auction in London c 1900, but its late 16C to 17C icons remain in situ. **Ayios Theodosius** is a cruciform building of perhaps the 12C, barbarously modernised in 1932, but retaining some 15C murals. The altar in the south transept is made from a piece of Roman marble with egg and dart moulding. Some 2km to the south is a restored chapel dedicated to **Ayios Leonidas**. Roman columns and capitals, which once littered the area, are now in the Paphos Museum.

At **Timi** the former Byzantine church of **Ayia Sophia** was used as a mosque until 1975 and its frescoes were covered by layers of whitewash. Timi is famed for its cheese and sausages, *loukaniko*. Nearby is **Paphos International Airport**. At pebble strewn **Timi Beach** there are several tavernas.

Above the west door of **Mandria's** modern church of St Andronicos there is a curious marble capital with a female head in a wimple. This is believed to have come from a Latin convent. To the south west is the chapel of **Ayios Evresis**. Note the marble columns and other material from earlier structures. Between the chapel and the sea lies an ancient quarry, its rocks pierced by many vaulted tunnels.

Palaepaphos

A new approach road leads to the village of **Kouklia**, the site of **Palaepaphos** and the prominently positioned **Royal Manor of Couvoucle**.

History

The Birth of a Goddess. Idols of a fertility goddess dating from the Chalcolithic Period (3900/3800 to 2900/2500 BC) have been found at Palaepaphos. Artefacts discovered in tombs show that the place had achieved a degree of prosperity as early as the 16C BC. It appears that the worship of Aphrodite came to Cyprus from the east, but she was known as the 'Cyprian' as early as the 8C BC (Homer) and as the 'Paphian' in the 6C BC. Inscriptions at Palaepaphos call her simply 'Wanassa', the lady. This name is of great antiquity and widespread use. Found in Mycenaean Linear B texts, it was used on a 5C BC stele dedicated to Wanassa Preiia, Artemis of Perge, in Pamphylia Southern Turkey.

According to the 1C BC and 1C AD geographer Strabo (14.6.3) and the

2C AD traveller Pausanias (VIII.5.2) the sanctuary of Aphrodite at Palaepaphos was founded by Agapenor, leader of the Arcadian contingent, on his way home from Troy. However, an alternative tradition would accord that honour to the pre-Greek king Cinyras, son of Adonis, who is believed to have come to Cyprus from Syria (see Amathus). The priests of the sanctuary claimed to be descended from him (Tacitus. *Histories* 2.3). There is archaeological evidence in support of both legends. The existence of 11C chamber tombs and the discovery of a grave gift inscribed with the Greek name 'Opheltes' indicate the presence here of Achaean colonists. It may be that they adopted the worship of a native fertility goddess named Astort, the Canaanite form of Ishtar, which they Hellenised as Aphrodite. What is certain is that this place was the centre of the Cult of Aphrodite, the goddess of love, generation, and fertility from an early date.

In the *Theogony* (178 to 206) Hesiod gives a dramatic account of Aphrodite's birth:

> ... 'the hidden boy (Chronos) ... took
> The great long jagged sickle; eagerly
> He harvested his father's genitals
> And threw them all off behind.
> ... The genitals........
> Were carried for a long time on the waves.
> White foam surrounded the immortal flesh,
> And in it grew a girl ...
> Her name is Aphrodite among men
> And gods, because she grew up in the foam'. (Gr. αφρίζω, to foam)

Aphrodite was borne ashore on a shell by the soft breezes of the Zephyrs at the traditional place of her birth, the rocks known as Petra tou Romiou (see below). This myth, beloved by poets and painters alike, is memorably depicted in Botticelli's *Birth of Venus* in the Uffizi Gallery, Florence.

Homer, less dramatically, made Aphrodite the daughter of Zeus and the fresh water nymph, Dione, at whose bosom she would sometimes seek solace. (Il. 5.370–417).

The Sanctuary

■ Open from Monday to Friday 07.30 to 17.00 (summer 07.30 to 18.00); Saturday and Sunday 09.00 to 16.00 (summer 09.00 to 17.00).

Like Artemis of Perge, Aphrodite was worshipped in the form of a cone-shaped aniconic stone. This has survived and is now in the Cyprus Museum, Nicosia. Fragments of smaller marble cones, which may have been votive offerings, were found when the site was explored in 1888. A representation of part of the sanctuary appears on a bronze coin kept in the British Museum. Issued during the reign of Caracalla, AD 198 to 217, this shows the cult stone under a tower like-structure. A dove feeds in the foreground, others perch on the roof.

At the annual festival of the goddess there were games, musical and poetry contests. Participants, spectators and worshippers processed along the Sacred

Way from Nea Paphos to the sanctuary. It is believed that ritual prostitution took place at Palaepaphos. It was said that every young maiden went once in her life-time to the sanctuary to make love with a stranger. When a man had made his choice, he threw some money—the sum was not important—at the girl's feet and pronounced the ritual formula, 'I invoke the goddess upon you'. The beau-tiful and comely fulfilled their duty quickly, but ugly and ill-formed girls had to wait sometimes as long as four years! Pompeius Trogus, a Roman historian in the age of Augustus, mentions the existence of similar rites in Cyprus, but these took place on the seashore. (*Historiae Phillipicae.*) Memories of the sanctuary's lurid past remained in men's minds and continued to give rise to prurient stories. The mid 14C German priest Ludolf of Suchen wrote of pagan pilgrimages, where '....all ladies and damsels before their betrothal yielded themselves to men; for in Cyprus above all lands men are by nature most luxurious. For the soil of Cyprus....if a man sleep thereon, of its own self will all the night through provoke a man to lust'. This echoes the aphorism of the 1C AD Roman poet Martial, *Infamem nimio calore Cyprum,* 'Cyprus infamous through too much heat'.

The Sanctuary of Aphrodite flourished under the *Pax Romana.* It was honoured by several Roman emperors and visited by one who would later wear the purple. Titus, then quaestor en route to Egypt, consulted the oracle of Aphrodite in AD 69. He was told that he had a great future. The text of a Cypriote oath of allegiance to Tiberius has been found in the sanctuary.

With the spread of Christianity things began to change in the Empire. Many laws to discourage pagan practices were introduced. In November 397 the Count of the East was instructed to use the stones of destroyed pagan temples and shrines for the repair of bridges, roads and aqueducts and in 405 an impe-rial edict ordered the destruction of pagan temples, 'if there are any still untouched'. It is not known when the cult of Aphrodite at Palaepaphos was suppressed or if any resistance was made by the remaining pagans. The site appears to have been occupied up to the time of the Arab raids in the 7C. Once abandoned, it became, like so many others, a useful source of cut and shaped stone. During the Middle Ages building material taken from here was used to construct a sugar refinery near the Château de Couvoucle.

William Turner, who visited Kouklia in October 1815, observed that the village was 'nothing but a mass of ruined churches and houses, of which latter about thirty are inhabited, half by Turks and half by Greeks'. With good stone houses they were, he thought, undoubtedly happier than the people of Larnaca and of the capital whose homes were made of mud brick. Of the churches 'one only remains sufficiently entire to be still used'.

The Site

The site of the **Sanctuary of Aphrodite** lies immediately south of the modern village on a spur now dominated by the Château de Couvoucle. The sanctuary, hardly touched by Cesnola, was first excavated systematically in 1887 by the Cyprus Exploration Fund which presented some of its finds to the British Museum. Since then it has been dug, intermittently, by the British Kouklia Expedition in 1950 to 55 and by a Swiss–German expedition since 1966. Many of the artefacts unearthed are displayed in the museum housed in the château.

The ruins of Palaepaphos, which date mainly from the Roman period, offer little to the non-specialist observer. They are spread over a wide area and it requires a lively imagination to conjure up an image of the sanctuary's appearance. When it was rebuilt after the earthquake of AD 76/77, all or part of the Late Bronze Age shrine was incorporated into the new complex. The Roman reconstruction preserved the oriental layout of its predecessors. This differed from Graeco-Roman temples by having the shrine of the deity in the open air. It is not known whether the conical stone, which represented the presence of the goddess, was kept in the temenos of the earlier Sanctuary I or was moved to the newly constructed Sanctuary II to the north. Steps or a ramp led from Sanctuary I to the South Stoa of Sanctuary II. Sanctuary II consisted of a large open courtyard with stoas on its south and north sides and with several rectangular rooms on the east side where the entrance was sited. Modern buildings on the west side make it impossible to discover what lay there. Beyond the north stoa there was a rectangular hall which appears to have been used for banquets, perhaps of a ritual nature. Because the ground rises steadily, the sanctuary was built on different levels. It must have presented a magnificent spectacle to pilgrims arriving from Nea Paphos.

Some 40m to the west there are the ruins of a **Roman peristyle house** dating from the 1C AD with later reconstructions. Its eastern foundations lie over a *bothros* in which votive offerings were found. These included terracotta figurines of female worshippers with uplifted arms and fragments of pottery, mostly Archaic and Classical, some of which retained their original polychrome decoration.

A **Late Roman building** with a plain mosaic floor, lies to the north east of the main temenos. In 1978 a large square capital with stepped sides, typical of Late Bronze Age sanctuaries in Cyprus, was discovered by chance in the yard of one of the village houses.

The fortified **North East Gate** of the city was on the slope of Marcello Hill above the village. First erected c 700 BC, it was later strengthened and guard rooms were added in the 4C BC. Palaepaphos, the capital of one of the first Cypriot kingdoms, was attacked by the Persians in 498 BC. Their **siege ramp** located immediately to the east of the gate was mined by the defenders who dug three tunnels beneath the city wall in an attempt to topple the wooden towers used by the enemy. Several hundred fragments, including columns, altars, stelae and a finely sculpted head of a Priest King of Paphos from an extramural sanctuary, which had been used to build up the ramp, have been uncovered. Almost 500 bronze and iron arrow-heads and spear-points and a Greek bronze helmet have also been unearthed in the surrounding area. The Paphians, when rebuilding the fortifications at a later date, erected a revetment wall around the siege ramp, making it part of their defences. This left it in a relatively undisturbed state for the archaeologists. It has been partially reconstructed behind a modern retaining wall.

During the Roman period many fine private houses were built in the city. In one large villa the archaeologists found a superb mosaic depicting the story of **Leda and the Swan**. (This was stolen from the site and later recovered in London. It is now in the Cyprus Museum at Nicosia.) Leda, the daughter of the king of Aetolia, was pursued by Zeus in the form of a swan. After copulating with him, she laid two eggs. From these emerged two pairs of children, Castor and Pollux and Helen and Clytemnestra. The composition of the mosaic is unusual. It shows Leda, semi nude, emerging from a stream. She looks over her shoulder at the swan which is tweaking her garment in its beak, obviously anxious that she should undress as quickly as possible.

Other excavations have been conducted at the necropolis at **Skales** c 1km to the south east. Several chamber tombs have yielded objects dating from the 11C BC to the Hellenistic period.

Before leaving Kouklia find time to visit the **Katholiki church**, formerly Panayia Chrysopolitissa. On the west wall part of a Last Judgment fresco shows the rivers Tigris and Euphrates emerging from lions' masks. There is a painting of Christ Pantocrator on the dome. It is believed that this church was called Panaya Aphroditissa at one time. Certainly a memory of the fertility cult persists here. Young mothers still light candles in honour of Panayia Galatariotissa, the milk giving Virgin, at a large limestone corner block in the north stoa of the sanctuary.

The Frankish **Château de Couvoucle** dates partly from the 13C—it suffered considerably from the attentions of the Mamelukes in 1426. The north wing and gate tower, the west wing and half of the east wing are from the Turkish period when it was used as the manor of a large farm or *çiftlik*. Its name may be derived either from 'covouculeris', a Byzantine word for the bodyguard of rulers, who were sometimes rewarded by the gift of a country-house or from the Greek for sepulchre or pavilion.

The present courtyard is at a higher level than the medieval one. A flight of steps descends to a large cross-vaulted **hall**. This is over 30m long and 7m wide and is lighted by small pointed windows. The upper storey, which once had a flat roof, commands a fine view. Approached by an external ramp, which replaces the original stairs, it has rectangular windows and has been reroofed.

There are substantial remains of the medieval **sugar cane mill** below the road leading from the coast to the château. Sugar made a considerable contribution to the coffers of the Lusignan kings. Palaepaphos was the administrative centre of the industry.

The château houses the reorganised **Palaepaphos Museum**. Opening times are the same as for the site. Material found in the area includes terracotta figurines, ivories, white painted ware from Skales, Hellenistic and medieval pottery and glass, mosaics, a 12-sided colonnette with incised letters filled with bitumen dating from 550 to 500 BC, the 6C BC painted wing of a marble sphinx, stonemortars and pestles, a Chalcolithic shell necklace with picrolite pendant, a limestone head with a wide necklace and four rings in each ear, weapons found in the siege ramp, a stone bath, a limestone relief of the Annunciation from the Katholiki church, a large conical stone found in the Sanctuary of Aphrodite and an epigraphical collection.

Petra tou Romiou

The scrub covered hills north of the main road to Limassol are, rather exaggeratedly, called the **Randi Forest**. On the seashore below the forest is **Petra tou Romiou**, the Rock of the Greek. The rocks, there are several, get their name from the activities of the legendary Byzantine hero Dighenis who threw them into the sea to protect his lady. However, they have much older associations. According to an oral tradition it was here that Aphrodite was born from the waves. It is said that in certain weather conditions the waves rise, break and make a column of water that dissolves into a pillar of foam. To the imaginative eye this looks —for just a moment—like an ephemeral, evanescent, translucent human shape. And so perhaps it was at this beach that

> '…laughter-loving Aphrodite came to Cyprus to
> Paphos, where is her precinct and fragrant altar.'

There is a small pebbly strand at Petra tou Romiou. During the holiday season a kiosk sells soft drinks.

Paphos

Highlights
Paphos District Archaeological Museum, Byzantine Museum, Ethnographic Museum, The Tombs of the Kings, Ayia Kyriaki or Khrysopolitissa, The Pillar of St Paul, Saranda Kolones, House of Dionysus, House of Aion, Villa of Theseus, House of Orpheus, Ottoman Castle

Paphos is made up of two towns, **Ktima** built along an escarpment and **Kato Paphos**, often called **Nea Paphos**, which is near the sea. Most of the local people live in Ktima where the museums are located and where the neo-classical town hall rubs shoulders with the covered market, smart shops and banks. Many of the hotels and the principal archaeological sites are at Kato (Κάτω, below, underneath) Paphos. The combined population of the two towns is about 30,000, but this figure increases considerably during the holiday season. Before 1974 approximately one third of the population was Turkish-Cypriot. Paphos should not be confused with Kouklia-Paphos or Palaepaphos, the centre of the cult of Paphian Aphrodite, which is c 16km to the south east. Paphos, Pafos in Greek, Gazibaf in Turkish, was known as Baffo or Basso at various times in the past.

■ Practical information

Tourist information
The principal office is at Odos Gladstonos 3, Ktima. (There is a branch office at Paphos International Airport.) **Open** every day in the morning (except Sunday) and on Monday, Tuesday, Thursday and Friday afternoons.

Post office
The main post office is at Odos Nikodimou Mylona, also in the upper town.

Accommodation
Visitors have a wide range to chose from. There are six 5-star and nine 4-star hotels and various establishments in other categories in Paphos and its environs.

smaller scale by the Turks. The **baths** on Paphias Aphroditis street are Ottoman.

In the ruined church of **Ayios Yeoryios** there are two medieval tombstones. One is the memorial of Hariot Beduin and his father. The Beduins were among the earliest Latin families to settle in Cyprus. A Thomas Beduin held a position at Court in 1223. The diminutive domed church of **Ayios Antonios** was originally a double aisled building in the Byzantine style. The south aisle was removed, at some point, and a common narthex added. Catholic Mass is celebrated here on some weekdays (see above). Near the site of the North East Gate of the Roman city is the 15C church of **Ayia Marina**.

On or near the site of the city's ancient **East Gate** is the unattractive early 20C church of **Panayia Theoskepasti**, ie, the church of the Blessed Virgin Mary Shrouded by God. The church gets its name from a pious tradition. This claims that the original building was miraculously hidden by mist when a marauding Arab force attacked the city in the 7C. Divine intervention preserved the church from damage then, but not, alas, from the hands of modern, insensitive builders. It has one of the icons which, it is said, were painted by St Luke.

The 15C church of **Ayia Kyriaki** or **Khrysopolitissa**, Our Lady of the Golden City, as it is sometimes called, has three aisles, an octagonal lantern and an extended west bay. It replaced an 11C church which was destroyed by an earthquake in 1159. The earlier church was considerably larger. The foundations of its apse encircle the bema of the present building. It belonged to the Latin Catholics at the time of the Turkish invasion, but was taken from them by the Turks and given to the Orthodox in 1571. In a gesture of ecumenical friendship it was recently restored by the Bishop of Paphos to the Catholic Church which now shares it with the Anglicans.

The first Christian building on this site was a seven aisled basilica constructed towards the end of the 4C. It had a double apse, a feature not found anywhere else in Cyprus. According to a mosaic inscription alterations made by Bishop Sergios in the 6C reduced the number of aisles to five. A large paved courtyard was added. Excavations have revealed much of this magnificent church including a part of the apse and two of its monolithic granite columns. Green and white **Cipollino marble columns and capitals** from Karystos in Southern Euboea, Greece lie scattered on the ground. A considerable area of late 4C mosaic pavement has been exposed both inside the church and west of the narthex. Inscriptions referring to passages from the New Testament are juxtaposed with representations of a deer drinking from a rivulet and of a sheep's head by a vine. The east and south porticoes of an atrium, a central fountain and more columns and finely carved capitals have also been laid bare. The bishop's palace, with its deep vaulted basements, lay to the south. The entire complex was demolished by the Arabs in 653.

Khrysopolitissa is surrounded by a large area which, at present, is under excavation. This is not open to the public.

The ruined **Gothic church**, the church of the Franciscan Friary, sometimes called the Frari (Italian, 'Frari', the Friars), was built in 1312 and restored in the late 15C or early 16C. Three of the bishops of Paphos were Franciscans. The church had three aisles. The ceiling was probably rib vaulted. There were two rows of columns. Their capitals had an unusual decoration of rosettes, flowers and grapes. Four near life size angels carved from limestone, now in the Paphos Museum, supported a canopy. This may have been a baldacchino over the throne of the presiding cleric or over the altar. The walls were limewashed, probably to cover frescoes. This suggests that the church was being used as a mosque when it collapsed c 1600.

To the west of the church a column, previously railed off to stop the devout from stealing small pieces, was known as the '**Pillar of St Paul**'. According to an ancient, but unsubstantiated, tradition the apostle was bound to this column and suffered 39 lashes before he converted the Roman governor Sergius Paulus to Christianity.

Many of the most interesting remains of Nea Paphos are to be found in the rectangular area delimited by Leoforos Apostolou Pavlou on the east and south, and by the line of the ancient walls on the west and north.

The first church dedicated to **Panayia Limeniotissa**, Our Lady of the Port, was built towards the beginning of the 5C. All that remains of this building are parts of the coloured geometric patterned floor mosaic. It was a three aisled church, measuring 52m by 19m, with a single apse and a narthex on the west side. Inscriptions in Arabic on columns from the church found nearby suggest that it was destroyed during the Arab sack of Paphos in AD 653. The second church on the site, destroyed by the earthquake of 1159, was replaced by a small chapel. This appears to have been abandoned sometime after the Turkish conquest of the island, possibly because of the gradual depopulation of Nea Paphos.

The site of the **Sanctuary of Apollo Hylates**, c 1km to the east of the town centre near the Limnarka river, is likely to attract only the most dedicated and enthusiastic travellers. A rectangular underground chamber precedes a circular domed room. The sanctuary has been dated to the late 4C BC by two syllabic inscriptions. Now in private hands, the site is guarded by dogs. Sadly, a part is used as a rubbish dump.

Saranda Kolones

Built by the Lusignians at the end of the 12C to protect the harbour, the castle usually known as Saranda Kolones, the Forty Columns, acquired its sobriquet from the many granite columns scattered about its ruins. Taken from a colonnade which surrounded the Roman agora, these had been built into the outer walls. As a consequence, it was believed for some time that the ruined structure had been a temple dedicated to Aphrodite.

The castle had a very short life. It was destroyed by an earthquake in 1222 and not rebuilt. A systematic investigation of the site, begun in 1957, continued for about 30 years. Some restoration has been done.

The castle had a square keep protected by a curtain wall on the east and south, and by a ditch on the east and north. There were eight towers of different shapes. A wooden bridge over the ditch led to the original entrance in a gate tower on the east side. Access is now on the west. Staircases led down to sally-ports opening into the ditch. The castle was surrounded by a 3m thick outer wall. The keep was built around an open courtyard. Here massive piers rose to the vaulted ceiling and supported an upper storey. Excreta from latrines in three of the piers was conveyed by a drain to the ditch and thence to the sea. There were mangers and water troughs fashioned from ancient columns and a mill operated by donkey power on the east side of the keep. The garrison was housed on the west side of the outer courtyard. In a corner near the northwest tower there was an oubliette.

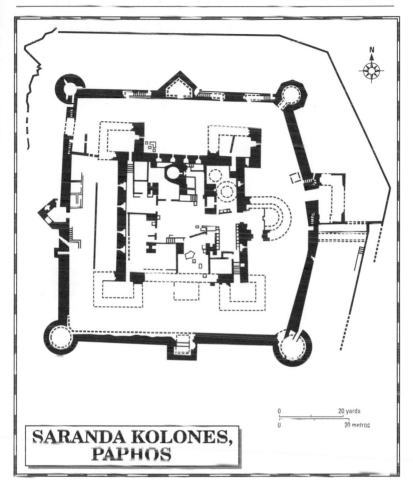

SARANDA KOLONES,
PAPHOS

The **Asclepieion** and the **Odeion** date from the early 2C AD. They may have been part of a reconstruction of the civic centre destroyed by the earthquake of 76/77 AD. The Asklepieion was aligned on an east/west axis with the Odeion. A corridor, which may have been colonnaded, connected the two buildings. In the Asklepieion two square rooms flanked an apsidal chamber. Substantial remains of the painted decoration of the walls of the building have been found. Demolished by earthquakes in the late 4C AD, it was never restored.

The Odeion lies below the acropolis. This semicircular structure has an overall diameter of 47.5m, two parodoi and 11 rows of restored seats. The upper rows were reached by a vaulted passage at the back of the cavea. Only fragments of the *scaenae frons* remain. Audiences in this theatre may have enjoyed the plays of the celebrated Greek parodist Sopater of Paphos who flourished during the reign of Alexander the Great and Ptolemy I. Only a fragment of his play *The Gauls* remains. This suggests that his work approached the best of Attic comedy.

The **agora**, which measured 95m by 95m, was surrounded by a raised colonnade. Some of the grey granite columns of the colonnade, which were surmounted by elaborately carved marble Corinthian capitals, were built into the walls of the 12C castle, Saranda Kolones.

The lighthouse rests on the remains of an ancient temple. To the north there are extensive remains of the Roman **city walls**. Note the ramp and a rock bridge leading across the excavated moat.

Paphos Archaeological Park

There are plans to enclose the Houses of Dionysos, Orpheus, Theseus and Aion in an Archaeological Park. Raised paths will link the houses and information will be provided by improved signs. There will be a visitors' centre, a small museum, a bookshop and a lecture hall where audiovisual presentations will be given and special exhibitions held.

The **House of Dionysos**, which dates from the end of the 2C AD, occupies an area of 2000 sq. m. Discovered by chance in 1962, it was excavated by the Department of Antiquities during the following three years. It was, perhaps, the home of a rich merchant or of an important official. Floor mosaics cover an area of 556 sq. m. As many of these feature the god of wine, it has been given the name House of Dionysos. A roof has been placed over the mosaics to protect them from the weather. Only this covered part of the building is open to the public. Several structures stood on the site. In the earliest, which may have been a sanctuary, the archaeologists found a fine bone knife handle. Now in the Paphos District Museum, this shows the Egyptian god Horus/Harpocrates, the son of Isis, to whom the sanctuary may have been dedicated. An amphora containing 2484 silver Ptolemaic tetradrachms, most from the mints of Paphos, Kition and Salamis, dating from 204 to 88BC was discovered under a plain mosaic floor.

Unfortunately most of the walls of the Roman house have disappeared—the cut stone was reused in later structures. As a result of this spoliation few traces of its elaborate pictorial and geometric wall paintings remain.

The mosaics, made by local craftsmen, were probably chosen from pattern books and adapted to fit the floor area of the house. Sometimes this meant that the design had to be cut, as in the case of the mosaic of the Rape of Ganymede where the edges of the eagle's wings have been trimmed. The most elaborate and decorative mosaics were in the rooms around the atrium, ie, those most likely to be used by visitors. The floors of the private apartments had simple designs of pebbles, while the kitchens and servants' quarters had floors of beaten earth.

The **Scylla Mosaic** does not belong to the Roman house. It was found about one metre below the south west corner of the atrium. The subject of this Hellenistic pebble mosaic is Scylla, the sea monster. According to Ovid, Scylla was a beautiful young maiden, the beloved of Glaucus, who was transformed by the magic potions of jealous Circe into a terrifying hybrid. The top half of her body remained the same, but six ravening dogs protruded from her groin. In rage and despair she spent her life luring ships to their doom. In the mosaic Scylla holds a trident in one hand and a ship's mast in the other. Apart from her hair, rendered by reddish brown stones, the mosaic is composed of black and white pebbles carefully selected for their size. Dated to the late 4C or early 3C BC, this is the earliest mosaic discovered in Cyprus. It compares, not unfavourably, with the c 330 BC pebble mosaic of the lion hunt of Alexander the Great found in the royal palace at Pella.

The **Triumph of Dionysos** depicts the return of the god from India. Crowned with ivy leaves, he is seated in a chariot drawn by panthers and holds a thyrsus in his right hand. In his entourage are Pan, Silenus, satyrs, maenads and Indian captives.

The **Dioscouroi**, Castor and Pollux, fathered by Zeus in the guise of a swan on Leda, are depicted in military costume. This was probably an apotropaic image, ie, to keep evil away from the household.

The damaged mosaic of **Narcissus** shows the youth looking longingly at his reflection in a pool. The 16 year old son of the river god Cephisus and the nymph Liriope was so handsome that girls and boys alike fell madly in love with him. However, he repulsed all their advances and caused them much suffering. His punishment was to fall in love with his own reflection 'so he was worn and wasted away'.

One of the most interesting mosaics in the House of Dionysos depicts **Phaedra and Hippolytus** at the moment when the surprised and embarrassed young man receives a letter from Phaedra, his step mother, in which she declares her sinful passion for him and proposes that they sleep together. He is shown naked, but for hunting boots and a mantle draped over his left shoulder. He holds a spear in one hand, the fateful missive in the other. Phaedra looks pensive. Eros holds a downturned torch, possibly signifying disapproval of her incestuous passion.

Under this mosaic the archaeologists found about 11,000 clay seal impressions which had once been attached to documents in the Nea Paphos Archive. These showed various gods, Ptolemaic kings and Roman emperors. They were mixed up with detritus and ash from the burned Archive which had been used by the ancient builders to provide a level surface for the mosaic.

Zeus, having fallen for the handsome Phrygian shepherd Ganymede, and always vigorous in the pursuit of his amours descended on Mt Ida in the Troad in the form of an eagle and carried the barely adolescent boy off to Olympus. The mosaic of the **Rape of Ganymede** shows a triumphant king of the gods holding the youth firmly with his claws. Ganymede grips a spear in his right hand—in his excitement he has dropped the accompanying pelte—and with his left clutches the eagle's neck. Note the trimming of the eagle's wings to fit the design into the available space.

The mosaic of the Babylonians **Pyramus and Thisbe** shows a condensed version of their tragic love affair. Depicted are the distraught Thisbe; a leopardess carrying away the bloodstained cloth, which caused all the trouble, and Pyramus after his transmogrification into a river god in Cilicia.

The theme of wine is continued in the mosaic of **Icarius and Dionysos**. Icarius was a gardener who entertained Dionysos. The god repaid his hospitality by teaching him how to make wine, telling him to hide it. Unfortunately, Icarius ignored the warning and gave it to some shepherds. Experiencing the effects of alcohol for the first time, they thought they were being poisoned and killed Icarius. The mosaic shows the drunken shepherds on the right, Icarius in the centre with an ox cart laden with wine skins and Dionysos on the left with a female figure who is drinking from a wine bowl. She bears the name Akme or Age, Perfection. The mosaic may be read as an allegorical representation of the effect of using and misusing the gift of Dionysos.

The mosaic of **Neptune and Amymone** depicts the moment when Amymone, who has been desperately searching for water in arid Argolis, is about to succumb to Neptune's amorous advances. Afterwards the grateful god showed her the spring of Lerna, so ending the drought.

Daphne, sworn to chastity, was pursued by lustful Apollo. To escape his clutches the nymph prayed to her father Peneus, who turned her into the laurel tree or daphne. The mosaic of **Daphne and Apollo** shows the moment of the metamorphosis. Peneus, the river god, is in the bottom left hand corner, Daphne stands behind him her legs already covered with bark while an astonished Apollo runs towards her.

A badly damaged **Four Seasons** mosaic has the customary iconography— Spring is crowned with flowers, Summer holds a sickle, Autumn has a pruning knife and behind old, bearded Winter there is a jug from which water pours. Two inscriptions 'XAIPEI', 'Rejoice', and 'KAI CY', 'You too', traditional greetings on entering or leaving a house, suggest that this was an antechamber.

Other mosaics include that of a glittering **peacock**, an effect achieved by the use of blue and green glass tesserae, and a stylised **hunting scene** with moufflon, leopard, bear, boar and tiger, reminiscent of those found in Roman houses at El Jem, Oudna and Thuburbo Maius in Tunisia.

The House of Dionysos was probably destroyed by the earthquakes that devastated the cities of Cyprus in the 4C AD. It would seem that the ruins were then abandoned.

In 1983 investigations carried out by a team of Polish archaeologists led to the discovery of the so called **House of Aion**. This gets its name from pictorial mosaics found in one of the three rooms which have been excavated so far. Dating from about the middle of the 4C AD, they are considered by some to be a confident exposition of pagan beliefs and values at a time when the influence of paganism was waning and Christianity was beginning to establish itself as the dominant religion. The god Aion, regarded at that time as the eternal judge 'ever remaining by divine nature the same', is depicted in the centre panel.

The pictorial mosaics are surrounded by a geometric design shaped like the Greek letter Π. The panel on the top left shows Leda about to bathe in the Eurotas river, where she will copulate with Zeus who has assumed the form of a swan. This liaison will produce Castor and Pollux and Helen of Troy. The top right hand panel shows the divine infant Dionysos being entrusted by Hermes to the care of his tutor, Tropheus. On the left, the nymphs of Mount Nysa prepare the infant's bath and on the right, female personifications of Nectar and Ambrosia, the food of the gods, greet the child. The centre panel shows the judgment of Aion in a beauty contest held between Cassiopia, the wife of Phoenix, king of Tyre, and mother of Andromeda, and Thetis, Galatea and Doris, three of the daughters of Nereus, the archetypal Old Man of the Sea. On the left side of the panel Cassiopia, proudly displaying her nude body, is being crowned by a female figure Krisis, the personification of Choice or Judgment. On the right the disappointed Nereids, accompanied by a downcast Eros riding a bull, are being carried away on the backs of sea monsters. Above their heads Zeus and Athena indicate their approval of Aion's decision to give the prize to Cassiopia. The bottom right hand panel shows the outcome of the musical contest between Marsyas and Apollo. The unfortunate Marsyas, who unwisely challenged the god, is being led away by two Scythians to pay the penalty for his temerity. He will be flayed alive. The damaged left hand panel shows the triumph of Dionysos. His car, drawn by a pair of centaurs, is preceded by a maenad *en déshabillé*. The god is offered a dish of pomegranates, apples and grapes by a young satyr named Skirtos. Tropheus, the tutor of Dionysos, rides behind the triumphal car.

The mosaics have been interpreted in the following manner. The Dionysos portrayed here is not to be confused with the traditional god of wine. He is the young god who has come to make the earth fruitful and to save mankind. The contests between Marsyas and Apollo and between Cassiopia and the Nereids symbolise the struggle between untamed Nature and Divine Cosmic Order. In effect, the mosaic is a late defiant challenge by paganism to the new faith symbolised by the churches which were beginning to be built in Paphos.

The **Villa of Theseus** was probably the official residence of the Roman governor of the island. It measured 120m by 80m and is the largest house found so far in Cyprus. Occupying the site of earlier Roman and Hellenistic buildings, the oldest parts of the villa date from the second half of the 2C AD. It was a peristyle building constructed around a central, unpaved courtyard which had porticoes, ornamented with geometric floor mosaics, on the east, west and south sides. The villa continued to be occupied until the 7C. However, it went down hill in its final years. It appears to have been used by artisans and others who introduced lime kilns, ovens and partitions into some of its rooms.

The principal entrance to the villa, which was on the east side, led to an atrium. This, in turn, provided access to the courtyard. In the centre of the south side of the building a large room fronting a raised apse served as an audience chamber. The mosaic showing the Bath of Achilles was found here. There was a luxurious private bath complex in the south east corner. The mosaic of the defeat of the Minotaur by Theseus, which gives its name to the villa, was in a nearby room. The private residential apartments occupied much of the west side. Late 2C or early 3C AD marble statues of Asclepius, Persephone, Dionysos, Aphrodite, Hephaestos, Artemis, Hercules, Silenus and a satyr, now in the Paphos District Museum, were found here. The servants quarters and various workrooms were on the north side of the villa.

Most of the mosaics in the villa have elaborate geometric patterns.

The most interesting of the pictorial mosaics tells the story of **Theseus and the Minotaur**. This has been dated to the late 3C or early 4C AD. Minos, king of Crete, imposed a tribute on Athens. Every nine years the city had to send seven youths and seven maidens to the island where they were eaten by the Minotaur, the Bull of Minos. This monster, half man, half bull, was the fruit of the illicit union of Pasiphae, the wife of Minos and a sacred bull. The Minotaur lived in a labyrinth on the island. Theseus, the son of Aegeus king of Athens, volunteered to be one of the youths. Ariadne, the daughter of Minos, fell in love with the young hero and gave him a ball of thread which helped him to find his way through the labyrinth to the Minotaur whom he killed.

The mosaic was partially damaged, perhaps during the 4C earthquake, and later repaired. Within a circular border the youthful hero is shown, with raised club, about to strike the decisive blow. On the left a cowering male figure represents the labyrinth. On the top left there is a rather complacent Ariadne. She is balanced on the top right by a solemn crowned female figure representing Crete. Unfortunately, the area showing the Minotaur has been badly damaged. The head and upper body of Theseus, part of the late repair, shows him gazing serenely into the distance. The pose is strikingly reminiscent of that of the Theseus in a fresco of the same subject from Pompeii now in the Museo

Archaeologico in Naples. The head and upper body of Crete were also restored. A semicircular area at the top of the mosaic, which, too, has been repaired, may have shown the peering heads of the fearful members of the tribute who have been saved by Theseus.

The 5C AD mosaic of the **First Bath of Achilles**, one of four, is in the square audience chamber on the south side of the villa. Enough remains of the other three to suggest that they also portrayed episodes in the life of the hero. The pictorial panels were enclosed by a Π shaped geometric pattern which was separated from them by a frieze showing Erotes in pursuit of wild animals. Dated to the 5C AD, it is markedly inferior in workmanship to the Theseus mosaic. The faces of the protagonists are lifeless, the bodies stiff and unreal and there is little impression of perspective. Achilles, the son of Peleus king of Phthia in Thessaly and Thetis one of the Nereids (see the House of Aion above) is seated on the lap of his nurse Anathrope. Behind them a servant named Ambrosia (Ambrosia was the food of the gods) brings water in a golden jar. In the centre Thetis reclines on a padded couch. Peleus is seated on a throne by her side. Behind him are the Moirae, the Fates, Atropus, Clotho and Lachesis who regulated the length of each person's life by means of a thread which one of the Fates spun, the second wound and the third cut at the moment of death.

In a rectangular room in the south west corner of the villa there are the remains of a finer mosaic which has been badly damaged. This may not be on show to the public. It shows **Poseidon and Amphitrite** and has been dated to the second half of the 4C AD. Poseidon holds a trident in his left hand and rides on the back of a sea monster. The faces of the gods have been rendered with great delicacy and charm.

Only part of the building called the **House of Orpheus** has been excavated. Dated to the late 2C early or 3C AD, it takes its name from a fine rectangular mosaic which shows Orpheus charming the beasts. Seated on a rock, and surrounded by the animals, he holds a lyre in his left hand and gestures with his right hand. An interesting inscription above his head reads: [ΓΑΙ] ΟС or [ΤΙΤ] ΟС ΠΙΝΝΙΟS ΡΕСΤΙΤΟΛΤΟС ΕΠΟΙΕΙ, '(Gaius) or Titus Pinnius Restitutus made it'. This may be the name of the artist or of the person who paid for the mosaic. Note that the name, although written in Greek letters, is in Latin.

The mosaic of **Hercules and the Nemean Lion** is an unusual portrayal of the story of the first of the 12 labours imposed on the hero by his cousin Eurystheus. When Hercules tried to kill the mythical beast with his club, it retreated into a cave, so he strangled it with his bare hands.

The rather formal portrayal of the **Amazon** shows her standing by her horse wearing a Phrygian cap and a transparent garment. She holds a double headed axe in her right hand. The Amazons were a mythical, warlike tribe of women who were believed to live by the river Thermodon in Pontic Asia Minor. Their name is said to mean 'breastless' from αμαζός, breast, as it was thought they pinched out or cauterized their right breast to make it easier for them to throw javelins. They mated once a year with men from neighbouring tribes. Girls born from these encounters were kept by the Amazons. Boys were castrated, killed or returned to their fathers.

Do not miss the unusual **Monochrome Mosaic** found in the south east of the excavation. This has a geometric pattern of octagons formed by the grey green tesserae.

After the destruction of the castle, later known as Saranda Kolones, by the earthquakes of 1222, the Lusignans built a new fortress at the western end of the breakwater on the ruins of an earlier structure. This was blown up by the Venetians and rebuilt by the Turks between 1580 and 1592, as recorded in an inscription over the entrance. For most of the period of British rule the castle was used as a salt store. Only in 1935 was it declared an ancient monument.

The moated **Ottoman castle** has a vaulted central hall. Beyond are small courtyards with rooms on either side. In the upper storey there is a *mescid*.

At the end of the breakwater there are the submerged remains of its ancient extension towards the **Moulia Rocks**. Relics of an inner mole, a continuation of the city wall, lie to the north east of the present breakwater.

North west of Paphos

Highlights
Emba, Monastery of Ayios Neophytos, the Lemba Project, Coral Bay, Maa Palaeokastro, Peyia, Cape Drepanon, Yeronisos, Avgas Gorge, Lara Beach

Leave Paphos by Tafon ton Vasileon and continue past the Tombs of the Kings and the Venus Beach Hotel. At the little fishing hamlet of **Ayios Yeoryios** Colonel Grivas made a clandestine landing from Greece in November 1954 to lead EOKA guerrillas against the British.

Emba

To visit the Monastery of Ayios Neophytos take Thermopylon from Ktima and continue in the direction of **Emba**. This village is famous for its wild flowers. In spring the fields around it are ablaze with anemones. Their colours range from a ghostly white to a red so deep as to be almost black. On roadside banks the pallid blossoms of *Asphodelus albus*, Homer's flowers of the dead, gleam like ghostly lanterns, while the rocky land south of the village near the church of **Ayios Yeoryios** is carpeted with cyclamens. The barrel-vaulted Byzantine church has been largely rebuilt. It has two layers of frescoes, the later dating from the 16C. Note the unusual square apse with the founders' tombs on the east, south and north sides. The principal church in Emba is dedicated to **Panayia Khryseleousa**. Dating from the 12C, this twin domed structure had a narthex added to it in 1744 and was further repaired in 1955. Its frescoes were not improved by the attentions of a local artist in 1886. (This overpainting is being removed.) Only the fine 15C representation of Christ Pantokrator on the dome escaped the restorer's attentions. It was out of his reach. It is untouched except for the effect of candle smoke. Note the early 16C double panel icon showing the Twelve Apostles. The church also possesses a copy of the Gospels printed in Venice in 1539.

Ayia Ekaterina in **Tala** is a domed Byzantine style building with an added narthex. Among the surviving frescoes on the west wall is one of the Last

Judgment. An Early Cypriot cemetery was discovered in 1963 some 5km to the north west at **Spilia tou Mavrou**.

The Monastery of Ayios Neophytos

The Monastery of Ayios Neophytos nestles in a secluded wooded valley about 9km north of Paphos. St Neophytos, an autodidact, was born the son of poor parents in 1134 at Lefkara. Thwarted in his efforts to join a group of anchorites in Asia Minor, he retreated to this valley and began to live in an isolated cave which he called the Enkleistra. In time he was joined by others and a monastery was established near the cave. During his long life he drew up a Rule for the Enkleistoi, as he called his followers, and issued a stream of letters, instructions, commentaries and theological writings. Like many other holy men living in isolation he did not hesitate to comment on matters of state. In a celebrated letter he denounced Richard Coeur de Lion, 'the wicked wretch' from 'England ... a country beyond Romania to the north' for selling Cyprus to the Latins for 100,000 bezants. St Neophytos made his own shroud and coffin and instructed his monks to hide his body away after the burial so that 'it should stay in quietness until the common Resurrection ...' His remains were found in the middle of the 18C and, despite his wish, were moved to the main church where they are still kept.

In the **Enkleistra**, which measures c 4m by 3m, are the stone bench on which Neophytos slept, the table at which he wrote and the rock cut tomb in which he was buried. The wall paintings, the work of one Theodore Apseudes, are dated by an inscription to 1183. Note the fine rendering of the Crucifixion in the tomb. In the adjoining sanctuary there is a magnificent depiction of Neophytus being carried to Paradise by two Archangels. In the nave, the paintings depict various incidents from the life of Christ. Neophytus is shown in several of them.

The **abbey church** has a high dome, a triple apse and barrel vaulting. The nave is separated from the side aisles by columns with acanthus ornamented capitals. The wall paintings are believed to date from the mid 15C. The chest containing the remains of the saint is 19C, the reliquary holding his skull mid 18C. Of the icons, the mid 15C depiction of the Blessed Virgin Mary of the Enkleistra is the oldest.

At the southern entrance to **Khlorakas**, a market-gardening centre, is the toy-like Byzantine church of **Ayios Nikolaos**. It could scarcely hold a congregation of more than a dozen people. There are traces of murals on the north wall and a coat of arms above the north door. Adjoining the large modern church is the 13C **Panayia Khryseleousa**. Its wall paintings have been ruined by unskilled attempts to restore them. This church has the same coat of arms above its west door.

Before the events of 1974 **Lemba** was mainly occupied by Turkish Cypriots. Recently it has become the home of the Cyprus College of Art. Lemba is the centre of an area which was heavily occupied in the 3rd millennium BC. Excavations have been conducted at the local sites of **Lakkous** to the north, and at **Mosphilia** and **Mylouthkia** where 28 graves and 11 circular stone buildings have been uncovered. At the **Lemba Project** archaeologists have built a number of huts based on information garnered at various prehistoric sites.

Four icons of 1775 are kept in **Kissonerga's** modern church. Water from a holy well in the ruins of a chapel dedicated to SS Zenais and Philonilla, two holy women, perhaps sisters, relatives and companions of St Paul, is reputed to cure various female ailments.

Coral Bay

Coral Bay has, in fact, two bays. It gets its name from minute fragments of coral which give the sand a delicate pink hue. Recently developed as a resort, it has the usual clutter of snack bars and boutiques, the inevitable concomitant of tourism. For a decent meal go to Peyia (see below) or try the taverna on the peninsula which separates the two beaches. Just west of the taverna are the remains of the Mycenaean fortified town of **Maa Palaeokastro** which appears to have been occupied for a very short period. It may have been an Achaean stronghold established before the second wave of Achaean invaders arrived in the 12C BC. Recent excavation confirmed its violent destruction c 1200 BC.

In the **Cave of Ayii Phanentes**, ie, the Cave of the Discovered Saints, to the east of Maa, fossil bones of pigmy hippopotami found by the inhabitants of Kissonerga in medieval times were believed to be those of early Christian martyrs.

Peyia, attractively sited on a hillside, was probably founded by the Venetians, although claims are also made for a Byzantine establishment. It has a number of good restaurants. About 7km to the west is the site of **Ayios Yeoryios**, with the ruins of a 6C **basilica**—in fact three superimposed churches—discovered in 1951. The ruins, and those of another 11C to 14C edifice with adjacent baths await further excavation. Note the finely carved capitals of Proconnesian marble with their spare decoration of carved crosses. There are some fragmentary mosaics. Appropriately, these depict sea creatures and sea birds as well as a wild animal hunt. Near the harbour there are some 20 rock-cut tombs, some Christian burial places as very early forms of the cross on them evince.

Cape Drepanon

At Cape Drepanon, which perhaps derives its name from its curved shape, (δρέπανον, a scythe or scimitar) the extensive ruins of a late Roman and early Byzantine city await systematic excavation.

Just offshore, the island of **Veronisos** rises abruptly from the sea. There are remains of a Neolithic settlement on the south side. The ruined Roman buildings on the west are now the haunt of pigeons.

The Akamas Peninsula

A rough road continues northward towards Cape Lara, Cape Arnaoutis and the **Akamas Peninsula**. To explore this area thoroughly you need a four wheel drive vehicle, iron nerves and considerable stamina. Places not be missed include the **Avgas Gorge** where the Kouphon and Avgas rivulets meet, **Lara Beach** where the loggerhead turtles lay their eggs and the 12C monastic church of **Ayios Minas** near Neokhorion. Paradoxically, this beautiful wilderness has been saved from the hands of greedy developers by the British Army. For a number of days each year part of it is used as a firing and military exercise range! Currently there are plans to turn the Akamas into a national park. The Cyprus Forestry Department has prepared two nature trails—Aphrodite and Adonis. These start

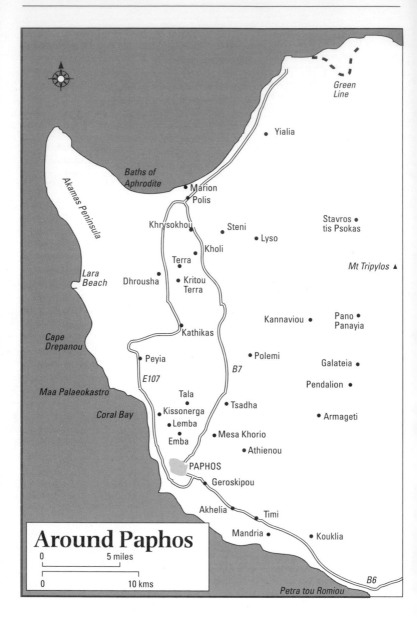

Green
Line

• Yialia

Baths of
Aphrodite

Akamas Peninsula

• Marion
• Polis

Khrysokhou •
• Steni
• Lyso

Stavros •
tis Psokas

Mt Tripylos ▲

Kholi •

Terra •

Lara
Beach
Dhrousha •   • Kritou
              Terra

Kannaviou •   Pano •
                Panayia

• Kathikas

Cape
Drepanou

• Peyia
E107

• Polemi

B7

Galateia •

Pendalion •

Maa Palaeokastro

Coral Bay

Tala •
• Kissonerga
  • Lemba
  Emba

• Tsadha

• Armageti

• Mesa Khorio

• Athienou

PAPHOS
• Geroskipou

Akhelia •   • Timi

Mandria •   • Kouklia

Around Paphos

0   5 miles

0   10 kms

B6

Petra tou Romiou

from the Baths of Aphrodite (see below). The walks are about 7.5km and should take no more than 4 hours. A booklet describing the varied flora and fauna of the Akamas is available from the Cyprus Tourism Organisation.

NOTE. When military exercises are carried out in the Akamas Peninsula parts of it are out of bounds to the public.

Exalt Tours, 24 Ayios Kyriaki St., Kato Paphos organise excellent guided day tours of the area. Small groups led by English or German speaking guides, who are thoroughly versed in the history, archaeology and natural history of the area, set out in jeeps several times each week during the holiday season. The combination of pure air and moderate exercise produces healthy appetites and these are satisfied by an excellent lunch of typical Cypriot food in one of the isolated villages of the Akamas.

North of Paphos

The hill villages of Akamas

Highlights
Khrysospiliotissa, Ayia Ekaterina, Marion, Panayia Khryseleousa, Stavros tis Psokas, Mt Tripylos, Baths of Aphrodite, Fontana Amorosa, Fontana Amorosa, Kato Pyrgos

Near the little village of **Mesa Khorio** there is a ruined medieval chapel dedicated to **Ayia Marina**. A popular belief holds that a man cursed with a nagging wife may obtain peace by collecting dust from the floor of this chapel and sprinkling it, surreptitiously of course, in his house!

In the village church of **Tsadha** there is a mid 16C icon of the Blessed Virgin with two donors, the priest Gideon and his wife. According to an inscription this was 'Painted at the expense of and by the sinner Titus'. Not far from Tsadha is the **Monastic Church of Stavros Mithas**, the Holy Cross of the Wild Mint. This houses a relic of the True Cross.

Before the events of 1974 Turkish Cypriots lived in many of the villages between Stroumbi and Dhrouska. High in the mountains, they offer magnificent views of the surrounding countryside. The area around **Kathikas**, which rather unflatteringly means 'chamber-pot' in Greek, produces grapes and sultanas. The names of **Pano** and **Kato Arodhes** recall the fact that they were once the property of the Knights Hospitaller of St John of Jerusalem whose headquarters were, for a time, in Rhodes. Near Pano Arodhes is the shrine of **Khrysospiliotissa**, a Hellenistic or Roman tomb which was used for Christian worship. There is an altar and traces of a fresco of the Blessed Virgin between angels. It was used by Linobambakoi (literally 'flax cottons') Orthodox Christians who, for tax purposes, pretended to convert to Islam but who

named 'Caledonian Falls' and the distinctive colonial appearance of some of the older villas. The former summer residence of the British High Commissioner, eccentrically built in the style of a Scottish shooting lodge, was constructed under the supervision of the French poet Rimbaud. Sailing from Alexandria, Rimbaud landed at Lanarca in December 1878. Having contracted typhoid while directing labourers quarrying stone near Voroklini, he went to France to recuperate before returning to Cyprus in 1880 to work on 'le palais du Gouverneur'. In the 1940s a plaque was affixed to the building to commemorate the poet's contribution to its construction. It is now the summer residence of the President of the republic. The British military chapel in Pano Platres has been turned into a police station.

Good roads from Nicosia and Limassol bring a constant stream of visitors to Pano Platres. It is a popular destination for bus tours from the coastal resorts during the holiday season. Walkers enjoy its woods of Troodos Cypress and Black Pine.

■ Practical information

Tourist information office
The Tourist Information Office is in the centre of the village near the **post office**.

Accommodation
Accommodation is offered by the 4-star **Forest Park Hotel**, ☎ (05) 421751; the 3-star **Pendeli**, ☎ (05) 421736; and three 2-star hotels, **New Helvetia** (☎ (05) 421348, **Petit Palais** ☎ (05) 422723, and **Edelweiss**, ☎ (05) 421335. The New Helvetia and the 1-star **Minerva**, ☎ (05) 421731 are recommended.

Other facilities
Pano Platres has a number of **restaurants**. All have rather unexciting menus. There is a supermarket and a shop which hires out **bicycles**. A **rural bus** leaves for Limassol very early every weekday morning. The Tourist Office will have the departure time of this and other bus services. Apart from a single disco, which functions only during the holiday season, there is no evening entertainment.

The **Caledonia Trail** starts near the Presidential summer residence and ends at the waterfall which gives it its name. About two kilometres long, if taken at a leisurely pace, the trail requires about one and half hours.

Phini (910m) was the birthplace of Archbishop Sophronios II (1825 to 1900) who welcomed the first British High Commissioner to Cyprus in 1878. The village is noted for its pottery and chairmaking. Near Phini is the abandoned **Monastery of Ayii Anargyri**, ie, the Monastery of the Penniless, a title often given to SS Cosmas and Damian. The late 15C church is said to be haunted by the ghost of a youthful horseman who rides out of the west door at dusk and disappears into the gathering darkness. The iconostasis dates from 1697, some of the icons and the furniture from the 17C to early 18C. The names of earlier visitors, among them a German named Rohr and Porry an 18C French consul are cut into the walls.

There is a tradition that the **Monastery of Troodhitissa**, at 1300m the

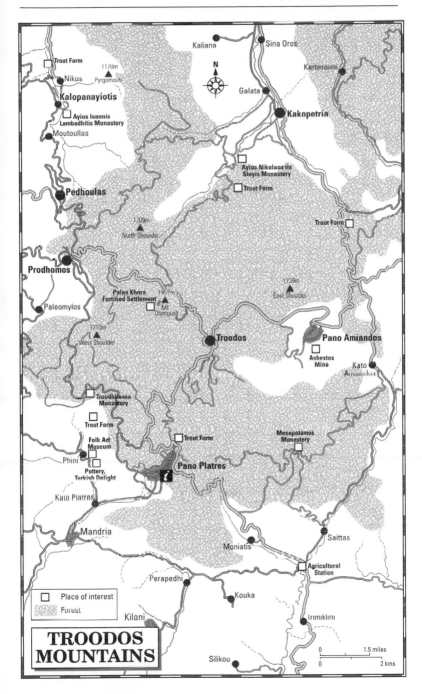

Kaliana
Sina Oros
Karteroimi
Trout Farm
Nikos
11/0m
Pyrgomouti
Galata
Kalopanayiotis
Kakopetria
Ayios Ioannis
Lambadhitis Monastery
Moutoullas
Ayios Nikolaos tis
Steyis Monastery
Trout Farm
Pedhoulas
Trout Farm
1709m
North Shoulder
Prodhomos
1739m
East Shoulder
Palea Khora
Fortified Settlement
1952m
Mt
Olympus
Paleomylos
1710m
West Shoulder
Troodos
Pano Amiandos
Asbestos
Mine
Kato
Amiandos
Troodhitissa
Monastery
Trout Farm
Mesapotamos
Monastery
Folk Art
Museum
Trout Farm
Phini
Pano Platres
Pottery,
Turkish Delight
Kato Platres
Mandria
Saittas
Moniatis
Perapedhi
Agricultural
Station
Kouka
Irimiklini
□ Place of interest
Forest
Kilani

TROODOS
MOUNTAINS

Silikou

0   1.5 miles
0   2 kms

highest monastery in Cyprus, was founded in 1250 to house an icon of the Blessed Virgin which came here from Asia Minor under mysterious circumstance during the 8C iconoclastic controversy. Hidden in a cave by two monks, the icon remained undiscovered after their death until 990. The present church, the third constructed on this site, dates from 1731. Several dependencies added in 1780 were destroyed 20 years later by a forest fire.

The unremarkable three aisled **church** was restored in the 1960s and its ugly corrugated roof replaced with tiles. The icon of the Blessed Virgin was covered with silver-gilt repoussé work in 1799. Copies show Our Lady, crowned, with the Christ Child sitting on her right arm. There are several 16C icons and a belt with silver buckles which is believed to cure female infertility. Barren woman have the belt fastened around the waist. If, subsequently, they conceive and bear a male child, it is customary for him to become a novice at the monastery.

Cypriots come to the Monastery of Troodhitissa in their thousands on 15 August to celebrate the Feast of the Assumption of the Blessed Virgin.

Tris Elies was the birthplace of Archbishop Khrysanthos who held office from 1767 to 1810. It was also the place of martyrdom of St Charalambos in 198 during the reign of the Emperor Septimius Severus. The bones of the saint are preserved in a circular bronze reliquary in the rebuilt church of **Panayia Eleousa**. The mid 18C church of **Arkhangelos Michael** has a Gospel of 1590.

Troodos (1725m) has few attractions. A meagre collection of souvenir shops, quick food restaurants and hotels, it is the highest place in the island to be inhabited throughout the year. It is popular with skiing enthusiasts—the north and south slopes of Mount Olympos enjoy a brief but unpredictable season between January and March. The **Atalanta Trail** starts at the Troodos Post Office and finishes at the Chrome Mine camp. About 9km in length, the trail takes four hours at a moderate pace.

During the Ottoman period Troodos was visited by few except the carriers of snow to the capital's ice houses. Shortly after the arrival of the British, Sir Garnet Wolseley set up a summer camp for his troops to the south of the village.

Mount Olympos (1952m), the highest peak in the Troodos range, is also the highest point in the island. According to a late 18C visitor to Cyprus, Constantius, Archbishop of Sinai, there was a temple on the summit '...dedicated to Aphrodite Acraea. By a law strange indeed in a country so devoted to this goddess, this temple might not be approached, nor even seen, by women.' There are the remains of a Venetian fort at the nearby settlement of Palea Khora. No longer bare, the summit now has globular radar installations, a TV tower, observation posts and other modern excrescences.

The church of the Holy Cross in **Paleomylos** has an unusual icon of Christ and the Apostles on the iconostasis and a bust of Christ Pantokrator on one of the beams.

The village of **Prodhromos** is a good centre for visiting some of the more remote mountain hamlets. It has an agricultural station and boasts a bank and post office. There is one small, cheap hotel.

The road from Prodhromos to the **Monastery of Trikoukkia** skirts the west flank of the Troodos massif and, passing through apple orchards heavy with fruit in the autumn, offers wonderful panoramic views. The three aisled 13C **church**, rebuilt in 1761, has a much-venerated 17C icon which is believed to bring rain. The lowest temperature ever recorded in Cyprus—5°F (-15°C)—was noted here in December 1941.

In **Lemithou** is the small early 16C church of **Ayios Theodhoros**, the patron saint of Venice until 827 when the body of St Mark was brought to that city from the East. The 4C St Theodore Tyro was a Roman army recruit who converted to Christianity. He set fire to the temple of Cybele at Amasya in Pontus, Turkey and was burned alive there. With SS George and Demetrius, he is greatly honoured by the Eastern Churches as one of the Three Soldier Saints. The church has some well preserved murals including a fine head of the saint.

In the village of **Kaminaria** there is a restored early 16C chapel dedicated to the Blessed Virgin. This has an interesting donor painting of a lady elegantly attired in a red and blue gown, veil and apron accompanied by two male figures. Underneath there are traces of an inscription and some mystic, occult symbols. Note the splendidly martial figures of SS Demetrios and George on the north wall.

The ancient church of **St George** in the village of Milikouri was rebuilt in 1811. Most of its icons were badly repainted at the beginning of this century. An icon of the Blessed Virgin dating from 1523 is partially covered with gilt repoussé.

Monastery of Kykko

The Monastery of Kykko, said to be the richest in Cyprus, has one of the surviving icons attributed to the apostle St Luke. Of the others, one formerly in the Sumela Monastery near Trabzon, Turkey, is now in Athens, another is in a monastery in the Peloponnese. The word Kykko is derived from κόκκος, the acorn of a species of oak which once grew in profusion in this area.

Kykko is popular with foreign visitors and many bus tours call here. Cypriot Orthodox Christians come for weddings, baptisms and to celebrate religious feasts. There are gift shops, a restaurant and accommodation, in some 70 rooms, for genuine pilgrims. In the monastery treasury there is a collection of vestments, carved crosses, church plate including chalices, Gospels and reliquaries. Most date from the 19C.

According to the Chronicle of Makhairas, Kykko was established c 1092 by a hermit named Isaias to house the precious icon known as the **Eleousa**, the Compassionate said to be painted by St Luke. This was given to him by the Emperor Alexios I Comnenos as an expression of gratitude for curing his daughter. She was 'sick even unto death, and no physician could cure her, and she was lying thus for a year'.

The monastery has had a chequered history. It was burnt down in 1365 by a peasant in search of wild honey. He had lit a fire in its vicinity to scare off the bees. Rebuilt the same year by Eleanor of Aragón, the wife of Peter I (1359 to 1369)—a generous gesture by a Latin ruler to an Orthodox establishment—it was destroyed by fire again in 1541, 1751 and 1813. The monastery had close connections with imperial Russia and received many gifts from Russian pilgrims.

Kykko was visited by Richard Pococke in 1738. In his *Description of the East and some other Countries (London 1743–45)* he relates how he was received with great civility, served 'with marmalade, a dram, and coffee, and about an hour after with a light collation, and in the evening with a grand entertainment at supper'. Abbot Joseph of Kykko was a victim of the Nicosia massacre of 1821. It was pillaged the same year by the Turks. Frequently used as a sanctuary, even in this century, in 1956 its dependencies near a mountain hideout of Colonel Grivas were occupied by the Gordon Highlanders. Mikhail Khristodolou Mouskos, later Archbishop President Makarios, was a novice here.

An irregular pile of buildings of slight interest, roughly triangular in layout because of the shape of the site, surrounds two cloisters. According to Gunnis the carved marble panel over the south door of the domed, three aisled **church** may be a survival from the first building. Part of the apse dates from the late 16C, the belfry was added towards the end of the last century.

The **Icon of the Blessed Virgin**, considered too sacred to be exposed to public gaze, is enclosed in a tortoise-shell and mother-of-pearl shrine which stands before the iconostasis. The painting, which is said to be in encaustic, ie, pigment mixed with beeswax and fixed with heat after application, has been covered since the 16C. It is protected by a silver gilt plate stamped with a representation of the portrait beneath. This cover is believed to date from 1776. In times of drought, the icon is carried in procession to Throni (see below), as it is believed it can bring rain.

Among other relics is a bronze arm which, it is said, belonged to an impious heathen who tried to light his cigarette from one of the lamps illuminating the icon. His arm withered and was turned into metal. A swordfish's saw was given by a drowning sailor saved by the intercession of the Blessed Virgin of Kykko. Note the icon of the Crucifixion of 1520 and another of St Luke painting the Blessed Virgin. One of the church bells is said to have been rolled up to Kykko in a barrel from Lefka. This was an offering from the faithful in Russia.

The densely wooded hilly area to the west of Kykko is sparsely inhabited. Near the monastery on **Kykko Hill** (1318m), also known as **Throni**, is the **Tomb of Archbishop President Makarios III** (1913 to 1977). Approached by a fine new road the late President's grave is marked by a simple black marble slab protected by a stone cupola. On the summit of the hill stands a modern domed chapel.

Pedhoulas (1090m) is a pleasant little village whose mild climate provides a welcome escape from the oven like summer temperatures of Nicosia. It has a bank, a post office, several restaurants and four hotels, **Christy's Palace**, ☎ (02) 952655; **Mountain Rose**, ☎ (02) 952727; **Two Flowers**, ☎ (02) 952372; **Central**, ☎ (02) 952457, which offer simple, unfussy accommodation. It is famous for its Sunday market and for its springtime cherry blossom. Not far from the parish church is a diminutive chapel built in 1474 and dedicated to **Arkangelos Mikhail**. (The caretaker lives two doors away.) The chapel has striking contemporary frescoes in a naïve, slightly gauche but not unattractive style. Look for the depiction of the donor, the priest Vasilios, his wife and two daughters. Other paintings depict incidents from the life of Christ with an accompanying frieze of saints. The Lusignan arms appear above the holy doors of the iconostasis.

The tiny chapel of **Panayia tou Moutoulla** in Moutoullas dates from 1280. Apart from some 15C additions, this has changed very little. The donor John of Moutoullas and his wife Irene are depicted over the north door. St George does battle with a crowned harpy rather than the conventional dragon. The torments of the damned are depicted with considerable relish in the painting of the Last Judgment.

Kalopanayiotis (700m) is a small spa village with sulphur springs. Its three modest hotels, all without stars, **Helioupolis**, ☎ (02) 952451; **Kastalia**, ☎ (02) 952455 and **Loutraki**, ☎ (02) 952356 cater mainly for visitors to the spa. From the village centre a lane descends steeply to the valley floor where the **Monastery of Ayios Ioannis Lambadistou** is situated across the Setrakhos river. Restored in 1955, this is a complex of three churches—an 11C cross in square domed church dedicated to **Ayios Heracleidos**, the 12C church of **St John Lampadistis** and a **Latin church** which has been dated to the 15C. Unusually there is no division between the Latin and Orthodox churches. There is a **narthex** on the west side. The entrance is on the south.

St Heracleidos was the first Bishop of Cyprus. There is an ancient tradition that he was baptised by SS Paul and Barnabus in the river near here. The iconostasis in Ayios Heracleidos bears the Lusignan arms and those of other important Latin families—Damperre, Giblet, d'Ibelin etc. It was probably the rood screen in the Latin church. The earliest frescoes date from the early 13C and are to be found in the dome and central vaults. Note especially Christ's entry into Jerusalem and Ascension into Heaven. The second phase, early 15C, painting is mainly in the north vault.

St John Lampadistis, a young man from the village of Lampas near Galata, was engaged to be married, but decided to become a monk. Unfortunately for him, his rejected fiancée and her family were powerful sorcerers. They cast a spell on him which made him blind. He fell ill and died at the age of 22 and was buried in the monastery. His skull is preserved in a reliquary near his tomb. The icon of St John on the iconostasis dates from the mid 16C. Note the signatures of earlier visitors.

The paintings in the Latin church are much more sophisticated than those in the Orthodox church and it has been suggested that the artist had worked in Italy. Note the Tree of Jesse on the west wall. In the narthex there are paintings of the principal feasts of the Church and a portrait of the donor.

Some early icons survive in the monastic church of **Mesapotamos, Kalopanayiotis**, originally called **Prodhromos**. Founded in the late 14C, it was rebuilt in 1584 and again in 1774. It was the burial place of the mid 16C Theophanios, Bishop of Soloi and last of the saints of Cyprus. In 1955 it was a haunt of Colonel Grivas. The ruined church of **Panayia Saittiotissa**, a short distance to the south, commemorated a pious legend concerning the Blessed Virgin. Mounted on a white horse, she loosed an arrow and killed a dragon which was terrorising the district.

In the mid 14C **Pelendria** (865m) was in the fief of Jean de Lusignan, Prince of Antioch, Constable of Cyprus and son of Hugh IV. Of the village's many churches the most interesting is **Stavros** on its southern outskirts. A late 13C building with additions on the north (14C) and south (16C) sides, it was carefully restored earlier this century. The interior has some fine 14C murals. A large decorated wooden cross is enclosed in a shrine of Coptic mushrabeyeh lattice work. The roof of the large 16C church of the **Panayia** almost touches the hillside. Its icons have been over restored.

The ugly asbestos mines on the mountain side which give **Pano Amiandos** (990m) its name (αμίαντος is Greek for asbestos) have now been closed, much to the discomfiture of the Bishop of Limassol, it is said, who had invested heavily in them.

The important church of **Ayios Nikolaos tis Stegis**, St Nicholas of the Roof, is some 3km to the south west of Kakopetria. A 13C upper shingle roof protects the lower domed and tiled roof which was repaired in 1955. Fork left after a badly signposted small dam to a restaurant and ask there for the key. The building dates from the 11C. The narthex with its cupola was added in the 12C. Its interior is covered with frescoes of various dates. Those in the narthex are from c 1430. Frescoes of about 1320 are in the south aisle, the remainder date from the early 17C to the beginning of the 18C. Among the earlier murals note the Transfiguration of Christ, the Raising of Lazarus, a 14C Nativity, the Entry into Jerusalem and a Crucifixion.

Ayios Nikolaos tis Stegis

Attractively sited on the upper reaches of the Karyotis stream, **Kakopetria** (660m) is a busy summer resort. It has five hotels—**Hellas**, ☎ (02) 922450, and **Makris Sunotel**, ☎ (02) 922419, both 3-stars; **Hekali**, ☎ (02) 922501, 2-star; **Minaide's**, ☎ (02) 922421 and **Krystal**, ☎ (02) 922433, one star each. There have been good reports of the **Mylos** and **Maryland at the Mill**, ☎ (02) 922536, trout restaurants. Kakopetria is an excellent centre for exploring this part of the central massif. It was one of the many refuges of the EOKA leader Colonel Grivas. The older part of the village, on the far side of the river bank, merits a visit. Restoration and preservation work continues here.

The adjoining village of **Galata**, on the 'old' road, should be visited for the sake of its churches. Settled c 1515, it is said that Sir Henry de Gibelet kept his hawks in this village. The early 16C church of the **Panayia** is to the right of the road leading north into Galata. The key is kept in the garage opposite the Rialto Hotel. Note the frescoes of the Entertainment of the Angels by Abraham and of the Sacrifice of Isaac. The priest, who lives near the school, has the keys to most of the local churches. If collected by car, he will accompany visitors. Behind the modern church stands **Ayios Sozomenos** (1513) which is under restoration. Spirited frescoes by Symeon Axenti, a local artist, who also worked on the Arkhangelos church, include the Transfiguration of Christ and His Entry into Jerusalem. On the exterior wall there are murals depicting the Seven Councils of the Church recognised by the Orthodox. The last painting shows the **Triumph of Orthodoxy** when Iconoclasm was defeated at the Second Council of Nicaea in 787.

All that remains of the monastery of Podithou are the churches of **Panayia Eleousa** (1502) and **Panayia Theotokos** sometimes called **Arkhangelos**. In the former note the round windows of Byzantine origin. The painting of the Virgin and Child in the apse and those of Moses and of Joachim and Anne show evidence of Italian influence. Above the north entrance of Panayia Theotokos is a fresco of the donors by Axenti. There are also representations of St Helena and of the Emperor Constantine, her son.

The restored 16C church of **Ayii Joachim and Anna** at **Kaliana** has some late 16C and early 17C icons. Note the remains of an aqueduct near the main road. An Ottoman **han** is now a Folk Architecture Site. Most of the structure, apart from the front doors, is original. **Tembria** may occupy the site of the ancient Greek city of **Tembrus** where, it is said, enough gold had been buried to support the island for seven years!

On a hill near **Korakou** is the church of **Ayios Loukas**. According to an inscription over the north door this was founded in 1697 '... by the expenses of the priest Jacovos (and) built by the hands of Constantine and Dimitri Gavriel.' Another church dedicated to **Ayios Mamas**, also from the 17C, has acoustic vases built into the apse. This has a 16C icon of the Blessed Virgin.

North of the village of **Evrykhou** (430m), once the terminus of the Government railway from Famagusta and Nicosia, is the small, well-preserved 15C church of **Ayios Kyriakos**. The altar-tomb of this saint is in a side chapel. The iconostasis dates from the 16C.

The modest church of **Panayia Phorviotissa**, Our Lady of the Meadows, at **Asinou** (465m), is tucked away in an isolated pine clothed valley. According to an inscription it was built through the generosity of Nicephorus, a 'magistros', when Alexius I Comnenus was Byzantine emperor in 1099. It seems probable that this Nicephorus, a person of some importance, was married to one of the emperor's daughters. The domed narthex was added to the church c 1200 and in 1300 the barrel vault was reconstructed and the nave strengthened with internal and external buttresses. The 12C **frescoes**, which cover the interior, were repainted in 1333. They were cleaned and preserved between 1965 to 1968 under the auspices of the Centre of Byzantine Studies at Dumbarton Oaks, Harvard University.

In the dome of the narthex is **Christ Pantokrator** with a group of Apostles. There is a striking **Last Judgment** with the customary depiction of the pleasures of the blessed in heaven and the torments of the damned in hell. Note the **Deisis** on the right side of the door and the group of saints which includes a dashing St George on a white charger. Some of the early frescoes are to be found in the west bay of the nave. There is a representation of the **Forty Martyrs of Sebaste**. They were members of Legio XII Fulminata who refused to abjure their faith and were forced to stand naked on the ice of a frozen lake at Sebasteia, modern Sivas in Turkey. Others paintings include the **Last Supper**, **Christ's Triumphant Entry into Jerusalem** and the **Dormition of the Blessed Virgin Mary**. Look in the vaults of the centre bay for representations of the **Crucifixion** and of the **Entombment** and on the right of the **Transfiguration** and **Baptism of Christ**. Over the sanctuary there is a painting of the **Ascension** and in the semi-dome of the apse of the **Blessed Virgin with the Archangels Michael and Gabriel** on her left and right respectively.

A booklet available at the church provides detailed information about the frescoes.

The Mountain Villages Part II

Highlights
Agros, Kyperounda, Panayia Khrysokoudhaliotissa, Panayia tou Araka, Stavros tou Ayiasmat, Palekhori, Phterykoudhi, Monastery of Makheras, Phikardhou, Panayia Evangelistria, Pano and Kato Lefkara, Monastery of Prophitis Elias, Tamassos

The villages described in this chapter lie to the east and north of the Troodos area.

At **Louvaras**, one of several villages in this area dating from the 13C, the tiny mid 15C chapel of **Ayios Mamas** has interesting frescoes. Some of these, which have been carelessly restored, are attributed to Philippe Goul who was active towards the end of the 15C. Note the late 16C icon of the Blessed Virgin and early 17C icon of Christ.

Zoopiyi (880m) is one of the principal centres for the production of Commandaria wine. In the 19C **Zoodotospygi** church there is a 15C icon of the Blessed Virgin.

The much restored church of the **Panayia** at **Ayios Theodhoros** has an iconostasis of 1667 in a perfect state of preservation.

The large modern church in **Ayios Ioannis** (880m) has an iconostasis of 1757 from the previous church of 1725.

At **Agros** (1010m), a village surrounded by vineyards and almond groves, monks from Constantinople established the **Monastery of Panayia Eleousa Agrou** in the 9C. Rebuilt later, this had become much decayed by the end of the 18C. In 1889 a large church in the Byzantine style was erected on the site. The icon of the Blessed Virgin, after whom the monastery is named, is not hidden behind a silver protective cover. There are two hotels, the 3-star **Rodon**, ☎ (05) 521201 and **Vlachos**, ☎ (05) 521330, which has 1 star. Agros has several tavernas, a post office, banks and shops.

The small village of **Polystipos** (1060m), set among terraced vineyards, is noted for its almonds and hazelnuts.

Kyperounda (1650m) has a single guest house, the **Livadhia**, ☎ (05) 532014. This has nine rooms and serves meals. The village also has a taverna, the **Amazel**. With its neighbour **Khandria** across the valley, it is a good centre for walking holidays, particularly on **Mt Adelphi** (1610m). A church dedicated to the Holy Cross, which is believed to date from the early 16C, has some wall paintings of scenes from the life of St Helena who found the True Cross. Near Kyperounda are two villages which merit a visit, Dhymes, said to have been settled before 1200 BC, and Potamitissa.

Colonel Grivas had a hideout to the south of the village of **Spilla**. The **Marjay Inn**, ☎ (02) 922208, has nine rooms. To the north of **Kourdhali** is the early 16C church of the former monastery of **Panayia Khrysokoudhaliotissa**, the Dormition of the Blessed Virgin. This rectangular building has a central nave and two side aisles. The spring in the forecourt is used for lustral purposes. The icons on the iconostasis are in the Italo-Byzantine style. Note the **Deisis**, the

Christ in Majesty and the icon of **SS Joachim and Anna**, the parents of the Blessed Virgin. On the west wall to the right of the entrance there are the **Donor Portraits**. According to the inscription they were the deacon Kourdhalis, his wife and their children. It is said that the deacon came from Kurdistan. The presence of some hand written pages in a fine Arabic script bound into one of the early 15C manuscripts in the church lends some credence to this tradition.

In the church at **Sarandi**, which is believed to date from the 17C, there is an unusual mural of the **Last Supper**. This shows the Disciples sitting on the ground.

The mid 19C church of **St George** in **Lagoudhera** has some 16C icons. These depict the **Blessed Virgin and infant Child Jesus** and the **Deisis**. There is also an icon of **Christ** dated by an inscription to 1620. However, the principal attraction of Lagoudhera is the mid 12C domed church of the monastery of **Panayia tou Araka**, Our Lady of the Wild Vetch, located a short distance outside the village. The vaulted rectangular building has three bays and an apse. The 17C narthex replaces one built in the 14C. The protective tiled roof is probably from the same period. Originally the private chapel of the local overlord, it is not known when it became or when it ceased to be a monastery. A few monks still lived there in the early 18C. The decoration of the interior dates from 1192. This was a year of strife and turmoil in Cyprus, the year when Richard Coeur de Lion transferred the island to Guy de Lusignan, the founder of the Lusignan dynasty. The frescoes were restored between 1968 and 1973 by David Winfield. An impressive representation of **Christ Pantokrator** fills the dome. He is surrounded by an ornate frieze of **Old Testament Prophets**. Among a number of New Testament scenes note the beautiful **Dormition of the Blessed Virgin** in the lunette of the south recess, her **Presentation in the Temple** in the north recess, the **Nativity** in the south side of the west vault, the **Baptism of Christ** in the north west recess and the **Harrowing of Hell** in the north west vault. In the iconostasis is an **icon of Christ** painted on both sides.

Platanistasa (930m) is a pleasant village which dates from c 1200. The medieval church of **Ayios Ioannis**, which was rebuilt in 1740, was burnt to the ground in 1987.

The key to **Stavros tou Ayiasmati** is kept at Platanistasa. This monastery church is hidden away in a mountain valley some 3km from the village. Reached by a dirt track, which curls round the hill side, it is most attractively sited and commands fine views. Believed to date from c 1436, it has an almost complete cycle of Byzantine revival style wall paintings in two tiers. According to an inscription they were painted by Philippe Goul (fl. 1495) whose work is to be found also in the church of St Mamas at Louveras. Note particularly the **Baptism of Christ** on the south wall, the moving depiction of the **Nativity**, and **St Mamas** and his delightfully human looking lion.

The ancient, attractively sited village of **Palekhori** (900m) is famed for the quality of its red wine. It straddles the valley of the Peristerona river whose banks are lined with poplar trees. Part of the Commandery of the Templars in 1297, it passed later into the hands of the d'Ibelin family. The 16C church of **Panayia Khrysopantanissa** in the upper town, restored in 1863 and further modernised in 1948, has some **early 17C paintings** on the arches and pillars of the aisles. There is also an **icon of the Blessed Virgin** dated 1560. To visit the early 16C **Metamorphosis tou Soteros**, the church of the Transfiguration of the Saviour, which is above the village, you will need to get the key from the village priest. Note the **murals** of 1612 outside the west door. In the sanctuary there are frescoes depicting various events from the Old Testament, while the nave has a scenes from the New Testament. The paintings are attributed to Philippe Goul. Near the centre of the village are the medieval church of **Ayios Yeoryios** and **Ayios Loukas** which was built in 1925 to replace an earlier church. It has kept the modernised belfry of its predecessor.

The attractive village of **Phterykoudhi** (980m) was settled c 1575 after a battle between Venetians and Turks at nearby **Kalamithasa** in 1570 when that village was destroyed. To the east stands the early 16C church of **Ayia Paraskeva**, sometimes called **Ayia Khristina**. St Paraskevi is believed to have been a Roman maiden martyred during the reign of Marcus Aurelius for refusing to sacrifice to the pagan gods. The frescoes depict **St Mamas and his Lion**, **St George** with his youthful squire and portraits of the donors. The mid 16C church of **Ayios Ioannis Vaptistis**, St John the Baptist, at **Askas** was restored in 1763. Its remaining, age darkened wall paintings tell the story of the life of the Baptist.

The **Monastery of Makheras** (884m), the Monastery of the Sword, was founded c 1148 by Neophytos, an aged hermit who was expelled from Syria. He came to Cyprus with a companion named Ignatios and settled in this place because it was remote and had a reliable source of fresh water. After finding an icon, which was guarded by a sword, in a cave, the hermits decided to establish a monastery here. Following the death of Neophytos, Ignatios made the arduous journey to Constantinople and was granted an extensive tract of mountain land and an annual donation from the imperial treasury by the Byzantine Emperor Manuel Comnenos. Work commenced on the erection of suitable accommodation for the growing community which soon acquired a number of postulants. Among them was Nilos who became the first abbot, later Bishop of Tamassos and then Archbishop of Cyprus.

There is a story that in 1337 Alix d'Ibelin the impetuous wife of Hugh IV, insisted on entering the monastery church, something which was forbidden to women. As a punishment she was struck dumb and remained so for three years until a miracle at Tokni restored her speech. In 1393 James I and his court sought refuge here from the plague. The monastery was burnt down in 1530 and again in 1892. In the rebuilding, completed in 1900, few of the architectural features of the earlier structure were preserved. Some original masonry may be seen in the church. In 1957 Gregoris Afxentiou, second in command to Colonel Grivas in the EOKA uprising, died in a nearby cave.

The **miracle working icon**, covered by an 18C repoussé silver screen and, symbolically protected by a small silver knife, is on the iconostasis. The manuscript of Abbot Nilos' *Ritual Ordinance* together with some church plate is kept in the treasury.

The name of the monastery may come from the sword which was buried with the icon during the period of the iconoclastic controversy in the 8C as a token of protection or from the fierce winds which howl about this fortress-like structure in the winter.

There is a souvenir shop and a café which is open during the summer months. Overnight lodging is sometimes available. The views from the monastery are extensive—and beautiful—especially in February when the almond trees are in flower. Nicosia may be glimpsed in the distance. Walkers will enjoy the high upland forest around the monastery. To the south is **Mt Kionia** (1423m) which has a meteorological station on the summit.

Lazania (900m) has some well preserved 18C houses with fine carved windows and doors. Similarly ornamented houses are to be found in **Gourri** (730m). This village takes its name from one of the great medieval families of Cyprus. The Gourri coat of arms, a sun displayed, is to be seen in Famagusta and other places in the island. **Phikardhou** has been declared an Ancient Monument and is being looked after by those responsible for preserving folk architecture from further depredations. Two houses, open to the public, have been filled with the furniture and artefacts used by earlier generations. The village has a single taverna which serves a satisfying lunch and good local wine. Clitos Jacovides (1913 to 1975), owner of the taverna in Kyrenia frequently mentioned by Lawrence Durrell, was born at Gourri.

The large number of tombs around **Klirou** (455m) suggest that it was occupied from early times. It was the property of Sir Thomas de Montolif, a prominent member of the Cypriot nobility, in the 14C. During the Second World War it was, for a period, a British Army HQ. The ground plan of the predecessor of **Panayia Evangelistria** may be seen to the north. In the mid 18C iconostasis, which came from the old church, there is an **icon of the Annunciation** covered with silver gilt. It is believed that this can bring rain. If the suppliant's prayer is granted and he does not bring an offering to the church, disaster will follow. His crops will fail, his cattle will die and his children will fall ill. There are the ruins of a monastery of the **Blessed Virgin of Lakhni** to the south of the village.

At **Malounda** there is a badly restored **medieval bridge** which bears a defaced Lusignan coat of arms.

The 15C **Monastery of Ayios Minas**, rebuilt in 1754, has recently been taken over by a community of nuns. They paint and sell icons and excellent honey. There are paintings of SS George and Minas in the church.

The twin villages of **Pano** and **Kato Lefkara** are famed for their **handmade lace**, **Turkish Delight** and **jewellery**. In Pano Lefkara there are two modest hotels, the 2 star **Agora**, ☎ (04) 342901, and the 1 star **Lefkarama**, ☎ (04) 342000, several restaurants, a post office and shops. It is a good centre for walking holidays.

The Orthodox Bishop of Limassol was exiled here by the Latins from 1222 to 1470. A bishop's crown and other relics were found under the floor of the church of Arkhangelos Michael in 1865. According to Gunnis they were sold to one of the foreign consuls at Larnaca, probably General Cesnola. The villages were sacked by the Venetians in 1570 and many of their inhabitants massacred for supporting the Turkish cause. For this action the survivors were later exempted from the Ottoman poll-tax. The villagers once had the unenviable reputation of adulterating their olive oil by mixing mallow water with it.

The lace is of extremely high quality and therefore rather expensive. Its manufacture and marketing are in the hands of four main producers, each employing some 150 workers. The base material is now Irish linen. Beware of cheap imports which may be passed off as Lefkara lace by some unscrupulous shopkeepers. There is a tradition, ardently fostered by the villagers, that Leonardo da Vinci bought lace here in 1481 for the altar cloth of Milan Cathedral. However, there is no evidence that he visited the island in that year. Much of the Turkish Delight made here is exported. Try it and, if possible, see it being made. The villages' figs are famous. In the 18C a medicinal plant, *Cistus ladanifera*, a stimulant not to be confused with laudanum, was collected in the neighbourhood.

In Pano Lefkara there are several well constructed stone houses. In one of these, the **House of Patsalos**, is the **Museum of Folk Art**. This is largely devoted to the traditional embroidery, lace, and silverwork of the area. The large mid 19C church of **Stavros** has an iconostasis, icons and a large cross covered with silver plates showing scenes from the life of Christ. All date from the 18C. **Ayios Timotheos** is a well preserved medieval domed church.

The late 12C single aisled church of **Arkhangelos Mikhail**, which is some distance outside the village, has a modern extension at the west end. There are some fine 12C wall paintings.

The buildings of the post Byzantine **Monastery of Prophitis Elias**, restored in 1899 and again more recently, are now used by the Forestry Department. Date palms thrive here at an altitude of 608m! Only one monk was left in the monastery by 1735. Some monastic relics are kept in the 18C, but much restored, church of **Ayios Therapon** in **Lythrodhonda**. Many of the inhabitants of this village were *Linobambakoi*.

The **Monastery of Ayios Heracleidios**, near the village of **Politiko**, has had a long and chequered history. The first church on the site was built in the 5C. There were rebuildings in the 15C and early 17C. The monastic buildings are from the late 18C. Closed down during the troubles of 1821, the monastery was reopened by Archbishop Makarios and a community of nuns established here. Their rose jam, an almond preserve called *gliko amigdalou* and other succulent confections are justly famous.

The 15C south aisle of the **church** is dedicated to St Heracleidios, the early 17C north aisle to the Holy Trinity. The iconostasis, which incorporates earlier fragments, dates from 1774. Most of the icons are from the 18C. The icon of St John the Baptist, which dates from 1611, was painted in the monastery. The skull of St Herakleidios and one of his bones are in two ornamented reliquaries placed on a table in the east side of the church. Note the small section of the 5C mosaic floor, which has been exposed to view, and the wall paintings—St Heracleidios on the east arch, the Fathers of the Church on the south wall.

Adjoining the church is a small domed cruciform **mortuary chapel**, dating from the 14C. In it are the sarcophagi of St Heracleidios, of his successor St Mnason and of some other early saints from nearby Tamassos. The greater part of the unusual iconostasis of four large stone slabs carved with the Chi-Rho

---

St Heracleidios

Many miracles are attributed to St Heracleidios. Hackett, writing in *A History of the Orthodox Church in Cyprus*, tells a story of the exorcism of demons. A young boy, John Savas, from the Phaneromene quarter of Nicosia was possessed by devils. In 1769 he was brought here by his parents in the hope that intercession to the saint might alleviate his suffering. During a celebration of the Divine Liturgy the boy had convulsions and vomited forth 'a snake, a span long, and two crabs'. These were then hung up in the church to confirm the faith of believers and to silence the voices of the sceptics.

grilled lambs' testicles. Open for dinner is Kavouri at 125 Leoforos Strovolos. This specialises in fish dishes. It is usually necessary to book.

Transport
At Leoforos Stasinou: Paralimni-Deryneia Bus Co. Services to Paralimni-Protaras.
At Leoforos Omrou: Kallenos Buses, to Larnaca; KEMEK Buses to Limassol and Paphos; Zingas Bus to Platres
From near the Bayraktar Mosque: EMAN Bus to Ayia Napa; Kalrios Bus to the Troodos hill resorts
At Leoforos Stasinou near d'Avila Bastion: Shared taxis to Larnaca, Limassol and Paphos.

Religious services
Orthodox: Ayios Ioannis and Trypiotis Sunday 06.15 to 09.15.
Roman Catholic: the Franciscan Holy Cross Church near the Paphos Gate. Mass on Sunday in Greek at 08.00 and in English at 09.30, 18.30.
Anglican: St Paul's, Leoforos Lordou Vyronos. Sunday 09.30.
Maronite: Pyli Pafou. Mass in Aramaic Sunday 07.30, 08.30, 09.30.
Armenian: Odos Armenias, Akropolis. Mass Sunday 07.30 and 09.00.
Coptic: Odos Damonos, Kaimakli Sunday two weeks each month at 09.00.
Omeriye Mosque: Friday prayers 12.30 to 13.30.

The British Council at 3 Mouseiou, near the Cyprus Museum, has an excellent library of English books which may be borrowed by members. It also organises lectures and other cultural activities.

American Center is at Leoforos Omirou 33B.

The **Ledra Palace Hotel** is now occupied by the UNFICYP forces. The only crossing point into Northern Nicosia and North Cyprus is here. Bring your passport.
   A short distance to the west of the hotel is the **Pedieos River**, Measuring 74km, it is the longest river in Cyprus. Depending on the season it is either a raging torrent or a trickle of semi stagnant water in an arid, rubbish filled ditch. In the past, floods of the Pedieos drowned many in the city and its waters sometimes filled the moat.
   The **Church of St Paul**, a very English village church of 1893, looks somewhat out of place in its Cypriot setting. Enlarged in the 1950s, the interior was renovated in 1975. It is the cathedral of the Anglican diocese of Cyprus and the Gulf.

Cyprus Museum
The Cyprus Museum, headquarters of the Department of Antiquities, was established in 1883.

■ The museum is open from Monday to Saturday between 09.00 to 17.00; on Sunday between 10.00 and 13.00.

Claude Delaval Cobham, who translated, transcribed and collected the accounts of early travellers to Cyprus in *Excerpta Cypria*, was on its council. Captain Horatio Herbert Kitchener was the curator. The museum was maintained by private subscription until refounded in 1908 as a memorial to Queen Victoria. It was transferred the following year to a part of the present building. This brown stone structure, designed in the Classical style with a marble portico, was enlarged between 1913 and 1918. In 1942 the important **Louki Pierides Library** was donated to the museum. Between 1950 and 1951 the central courtyard was roofed to provide space for reserve collections and the building was further extended in the years 1959 to 1961. There is a plan to build an entirely new museum worthy of the collection, but it is unlikely that this will be realised for some years to come.

Photography is not allowed in the museum. Postcards, books, reproductions of some of the exhibits and videos on the archaeology of Cyprus are on sale at the shop by the main entrance.

Displays in the museum are not static and the objects described below may not be in the places mentioned. They may be on exhibition in another part of the museum, removed temporarily for conservation or study or on loan to other museums. You will find it helpful to refer during the visit to the Introduction to the Monuments and Early History of Cyprus, to the Chronological Table and the descriptions of the sites in the text.

Room 1. Artefacts of the Neolithic IA period, including stone, flint, and bone objects, from Petra tou Limniti, Mari, and Cape St. Andreas; of the Neolithic IB period from Troulli and Dhenia; and of Neolithic IA and II from Khirokitia, these include a small **andesite head**. There is a scale reconstruction of the settlement at Khirokitia. A ritual deposit from Kissonerga (Mosphilia), including cult objects of c 3000 BC, excavated in 1987; **a wall painting** of a human figure with upraised arms from Kalavassos Tenta; artefacts of the Neolithic IB and II periods from Philia and Sotira including andesite bowls, phalli, and pottery; Neolithic II and Chalcolithic I flints and ornaments from Kalavassos; obsidian and picrolite ornaments; Chalcolithic I artefacts from Erimi and shell and picrolite necklaces from Souskiou; Chalcolithic II artefacts from Ambelikou. Note the Chalcolithic I **stylised picrolite idol** with outstretched arms from Paphos, the jug of Red on White ware from Erimi of the same period, the limestone idol of c 2500 BC from Lemba.

Room 2. Glazed ware with combed design, clay figurines and the Early Bronze Age **clay models** of an **open air sanctuary** and of **ploughing** from Vounous. Also an Early Bronze Age alabaster bowl.

Room 3. Mycenaean crater from Kourion with female figures in 'windows'; another **krater from Enkomi** of c 1400 BC decorated with warriors going to battle in a chariot; others showing birds and bulls; a Mycenaean amphoroid crater with an octopus design; other important Mycenaean ceramics of the Late Cypriot II period; a **terracotta figurine** of a mother goddess with a bird like head; decorated ware of the Middle and Late Cypriot period, including Syrio-Palestinian and Egyptian imported pottery; artefacts of the Cypro-Geometric and Cypro-Archaic periods, including jugs with curious female figures, one winged, leaning on the shoulder near the spout, and holding miniature jugs. Cypro-Classical, Hellenistic and Roman pottery; imported Corinthian and Attic ware. An early 14C BC **silver cup with inlaid decoration of gold and niello**

from Enkomi. A 13C BC **conical faience rhyton** from Kition showing galloping animals and a bull hunt.

Room 4. 7C to 6C terracotta votive figurines excavated in 1929 near Ayia Irini, north of Morphou. Of the 2000 figurines found around the altar in the temenos only two were female. They included minotaurs, which might indicate the cult of the bull as a god of fertility, charioteers and hermaphrodites. Most of them wear a soft conical cap or helmet.

Room 5. Clay and limestone statuary and votive statuettes. Among them two female torsos each carrying a votive bull and wearing necklaces; a bearded head of c 450 BC from Troulli; a **female head** of 450 to 400 BC with a diadem decorated with sphinxes and palmettes from Arsos; a 3C BC stele of Bacchus; and a 3C BC marble head of Arsinoe II from Soloi.

Room 6. Roman period limestone female statue in ritual dress and the bronze head of a youth, both from Soloi. A bronze larger than life size **statue of Septimius Severus** (AD 193 to 211) discovered accidentally near Kythrea in 1928 and reconstructed in 1940.

Room 7. Bronze objects from Enkomi, including a wheeled stand decorated with bulls and gryphons; helmets, weapons, spearheads, mirrors, tripods, scales and weights, lampstands, and lamps. A 12C BC **bronze statue of a horned god**, possibly a representation of Apollo Keraiates, from Enkomi. Bronze objects from an 11 BC tomb at Paleapaphos; coins, including part of a **hoard of 2484 Ptolemaic silver tetradrachms** found below a mosaic floor at the House of Dionysos, Paphos; cylinder and other seals and impressions; an unusual Late Bronze Age relief pithos, peculiar to Cyprus. Note also the 5C Hathor type limestone capital from Vouni. The far end of this room is described below.

Room 9. Cippi and funerary stelae, one surmounted by a sphinx, from Idalion (4C BC). Terracotta and marble sarcophagi. Note the touching representation of a woman with an infant and a child.

Room 11. An ivory chair and bed and an iron chair and footstool from Salamis, 8C to 7C BC. Clay heads. An 8C BC bronze cauldron on an iron tripod from Salamis. Bronze accessories from chariots and harness.

The **library** adjoins this room.

Room 12 is devoted to the metallurgy of Cyprus.

From **Room 11** steps lead to a subterranean passage, **Room 8**, where there are reconstructions of rock tombs with the artefacts found in them.

Room 10. Funerary stelae and votive inscriptions, one in Cypro-Syllabic script.

Return to **Room 7**. **Mosaics** of a dog and partridge from Mansoura, 3C to 4C AD, and of **Leda and the Swan** from Palaepaphos. Hellenistic alabaster statuettes and vases and terracotta lamps. Bone and ivory objects, and glass amulets, beads, phalli, etc.

Room 13. 2C AD marble statues, including those of Asclepius, God of Healing, and of Isis. Both from Salamis.

Room 14. Terracotta figurines, statuettes from the Early Bronze Age to Roman times; the masks and the moulds used to make them. Note the Early Bronze Age square or plank figurine of a mother and child; votive figures, dancers and goddesses with uplifted arms; horned Baal Hamman and a comic figure with a big nose and a huge penis.

The Walled City

For the sake of convenience the entire stretch of the walls is described here although the northern half from the Roccas Bastion to the Flatro Bastion is in Northern Nicosia.

The **walls of Nicosia**, which encircles the old quarter of the city, are over 3km in length. In 1565 the Venetians dispatched an engineer, Ascanio Savorgnano, to report on the condition of the straggling medieval fortifications which stood, c 350m beyond the present circuit, all round the city except on the north west side. Two years later Francesco Barbaro laid out the present walls, based on Savorgnano's report and recommendations. They were strengthened by 11 bastions and pierced by three fortified gates, now known as the Famagusta Gate, the Kyrenia Gate and the Paphos Gate. Substantially the same as when built, although in some sections the stone casing has crumbled or has been taken for use elsewhere. At various times the walls have been breached and the moat filled in to provide additional entrances to the enceinte.

Famagusta Gate

The bastions and present entrances are described in clockwise order commencing with the **Caraffa** or **Garaffa Bastion** which faces due east and is immediately south of **Plateia Vasileos Georgiou II**. At the soutern side of the bastion is the **Famagusta Gate** which is now closed to traffic. A tunnel surmounted by a curious central dome, it was the principal entrance to the walled city. The most important monument of the Venetian period surviving in Nicosia, it was built in 1567 by Giulio Savorgnano, the brother of Ascanio. He copied Michele Sanmicheli's Porta del Lazzareto at Candia in Crete, constructed two years earlier. An aqueduct, which masked the façade, has been removed, revealing the six coats of arms mentioned by Mariti in 1791. The central domed chamber, with its oculus, echoes in miniature the Pantheon in Rome. It was briefly called Channel Squadron Gate to commemorate the entrance to Nicosia there of 50 British bluejackets and 50 Marines on 12 July 1878. It is now a cultural centre and is used for exhibitions, lectures and concerts.

On the ramparts nearby there is a modern statue by Costas Varotsos entitled *The Poet*. This is made of pieces of broken glass.

Next come the **Podocataro**, **Costanza** and **d'Avila Bastions**. The walls between them are now pierced by roads. On the **Costanza Bastion** are the remains of the **Mosque of the Standard-bearer**. This is said to mark the place where the first Turkish standard was planted at the siege of 1570. The tomb of the standard-bearer, the *Bayraktar* in Turkish, who was killed instantly, lies in a recess on the north side. On the **d'Avila Bastion** stand the Municipal Library, **Central Post Office** and the Town Hall.

Beyond the **Tripoli Bastion** was the tunnel of the **Paphos Gate**. This was originally known as the **Porta Domenica** after the royal château of St Dominic which stood nearby and was razed to the ground by the Venetians in 1567 when they constructed the new walls. The gate was closed in 1878, as it occasionally admitted floodwater from the Pedieos whose course originally ran along Hermes St.

The Cypriot Turkish flag flies above the **Roccas Bastion** which overlooks the Green Line that separates the two parts of the city.

The construction costs of the Franciscan church of the **Holy Cross** were largely met by a bequest of Queen Maria Cristina of Spain. Built in 1900, it replaced a Franciscan church of 1642. For several centuries the priors of the community have been Spaniards. The arms of Aragon and Castile are painted on the ceiling and appear on the cope of the Prior. It has a delightful **bas-relief** dated 1524 showing St Mamas and his lion in a landscape with palm trees. Below the saint is the donor supported by an angel. The relief was taken from an earlier Franciscan church destroyed in the siege of 1570. Access to the church is allowed although it is on the north side of the Green Line.

Beyond the **Mula** and **Quirini Bastions** is the **Kyrenia Gate**. This was originally the **Porta del Provveditore**, named after the Provveditore Francesco Barbaro. It was repaired by the Turks in 1821 when the chamber above it was added. The inscription over the arched doorway is of some verses from the Koran. It was repaired again by the British in 1931. Since then traffic has flowed past each side of the gate. It is the main entrance to Northern Nicosia.

Roads have been cut through the walls between the **Barbaro Bastion**, the **Loredano Bastion** and the **Flatro Bastion** which is divided by the Green Line. The old **Kaimakli Gate** has not been used for centuries.

The southern half of the enceinte is best explored on foot. It is here that many of the interesting old churches are to be found. The barricades of the soldiers on the Green Line are usually some distance south and north of the Line. These produce a dead area, normal life seems to peter out in their vicinity. Unfortunately the walled city has been allowed to decay. In southern Nicosia too many attractive traditional Turkish style houses with their latticed balconies have been allowed to disintegrate or have been deliberately dismantled. The situation is somewhat better in the northern part of the city where there are more old houses, more mosques, more stalls, more street kiosks and more bazaars. A busier street life still exists there. Although too many open spaces serve as dumping grounds for old cars and refuse, the character of some areas has changed little.

The area called **Laiki Geitonia** has been tastefully restored and refurbished. The **Tourist Office** is here, also bookshops, small restaurants, galleries, handicraft shops and a bank. Relax in one of the cafés after your visit to the old town.

The **Leventis Municipal Museum**, inaugurated in 1989, is devoted to the history of Nicosia. Essentially a didactic museum, it uses photographs, models, maps and costumes to explain the history of the city. A cutting shows the foundations of the medieval building over which the museum has been built. There is a small café and a shop sells cards, books and reproductions. It is **open** from Tuesday to Sunday 10.00 to 16.30.

Panayia Phaneromeni, the Church of the Blessed Virgin Discovered by Revelation, was built in 1872 with stones taken from the ruined Lusignan castle of La Cava at Athalassa. It rests on the foundations of an earlier Byzantine convent which, in turn, replaced a Cistercian convent. It incorporates fragments from its predecessors, including a number of gargoyles. Archbishop Kyprianos and the bishops of Larnaca, Paphos and Kition, who were executed by the Turks in1821, are buried here. Note the 17C iconostasis, the miracle working icon of the Blessed Virgin of Phaneromeni and a carved Byzantine cross, surrounded by 18C gilt filigree work, which holds a fragment of the True Cross.

The closed, diminutive **Arablar Mosque** was in Lusignan times the church of **Stavrou tou Missiricou**. The partly restored **Ömerye Mosque** was before the conquest the **Augustinian Church of St Mary**. It was converted by Mustafa Paşa, the victorious Turkish general, in 1571. He identified the early 14C church with the place where the prophet Ömer rested when he visited Nicosia in the 7C. The Latin archbishop of Nicosia retired here in 1469 and had a hospice built near the church to accommodate poor pilgrims who were on their way to the Holy Land. The west door and a rose-window survive from the original building. It was damaged during the siege, when it lost its roof. A small minaret was added to a turret on the north east side.

The church was a place of pilgrimage as it housed the shrine of the saintly Blessed John de Montfort. One of the most important Latin saints of Cyprus, Blessed John de Montfort was a Knight Templar. Wounded in a battle against the Saracens, he was carried to Nicosia where he died in 1248. His feast was long celebrated in Cyprus on 25 May. 'So great was his reputation, and so numerous the mircales attributed to his power, that pilgrims came from all over Europe to pray at his tomb, where his body lay unchanged and uncorrupted by time.' (Gunnis. *Historic Cyprus*). Many of the incised tombstones of the Lusignan period, which had been used to floor the mosque, were removed to the bedesten by Gunnis in 1935. Among them were the memorials of the Neville and Daubigny families.

The **House of the Dragoman Haji Georghakis Kornessios**, with its over-hanging latticed balcony, is a fine example of a traditonal 18C Turkish *konak* or town mansion. Kornessios was Great Dragoman of Cyprus from 1779 to1809. The word dragoman is derived from the Turkish *tercüman*, ie, interpreter. However, the Great Dragoman of Cyprus was much more than an interpreter. He was the link between the administration and the Greek Cypriots. He was always a member of the Greek Cypriot community and was appointed by the archbishop. It was said that Dragoman Kornessios was the richest and most powerful man on the island. In 1804 a mob protesting against high taxation attacked his *konak* and he was obliged to flee to Constantinople. Returning at the head of a detachment of Turkish soldiers, he quelled the revolt and resumed his duties. Accused of treason, he was beheaded in 1809 and his property was confiscated. Later his family bought back the *konak*.

His house has been tastefully restored. Note the carved escutcheon over the entrance. This features a very odd looking lion of St Mark above a shield which shows the Byzantine double headed eagle. The ensemble is completed by pomegranates and foliage. Some assert that this was a fictitious coat of arms invented by Kornessios, others that it was brought from an old building. A courtyard leads to a walled garden. Since 1987 the upper floors have housed an **Ethnographic Museum**.

■ Open from Monday to Friday between 08.00 and 14.00; and on Saturday between 09.00 and 13.00.

There is some interesting 19C furniture and Damascus glass. In the main reception room a cupboard conceals an escape route to the roof! Portraits of Kornessios show an apprehensive, shifty eyed man holding a document bearing the *tuğra* of the sultan.

The church of **Ayios Antonios**, itself architecturally unimpressive, is dominated by an intricately carved belfry. It was restored in 1743 by Archbishop Philothcos. The tombstone of a woman in 16C costume in the narthex was probably brought here from a Latin church in the neighbourhood. The carved baroque style iconostasis dates from the same period as the church. Note the grandfather clock with a ship on its pendulum.

The **Archbishop's Palace** is a three storey edifice in a grandiose, pseudo Venetian style. Begun in 1936, it is composed of superimposed loggias. Of great pretension and little architectural merit, even if displaying some fine workmanship, it has been the object of much well deserved criticism, not only for being entirely out of keeping with its surroundings, but also as gratuitous extravagance at a time of considerable economic difficulty. Archbishop Makarios escaped from the palace on 15 July 1974, when it was attacked and set alight in an attempted coup d'état by the Greek military junta five days prior to the Turkish invasion. A gigantic statue of Makarios dominates the site.

The north west part of the palace complex is a large building which houses part of the **Archbishop Makarios III Cultural Foundation**. This has public art galleries, a library, research centre and the **Byzantine Museum**, which houses more than 150 icons.

■ Open from Monday to Friday between 09.00 and 16.30; and on Saturday between 08.00 and 12.00.

The earliest icon dates from the 9C. Some 92 have been brought from churches in Nicosia alone. The collection was established by Archbishop Makarios III to stop the export of icons from Cyprus. The appreciation and enjoyment of icons, more than any other form of pictorial art, is a very personal matter. It is, therefore, with some diffidence that the following selection is proposed: 4. Christ's Descent into Limbo, 13C; 7. **St Nicholas**, late 13C; 8. the Blessed Virgin Kamariotissa with donors, late 15C; 17. the **Blessed Virgin**, 12C; 22. St Marina 13C; 29. St Mamas on his lion, c 1500; 36. St John the Baptist, 14C; 46. **Christ with angels and donors**, 1356; 50. an olive-coloured St John the Baptist, 16C to 17C; 65. the damaged double icon of the **Blessed Virgin Athanasiotissa** and the **Deposition of Christ**; 66. the Comnenian icon of **Christ**, c 1190; 70. the **Crucifixion** with a depiction the **Blessed Virgin** on the reverse, late 14C; 72. St Marina, second half of the 15C; 80. Christ's Entry into Jerusalem, 1546; 81. Christ's Descent into Limbo, 1563; 87. Christ, with donors, 1549; 88. the Blessed Virgin Hodegetria, ie, pointing at the Christ Child as the way to salvation, with angels and donors, 1529; 94. the Blessed Virgin *orans*, early 16C; 96. The Nativity, 16C; 100. the Last Judgment, 16C; 106. St Barbara, 16C to17C; 107. the Blessed Virgin Hodegetria, 1557; 118. the Burning Bush, 18C; 126. the **Blessed Virgin and the Christ Child** between SS George and Nicholas, 16C; 132. the Baptism of Christ, 16 to17C; 137. St George, 17C; 140. St Demetrius late 16C; 141, the Ascension of Christ, Pentecost and the Blessed Virgin *orans* between angels.

Note also the 14C wall paintings which were rescued from the Church of St Nicholas of the Roof and the **6C mosaics** from Kanakaria in the Karpas peninsula. The latter were removed illegaly from Cyprus, taken to the United States and subsequently recovered by legal action. They show the Blessed Virgin with the Christ Child attended by the Archangel Gabriel and ten of the apostles in roundels. John and Peter are missing. The mosaics compare in importance with the 6C mosaic in the church of Angeloktisti at Kiti near Larnaca.

On the first floor is the late Ethnarch's personal collection of 120 European paintings. Many of the attributions appear doubtful or the exhibits are poor examples of the work of the artists whose names appear on the labels. Two are notable: the Spanish School painting of St Bartholomew and an anonymous 18C portrait of the Duc de Penthièvre.

Of more interest is the collection of prints, engravings, watercolours, drawings and maps on the second floor. This is devoted to Greece and the Greek War of Independence. Of interest are: A girl of Chios by the Genevan artist Jean Etienne Liotard, 1702 to 1790, who travelled widely in the Near East and some works by Pierre Bonirote, 1811 to 1891.

In the **library** there are manuscripts and books in many languages about various aspects of Cyprus. The Foundation will house a **research centre** in the field of Cypriot studies and publish books and articles about the island.

The diminutive buttressed late 17C church dedicated to **Ayios Ioannis**, St John the Divine, is the Orthodox cathedral of Nicosia.

■ Open from Monday to Friday between 08.00 and 12.00 and 14.00 and 16.00; Saturday 08.00 and 12.00. Also during services.

It is believed to occupy the site of the Benedictine Abbey of St John the Evangelist of Bibi where a finger of St John the Baptist was preserved in the treasury. When the Benedictines left the island in 1426, the building passed into Orthodox hands. The vault and walls have paintings dating from 1730 onwards. These have become darkened by candle smoke. They include a graphic representation of the **Day of Judgment** above the south door. As the souls of the dead are being weighed the devils are pulling down the scales and conducting the damned to the fiery mouth of hell. Opposite is the **Creation**. On the right of the bishop's throne there are four scenes of the discovery of the relics of St Barnabas. Unusually for an Orthodox church **Pope St Sylvester** is included in the painting of the officiating Fathers of the Church in the apse. Note the marble slab on the floor with the double headed eagle of Byzantium and the 14C and 15C fragments of sculpture from the Benedictine abbey over the west entrance.

St Sylvester

St Sylvester (d. 335) baptised the Emperor Constantine and was the first pope to govern a church free from persecution. During his pontificate the first general council of the Church was held at Nicaea (now Iznik in Turkey). This dealt with the Arian heresy. He is usually shown in papal robes holding a small dragon in his hand or on a chain.

On the ground floor of the 14C to 15C monastery dependencies, which from 1730 were known as the Archbishopric and from 1961 as the Old Archbishopric, there is a **Folk Art Museum**.

■ Open from Monday to Friday between 09.00 and 17.00; and on Saturday between 10.00 and 13.00.

The buildings were restored between 1962 and 1964. At the top of the exterior staircase there is an early Byzantine carved marble panel of a pastoral scene—at the foot of three palm trees lies a sleeping sheep. This may be an early reference to the Lamb of God.

Like similar museums in Limassol and Paphos it houses a heterogenous collection of agricultural implements, peasant furniture and costumes, tools, embroidery, household linen, cooking utensils, basketwork and musical instruments.

Opposite the Archbishopric are the buildings of the **Pancyprian Gymnasium**. This was rebuilt after a fire in 1922 on the site of an earlier school founded in 1812 by Archbishop Kyprianos. Lawrence Durrell taught here for a short time. In the late 1950s under the direction of the passionately enosist headmaster, Dr Spyridakis, the gymnasium was a hot bed of youthful demonstrators.

The **Museum of National Struggle** has a collection of photographs, booby traps, arms and other lethal objects used in the anti British activities of EOKA during the troubled years of 1955 to 1959. It is open from Monday to Friday between 08.00 and 14.30 and 15.00 and 18.00.

The older part of the church of **Panayia Khrysaliniotissa**, Our Lady of the Golden Flax, dates from 1450 onwards. It is believed that Queen Helena Palaeologus, daughter of the ruler of the Morea and consort of John II, founded a Greek Orthodox monastery here at that time. The church was much rebuilt between 1735 and 1740, but the walls of monastery existed into this century. The exterior arcade and doorway of the elongated south transept are built of 15C materials. The icon of the Blessed Virgin, which was said to have been found in a field of golden flax on the site of the monastery and which gives the church its name, disappeared a long time ago.

Twenty eight icons from the church were collected by David Talbot Rice and Rupert Gunnis and cleaned. They are now in the Byzantine Museum.

Ayios Kassianos, a few paces to the north west, was erected in 1854. It is believed to occupy the site of a Latin church destroyed in 1570. In the wall of the narthex there is a small 15C bas relief of the Virgin and Child. The church is named after St Cassian who came from Germany in the 4C and was martyred here.

Ayios Yeoryios, a short distance to the north east and in the shadow of the

Green Line, is a small 17C barrel vaulted building. A panel from a 15C sarcophagus over the west door bears three coats of arms. The central blazon, a sun displayed, is that of the medieval family of Gourri.

The mid-19C church of **Ayios Savvas**, of little interest in itself, has furniture, plate and some repainted icons from an earlier building. These include a fine silver gilt chalice of 1501 and a curious early 16C panel showing a seated man wearing a long fur robe and a Persian head dress. According to the inscription he was named Demitrios and had made several gifts to the church.

An inscription of 1690 over the south door of **St Michael Trypiotis** states that the church was built by Archbishop Germanos. The exterior walls of the building are studded with fragments from medieval structures.The lintels over its three doors are from different periods. The lintel over the north door is Renaissance in design. That over the west door is 14C French. The most interesting and most difficult to date is over the south door. This shows a stylised human figure whose lower extremities turn into scrolls. It is undoubtedly very old. Over the east gable there is a shield with six fleur-de-lis. The interior is unusual. The iconostasis extends across the church and hides the three apses. Note the icon of the Archangel Michael to whom the church is dedicated. He is credited with having diverted a dangerous flood down a hole—hence the name of the church. Tripiotis means 'maker of the hole'.

South east and south west of Nicosia

Highlights
Idalion, Arkhangelos Gabriel, Panayia Khrysospiliotissa, Ayii Varnavas and Ilarion

---

South east

The village of **Athalassa**, now an outer suburb of the city, was once the gift of Peter I (1358 to 1369) to his mistress Echive de Scandelion. In 1888 it was a refugee camp for some thousand Doukhobors after their expulsion from Russia and before they made their way to Canada. Little remains of the Lusignan castle of **La Cava** which was built for James I (1382 to 1398) and later became one of two convents of the Poor Clares in Cyprus. It was used as a quarry for building the Phaneromeni church in Nicosia in 1870.

Near **Laxia**, set among orchards, a Middle Cypriot site was excavated in 1885. By the bridge over the river a curious deposit of fossil sea shells has been found. It is estimated that they have been here for 30,000 years or more. Some of the shells belong to species now extinct in the Mediterranean.

Nisou, a village given by James II (1460 to 1473) to Nicholas Morapiton a member of the Lusignan family in 1460, has an 18C church with a 16C icon of the Blessed Virgin Hodegetria and an icon of St Paraskevi, its patron saint.

The village of **Potamia** is near the Attila Line and some of the places described below may not be accessible. A castle built c 1380 by Peter II (1369

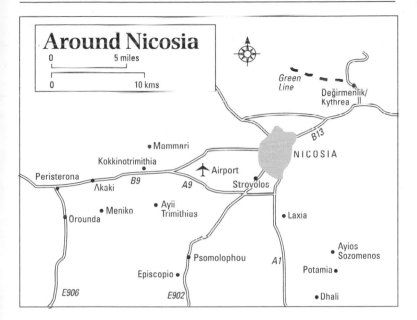

Around Nicosia

0 — 5 miles
0 — 10 kms

Green Line

Değirmenlik/Kythrea

B13

NICOSIA

• Mammari

Kokkinotrimithia

Peristerona

Akaki   B9

Airport

A9   Strovolos

• Meniko   • Ayii Trimithias

Orounda

• Laxia

• Ayios Sozomenos

Psomolophou   A1

Potamia •

Episcopio •

E906   E902   • Dhali

to 1382) became a refuge from the plague for the royal family in 1402. It was destroyed by the Mamelukes in 1426. Cesnola reported the discovery in the mid 19C of cache of gold and silver objects in the garden. Between Potamia and the hamlet of Ayios Sozomenos is the Bronze Age site of **Elinos**. A life size limestone **head of Apollo** of c 500 BC found here in 1933 is now in the Cyprus Museum.

The village of **Ayios Sozomenos**, once occupied by Turkish Cypriots, was the scene of fierce fighting during the early 1960s. Now abandoned, the clay walls of its houses are decaying and in a few years will have disappeared completely. This is a sad place, redolent of the suffering of its former inhabitants.

The tomb of St Sozomenos is in a rock cut cave decorated with wall paintings. Sozomenos was Syrian hermit who took refuge in Cyprus during the 5C Persian wars. The derelict early 16C church of Ayios Mamas had two Renaissance tombs and a finely carved west door. It now serves as a funerary chapel.

Near the village of **Dhali** is the small domed 12C or 13C church of **Ayios Dimitrianos** which was strengthened in 1964. There are the remains of some frescoes. On the west wall above the door is a painting of the donor and his wife. The inscription states that the church of Dimitrianos Andridiotis was renovated and painted by the 'donation and great desire' of Michael son of Katzouroubis, his wife and children in 1317. Gunnis speculates that the name Katzouroubis might be a corruption of 'Château Roux'.

Dhali, a corruption of Idalion, was on the camel route and was once a prosperous place, but by the mid 19C it had become a sad, impoverished village. Between 1866 and 1869 Cesnola spent his summers here and boasted that he had opened up some ten thousand tombs in the area. His looting and the depre-dations of others have meant that many of the objects found in Idalion are in foreign museums.

Immediately south of the village a lane leads left to ancient **Idalion**. The site is not signposted. At present, permission to visit it must be obtained from a nearby military post. Photography is **not** allowed. Built on the slope and in the valley between three limestone hills, it was discovered in 1850 and has not yet been fully excavated.

The first settlement of Idalion dates from the Bronze Age. It continued to be occupied until the Hellenistic period. Traces of its 5C BC walls remain. It was one of the ten kingdoms of Cyprus at that time. The city was said to have had as many as 14 temples. Those of Aphrodite Kourotrophos, found ransacked in 1883, and of Athena graced the sides of the two western hills, while that of Apollo was in the valley. According to an ancient legend it was near here that Adonis was killed by a wild boar. Among a number of important finds was a statue of Sargon King of Assyria of c 700 BC. This was sent by Robert Hamilton Lang, an employee of the Ottoman Bank, to the Berlin Museum. In the late 19C the British Museum bought a number of stone statues, statuettes of terracotta and bronze found by Hamilton in the sanctuary of Apollo. Later they purchased from him two hoards of coins found on the site.

Recent excavations have uncovered substantial sections of a massive, early 5C BC limestone ashlar wall. Built on the remains of earlier fortifications, this stands 6.5m high. The ruins of a large public building are being excavated by an American archaeological expedition.

South west

After a difficult reign Henry II of Cyprus (1285 to 1324) died at his favourite residence in **Strovolos** in 1324. This village was the birthplace of Archbishop Kyprianos, 1756 to 1821, who was hanged in Nicosia by Küçük Mehmed, the Ottoman Governor, because of his suspected sympathy for those fighting for the liberation of Greece. The dome and apse of the mid 14C church of the **Panayia Khryseleousa** were retained when it was rebuilt in 1817. In a chapel on the south side the capital of one exterior column is in the form of an archepiscopal crown. This may commemorate the martyred archbishop who was abbot of a monastery here in 1802. Little of the monastic buildings now remain.

Among farm buildings on low ground towards the river is the church of the monastery of **Arkhangelos Gabriel**. Dating from the late Byzantine period, it was ambitiously rebuilt in 1636 and in 1713 purchased by Kykko Monastery. In the narthex is the tomb of its founder Archbishop Nicephoros. The iconostasis dates from 1650 and there is a huge 16C or 17C fresco of the archangel holding a bust of the Christ Child. Graffiti on the right of the north door record the years—1685, 1813 and 1816—when the rain bringing icon of Kykko was brought down here break a drought. One of the more interesting but least known monuments in the vicinity of the capital, it deserves restora-tion.

To the north west is **Nicosia International Airport**. This is at present in the hands of UNFICYP.

The curious chapel of **Panayia Khrysospiliotissa** is a natural cave which has been enlarged to an area of 9m by 7m. As a refuge, it probably dates from the Early Christian era. Defaced by ancient graffiti and damaged by damp, little now remains of the wall paintings. Its icon of the Blessed Virgin had particular powers of producing rain in times of drought.

The ancient village of **Psomolophou**, once the goatskin tanning centre of the island, now concentrates on growing apricots. The 1847 church of **Panayia Theotokos** preserves parts of an earlier structure. It has a large icon frame made up of fragments of a 16C iconostasis.

Episcopio is said to be the village farthest away, 34km, from the sea in Cyprus. Here among the olive groves the bishops of Tamassos had their residence. Hence its name.

In the village of **Ayii Trimithias** the medieval church of **Ayii Anargyri** was rebuilt in 1900. Ayii Anargyri means 'without fees' and refers to the doctor saints Cosmas and Damian who did not charge for giving medical attention. The church has kept its original fine west door and part of the north doorway.

Kokkinotrimithia, a market gardening centre gets its name from the red earth, Greek *kokkini*, found here. It was on the old Cyprus railway line. The track was just south of the main street. East of the village is a UNFICYP camp. This was a British detention camp during the EOKA campaign. Outside the village is the chapel of **Arkhangelos Michael**. This dates from c 1525. It was probably a seigneurial chapel—the villagers sometimes refer to it as 'Venetico'. A well-constructed stone building, it has some interesting architectural details.

Beyond **Mammari** to the north, a village named after a Frankish owner, is the Attila Line.

The village of **Akaki**, apparently built on the site of a castle erected c 1300 by Henry II, has two churches of slight interest.

In **Meniko** the principal church, rebuilt on the site of a medieval edifice in the early 19C, is dedicated to SS Cyprian and Justina who, it was believed, were martyred at Nicomedia. Their silver plated skulls were said to have been buried in this church.

St Cyprian

According to an apochryphal story Cyprian was a necromancer who attempted to seduce the Christian maiden Justina. However, she turned him away from his evil ways and during the persecution of Diocletian they were both beheaded. This seems to have been just a pious story. Both were removed from the Catholic calendar of saints in 1969.

The area between Akaki and Avlona in Northern Cyprus has been a troublespot since 1974 and a number of 'incidents' have taken place between UNFICYP and its inhabitants.

Peristerona gets it name from the doves, which were once popular here. It is approached by the **Ana Bridge** which was probably thrown across the river in the Venetian period. Watermelons are extensively cultivated here.

The five domed church dedicated to **Ayii Varnavas and Ilarion**, SS Barnabas and Hilarion, somewhat over restored in recent years, dates from the early 10C with a later narthex. It has been the property of Kykko monastery since 1092.

Lapidarı Müzesi

It has some fine gilt woodwork in the Turkish Empire style and a collection of Turkish, Arabic, and Persian books. An important part of the principal Islamic college on the island, which stood nearby, it houses a number of rarities.

Close by is the **Lapidarı Müzesi**. This was formerly the Jeffery's Museum, named after George Jeffery who was responsible for the conservation of the island's monuments in the early part of this century. For access apply to the custodian of the Library of Sultan Mahmut II.

■ For access apply to the custodian of the Library of Sultan Mahmut II.

Housed in a charming 15C building is an interesting collection of sarcopahgi and architectural fragments. It has a Flamboyant Gothic window salvaged from the Lusignan palace which was destroyed by the British administration in 1904 and the white marble sarcophagus of Augustino Carlini, who died in 1553. He was a member of the Venetian Supreme Council that governed Cyprus from 1489 to 1570. Here also is the tomb of Adam of Antioch, Marshal of Cyprus, and the 14C bone chest of the Dampierre family. Note the fine carved corbels on the first floor.

The **Haydar Paşa Mosque**, formerly the **Church of St Catherine**, is, apart from the cathedral, the most important surviving Gothic building in Nicosia.

■ Open Monday to Friday from 09.00 to 13.00 and 14.30 to 17.00; Saturday 09.00 to 13.00.

During the Ottoman period windows were pierced in the façade at floor level. Two of the original doorways remain. The west doorway has a broken marble lintel decorated with a rose between two dragon repeated three times. The south doorway, heavier in style, is surmounted by a lintel on which there are three defaced shields. Note the unusual buttresses. Inside there are traces of the original paint near the piscina. North of the apse is the sacristy. Its vaulting is supported by corbels of carved human heads which survived the transition from church to mosque. This is now an office. The building has been turned into an art gallery.

All that remains of **Yeni Cami**, the New Mosque, originally a medieval church, is the south west corner turret staircase. The rest was pulled down by Menteş Haci Ismail Ağa, a rapacious governor of the 18C during a futile search for treasure. The staircase was spared because of the minaret erected on it. A modern prayer hall has been added. The governor's act of desecration attracted the attention of the Sultan and he was beheaded. He is buried in the grounds of the mosque.

The 18C church of **Ayios Loukas** was a casualty of the fighting in 1974 and now lies derelict.

The suburb of **Kaimaklı**, to the north east of the enceinte, has several streets of typical brown stone houses. In the past it was inhabited by the stone masons of the capital.

The Museum of Barbarism, 2 Irfan Bey St., is a quiet villa in the suburb of Kumsal. On Christmas Eve 1963 Mrs Ilhan, her three children and a neighbour, Feride Hassan, were murdered here by Greek gunmen. The bloodstained bath, in which the family sought refuge, bears eloquent witness to their fate. Photographs and newpaper cuttings record the massacres of Turkish Cypriots in the villages of Ayios Vasilios and Ayios Sozomenos. This is a sad and moving place. However, it is questionable whether its retention in this form will do anything to bring about the healing process that must take place one day between the Turkish and Greek communities.

■ Open Monday to Friday 09.00 to 13.00 and 14.30 to 17.00.

Girne ~ Kyrenia

> *Highlights*
> **The Castle, the Icon Museum**

It is believed that Achaean immigrants established a settlement here in the 10C BC and named it *Kerynia* after a mountain in the Peloponnese. To the Romans it was *Corineum* and in the 13C AD the pilgrim cleric Wilbrand von Oldenburg called the place *Schernae*. In the mid-15C a Spanish caballero, Pero Tafur, said it was *Aherines*, while to that mid-17C voyager, Le Sieur de Stochove of Bruges, it was known as *Gerines*. Today it is **Girne** or **Kyrenia**. But what is in a name? A 'Rose is a rose is a rose....' after all and this place remains what it has been for many years, a pleasant, unpretentious resort on the north coast of Cyprus.

Of course there have been changes in recent years. There are now more hotels, restaurants and smart shops than before and, although there is still a sizeable resident foreign community, it is no longer just a retirement haven in the sun. In the velvety darkness of summer nights visitors from many lands dine by candle light in the restaurants that overlook the horseshoe shaped harbour. During the day they visit the medieval castle, walk in the foothills of the Kyrenia range, even attempt to scale its peaks, and use the town as a base to explore the picturesque north part of the island.

■ Practical information

Tourist office
This is on the sea front near the Custom House at 30 Kordon Boyu. It is usually open in the daytime during the holiday season.

The harbour at Girne ~ Kyrenia

Post office
To the east of the main square in Cumhuriyet Avenue.

Accommodation
In and around Kyrenia there are nearly 50 hotels and holiday villages ranging from luxurious five star establishments to modest pensions. The following are recommended: in the town, the old established 4-star **Dome**, ☎ (90 392) 815 2453, the friendly 3-star **Dorana**, ☎ (90 392) 815 3521 and the **Atlantis**, ☎ (90 392) 815 2505/2242 and **British**, ☎ (90 392) 815 2240/5731 hotels, both 2-star, both a few steps from the harbour.

Good reports have been received of the small family owned **Ship Hotel**, ☎ (90 392) 815 6701/2/3/4 which is just one mile outside Kyrenia. At Alsancak, five miles to the west is the pleasantly sited **Deniz Kızı**, ☎ (90 392) 821 8024/8026, complex of two hotels (one 3-star, one 4-star), private beach and swimming pool. On the coast near the village of Lapta the 3-star **Club Lapethos**, ☎ (90 392) 821 8961, has individual apartments arranged around a pool. In winter, when the nights are often very cold in Cyprus, the fine open log fire in the residents' lounge is a welcome amenity.

Overlooking Kyrenia is the luxurious 4-star **Olive Tree Holiday Village**, ☎ (90 392) 824 4200. Its comfortable, air conditioned villas surround a large swimming pool. It has two restaurants and a pool bar. A courtesy minibus takes residents to and from Kyrenia. On the mountain slopes, set in extensive gardens, is the large, three star **Riverside Holiday Village**, ☎ (90 392) 821 8906/7, while just under the high peaks is the 3-star **Ambelia Village**, ☎ (90 392) 815 3655. This has breathtaking views over the coast. Within a few minutes of Bellapais village and abbey, its friendly Kangol dog will walk you there and back.

Restaurants
There is an *embarras de richesse* of restaurants in Kyrenia. Most of the old carob warehouses along the harbour have been converted into eating places and have tables set close to the water's edge. A lot of pleasure may be derived from a

leisurely evening stroll along Kordon Boyu Caddesi stopping from time to time to examine the proffered menus before finally making a decision.

Recommended are **Niazi's Restaurant and Bar**, which is just across the road from the Dome Hotel. Established in Limassol in 1949, Niazi's has been serving traditional Turkish Cypriot food for more than 40 years. Kebabs are cooked in the body of the restaurant. This is a place which attracts as many local people as foreign visitors. Dinner on the balcony of the **Harbour Club Restaurant** has always been a special event. Good reports have been received of **Ristorante Set** which is located behind the harbour near the Ağa Cafer Mosque. Nearby is the tiny, but very welcoming, **Cosy Corner Restaurant**. Book to make sure of a table. The **Saint Tropez** restaurant at Alsancak offers international cuisine in agreeable surroundings.

Transport

Minibuses leave at regular intervals from the **Garaj** which is outside the town on the Nicosia road. However, most **dolmuş** and minibus services to Nicosia, Famagusta, Güzelyurt and the villages around Kyrenia will pick up passengers near the fountain in the town square. The **main taxi rank** is by the Dome Hotel. Prices are fixed and are displayed at the rank.

There are **ferryboat** services several times a week to Taşucu, Turkey from the new harbour. Bring your passport. During the high holiday season a hydrofoil operates to Taşucu and a hydrofoil or boat service to Alanya.

There are several car hire firms in Kyrenia. Hotel reception desks and the Tourist Information Office will have up to date rates etc.

Church services

Holy Communion is celebrated each Sunday at 08.00 at **St Andrew's Anglican Church** which is a few minutes' walk from Kyrenia Castle. There is a Family Communion Service at 10.15.

Mass is celebrated on the first and third Sunday of the month at 12.30 at the **Catholic Church** in Ersin Aydın Street near the Dome Hotel. In an emergency a priest may be contacted at the Holy Cross Church which is in Southern Nicosia. Telephone through UNFICYP, 46-21-32.

British Residents' Association

This association was established in 1975. Its office behind the post office is open on Saturday between 10.00 and 12.00. Its address is PO Box 167, Girne-Kibris, Mersin 10, Turkey.

Information board

Information about local activities may be found on a notice board near the post office. This is the successor to the famous tree on which notices were pinned in the past.

Book shop

Books about Cyprus, periodicals and paperbacks from Britain, maps, prints, postcards and stamps may be bought at the air conditioned **Green Jacket Bookshop** which is at 20 Temmuz Street on the western outskirts of the town. The inner man and woman are not forgotten in this unusual bookshop. It also sells jacket potatoes with a selection of fillings and cold fruit juice!

Swimming

The local youth swim from the mole of the old harbour or from a beach to the east of the castle. In town the Dome Hotel has a private swimming area where you can hire chairs and sunbeds. There are showers and a bar. Several sandy bays to the east and west of Kyrenia are privately managed, eg, the Deniz Kızı hotel complex and the Mare Monte and Acapulco hotels. All of these have facilities for water sports.

Boat trips

Boat trips operate from the old harbour. Recommended are the day long excursions, with lunch, offered by the *Soli Queen*.

History

In the beginning. Excavations at Catalköy (Ayios Epiktitos-Vrysi) near Kyrenia have revealed the substantial remains of a Neolithic II settlement (c 4600 BC) while several Chalcolithic sites (c 3000 BC) have been found on the fertile north slopes of the mountain range. In the 5C BC Kyrenia was one of the ten kingdoms of Cyprus. In 312 BC it was absorbed by Salamis. Apart from the fact that the Romans called it *Corineum*, little is known about the place during the period of their rule. There is a legend that Simon of Cyrene, who helped Christ to carry the cross to Calvary, came from Kyrenia. Shortly after the arrival of Christianity in the island Kyrenia became an episcopal see. Although walled, like most coastal towns, it suffered from the Arab raids of the 7C and 8C.

The Lusignans. In 1191 the self-styled emperor Isaac Comnenos, fleeing from Richard Coeur de Lion and Guy de Lusignan, sought refuge near Kyrenia before retreating to the eastern extremity of the Karpas peninsula. In the same year Kyrenia castle surrendered to Guy de Lusignan. In 1220 it was besieged by the followers of Frederick II. Holy Roman Emperor and king of Sicily, Frederick, who had earned the sobriquet *Stupor Mundi*, Wonder of the World because of his 'insatiable artistic and intellectual curiosity' led the Sixth Crusade, 1228 to 1229, captured Jerusalem and stopped off in Cyprus on his way to and from the Holy Land. The castle became a residence and, sometimes, a place of refuge for the Lusignan kings and their families. In 1374 it was attacked by the vengeful Genoese angered by the massacre of their merchants at the coronation of Peter II (1369 to 1382).

The Ottomans. In 1570, after learning the terrible fate of Nicosia, the castle surrendered to the Ottoman Turks without a shot being fired. The sight of the severed heads of the Venetian defenders of the capital may have influenced their decision. The port was known as Gerina or Gerines during much of the period of Ottoman rule. When Le Sieur de Stochove, a gentleman of Bruges, visited the town in 1631, it was largely ruined. The Turks, he remarked, retired to the castle at night. In the early 19C Captain Kinneir East India Company, who called the place Cerina, said that the greater part of the defensive wall had fallen down and was blocking the harbour.

Communications with Nicosia were improved by the construction of a new road via Aş Dikmen (Dhikomo) in 1880 and by another road farther west through Gönyeli (Geunyeli) in 1902. The population, half Greek and half Turkish Cypriot, increased from 1200 in 1881 to 2900 in 1946. The

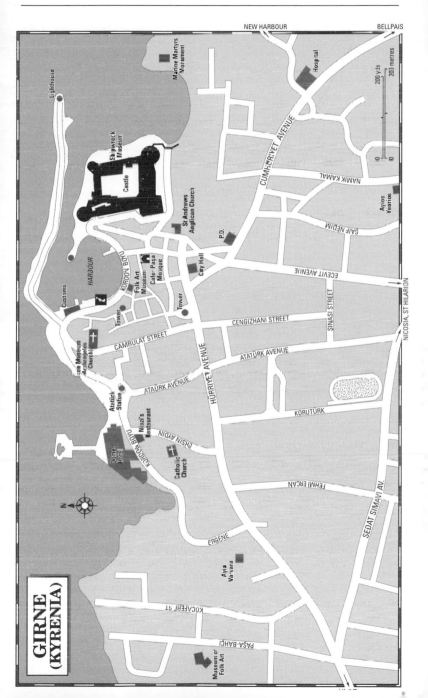

GIRNE
(KYRENIA)

NEW HARBOUR
BELLPAIS

Marine Martyrs Monument

Lighthouse

Hospital

CUMHURIYET AVENUE

NAMIK KEMAL

200 yds
200 metres

Shipwreck Museum

Castle

Ayios Yeorios

St Andrews Anglican Church

SAIF NEDIM

P.O.

HARBOUR

Customs

KORDON BOYU

Folk Art Museum
Cafe - Pasa Mosque

Cay Hall

ECEVIT AVENUE

NICOSIA, ST HILARION

Tower

Tower

Icon Museum
Archangelos Church

Tower

CENGIZHANI STREET

SINASI STREET

CAMBULAT STREET

ATATÜRK AVENUE

Atatürk Statue

HÜRRIYET AVENUE

ATATÜRK AVENUE

KORUTÜRK

Niazi's Restaurant

KORDON BOYU

EHSIN AYDIN NISHA

Dome Hotel

Catholic Church

FEHMI ERCAN

ERGENE

SEDAT SIMAVI AV.

Ayia Va*vara

KOCAFERE ST

PAŞA-BAHÇI

Museum of Folk Art

harbour, the only one of any consequence on the northern coast of the island, was greatly improved between 1886 and 1891.

The British. About the turn of the century Kyrenia became increasingly popular as a place of retirement for British Colonial officials. According to Lawrence Durrell, who settled here in 1953, the British community enjoyed 'what appeared to be a life of blameless monotony'. An anonymous and much more cynical commentator said that the lives of these expatriates were a giddy gavotte which took them from the Anglican Church to the Dome Hotel and thence to the cemetery! '*O tempora. O mores*', to misquote Cicero.

Independence. During recent years there has been a considerable amount of development in Kyrenia mainly designed to support the growing tourist industry. In the 1950s a new breakwater was built and a commercial port was constructed to the east of the town.

Museums

An **Icon Museum** is housed in the 19C church dedicated to the Archangel Michael. Most of the exhibits, which date from the 17C to the 19C, come from unnamed churches in the Kyrenia area. The most interesting is a 17C depiction of the **Entombment of Christ**.

■ Open daily. The hours are subject to alteration. Enquire at the Tourist Information Office.

Nearer the harbour is the **Museum of Folk Art**. This houses the usual assembly of furniture, domestic utensils and fabrics. Note the wine-press, looms and a **bride's coffer** among other furniture and fabrics from the Karpas peninsula, a brazier, a bed alcove and a collapsible bed with carved posts. Enquire at the Tourist Information Office about opening hours.

On the west side of the town, in Paşbahçe St., is the **Fine Arts Museum**. Sited in a pleasant garden, this has a heterogenous collection of objects. There are some interesting water colours. Enquire at the Tourist Information Office about opening hours.

Kyrenia Castle

■ Open from Monday to Saturday between 08.00 and 13.00 and between 14.00 and 17.00. Entrance is by a modern bridge which spans the dry moat. This replaced the original draw-bridge.

The Byzantine fortress may have been constructed on or around the ruins of a Roman fort some time in the late 12C. It surrendered to Guy de Lusignan in 1191 and changed hands frequently during the period 1228 to 1233 when the Holy Roman Emperor Frederick II was in Cyprus. Jean d'Ibelin, the uncle of the young Henry I of Cyprus, captured it in April 1233. The castle was remodelled considerably in the late 13C and then used as a state prison. In 1349 the two young sons of King Hugh IV were held here briefly as a punishment for trying to run away to see the world! Their tutor, Sir John Lombard, was blamed for the escapade and had a hand and foot cut off before being hanged. In 1368 during the absence abroad of Peter I, one of the two princes mentioned above, his mistress Joanna l'Aleman was confined here. This was done by his queen, Eleanor, in one of her many fits of jealousy. Under the future James I the castle successfully resisted all Genoese attempts between 1373 to 1374 to capture it. After the king's coronation in 1385 the castle became his favourite residence and further improvements were made to it. Cardinal Hugh de Lusignan, his sister and the royal children sought sanctuary here in 1426 when the Mamelukes were ravaging the island. In 1460 the last queen of Cyprus, Charlotte Lusignan wife of Louis de Savoy, took refuge in the castle which was then besieged by her step brother James the Bastard. It surrendered four years later when the occupants were beginning to starve.

The Venetians reconstructed and reinforced the stronghold considerably. The west wall was entirely rebuilt in 1544 and massive towers were raised at the north west and south east corners. In 1560 the huge rectangular south west bastion was constructed. It is possible that the fortifications had surrounded an inner harbour which was filled in at this time. The castle surrendered to the Turks without a fight in 1570.

In 1765 its commandant Khalil Ağa staged a revolt against the Ottoman government because of a special tax which was going to be imposed on both Turks and Christians. The revolt lasted a year. Eventually Khalil barricaded himself in the castle and held out there for two months. Tricked into surrendering, when food ran short, he was strangled with a bowstring and the heads of 200 of his followers were sent to the Sultan.

The castle was used as a prison during the period of British rule. Later it was converted into police barracks. In 1950 it came under the care of the Department of Antiquities. Largely refurbished in 1955, it was once more occupied by the military and used for the internment of members of EOKA.

A passage on the left of the covered entrance leads to the 12C Byzantine **Chapel of St George** which has been restored recently. Note the late Roman capitals and the small portion of *opus sectile* pavement in the right apse. Above the **gate house** there is a recent addition—the coats of arms of some of the Lusignan kings. The green covered **tomb of Sadik Paşa**, the Turkish naval commander who received the surrender of the the castle in 1570, is in a recess at the top of the slope. On the right there are some Hellenistic terracotta coffins.

From the large central courtyard a bewildering confusion of steps arise and descend to chambers, halls and dungeons. In the courtyard itself there are heaps of stone cannon balls, architectural fragments and a rather tired, dusty garden. On the right, steps lead to the **Royal Apartments**. Below these are an undercroft and oubliettes. The dungeons have been furnished with **wax figures** which depict in a very realistic fashion some of the tortures inflicted by the Lusignans on their prisoners. Just beyond the Byzantine south west tower a passage descends to the south west bastion. Nearby is the **South Ward** which was excavated in 1952 and 1953. The entrance is flanked by carved lions which are probably Roman. A passage leads down to dungeons below the South East Tower.

The remains of the famous **Kyrenia Ship** are housed in one of the halls on the east side of the courtyard. This was found at a depth of 18m c 1km offshore to the north east of Kyrenia. Archaeologists believe that it sank during a storm c 300 BC. The ship, the oldest vessel ever to be raised from the sea bed, was salvaged in 1969 by a team from the University of Pennsylvania which used modern techniques of underwater excavation. It was made of Aleppo pine sheathed with lead and was 14m long. The cargo included sacks of almonds, Rhodian wine in amphorae and mill stones from Kos. The remains of the vessel have been reassembled and immersed in a wood preservative and are kept in carefully controlled temperature and humidity. In an ante chamber there is a reproduction of part of the hull, also samples of the cargo and other objects—cooking utensils, fishing weights and drinking vessels—which were found by the archaeologists in the wreck. Around the walls there are photographs and a lucid, summary explanation of the salvage operation and the significance of the finds. Unfortunately, there is no guide book.

In the north east tower there is an exhibition of the various military forces which garrisoned the castle at different times. Lifesize **models of soldiers**—from the Byzantines to the British—are clad in the costumes of the period and carry the appropriate weapons. A large chamber on the north side is used for art exhibitions and cultural functions. The **view of the Kyrenia Mountains** from the battlements is spectacular.

The rock cut chapel of St Mavra

Near the new harbour there are three quarries which are now used as vegetable gardens. In one of them is the rock cut **Chapel of St Mavra**. Converted from an ancient tomb, this has an open air altar and some damaged 10C wall paintings. Note the **Hand of Christ** giving the traditional blessing, also the Ascension or Transfiguration of Christ with attendant angels and apostles. Very little is known about St Mavra. She is believed to have been martyred in the early days of Christianity and buried in one of the quarries.

South of Girne ~ Kyrenia

Highlight
Bellapais Abbey

It is a matter of great sadness that the extensive Early Bronze Age necropolis of Vounous, on a hillside between Özanköy (Kazaphani) and Çatalköy (Ayios Epiktitos-Vrysi), has been systematically looted. Its relatively remote situation did not protect it from the shameful thieving of modern grave robbers.

Bellapais ~ Beylerbeyi

The picturesque village of Bellapais-Beylerbeyi (220m), c 5km from Kyrenia, is visited mainly because of its magnificently sited ruined abbey and its associations with Lawrence Durrell. Between 1953 and 1955 Durrell lived here in a restored Turkish house and chronicled his stay in *Bitter Lemons*, a witty, sometimes mildly acidic book. A commemorative plaque marks his house which is a short distance up the hill from the village square. He also wrote *Justine*, the opening novel of the *Alexandria Quartet*, in Bellapais and held court to a select coterie of friends. They included writers, travellers and poets like Patrick Leigh

Fermor, Lord Kinross, George Seferis and Freya Stark.

The village, still largely cloaked in luxuriant vegetation, has lost much of its former unsophisticated character and over commercialisation has deprived it of a great deal of its charm. The origin of its name has provoked some controversy and many suggestions. I think is may be a corruption of the Italian 'Bel Paese', Beautiful Village.

■ Practical information

■ **Transport**. Unfortunately, there is no bus or dolmuş service to Bellapais. Taxis may be hired in Kyrenia for a day or half day. Agree on the price before starting out.

■ **Restaurant**. There are several restaurants in Bellapais. Recommended is the **Kybele Restaurant** in the abbey grounds. Confusingly, this has a drawing of Artemis of Ephesus—not Kybele—on the menu cover! There have been mixed reports about the **Abbey House Restaurant** which specialises in French inspired cuisine. Open daily from 08.00–17.00.

History of the Abbey

There is some suggestion that this place was the residence and—during the Arab raids of the 7C and 8C—a refuge of the Bishops of Kyrenia. The abbey was founded c 1200 by Aimery de Lusignan for the Augustinian canons who had custody of the church of the Holy Sepulchre in Jerusalem until the fall of that city in 1187 to the Saracens. The Augustinians came to Cyprus and were accompanied by or followed soon after by the White Canons of the Order of St Norbert. From 1206 onwards the canons adopted the Norbertine or Premonstratensian rule with the approval of Archbishop Thierry, the second Latin Archbishop of Nicosia. Their white habits gave the abbey one of its names. References to the 'White Abbey' appear in 15C and 16C documents.

In 1246 the abbey was given a fragment of the True Cross and the sum of 600 besants by Sir Roger the Norman who asked that the canons say masses in perpetuity for the repose of his soul and that of his wife the lady Alix. It grew in size and importance largely because of the pious patronage and generosity of Hugh III who died in Tyre in 1284 and who is believed to have been buried here. In 1373 its wealth attracted the attention of the rapacious Genoese and they carried away most of its portable treasure. The Mitred Abbots of Bellapais, who were given the privilege of bearing a gilded sword and wearing golden spurs by Hugh III, were frequently in dispute with the Archbishop of Nicosia. The pope had to intervene on several occasions to settle disagreements between them. When King Hugh IV lived in the abbey between 1354 and 1358 he added apartments appropriate to his state.

By the mid 16C the strict Norbertine rule had been largely abandoned. Many of the canons had taken wives, some more than one, and the only novices they would accept were their own children. After the Turkish conquest of Cyprus the abbey was handed over to the Orthodox Church. The buildings were neglected. Some were used as byres. The abbey church became the village church. In 1738 the English traveller Richard Pococke described it as 'a most magnificent uninhabited convent...almost entire' and in 1750 Alexander Drummond, HM Consul in Aleppo, was equally impressed by its 'palatial stile', but when Captain Kinneir of the East India Company passed this way in 1814 he saw cows grazing in the outer court.

The building became a useful source of cut stone for the construction of houses in the village. In 1878 the British Army cemented the floor of the great hall so as to turn it into a military hospital. The ruins were repaired in 1912 under the supervision of George Jeffery, the Curator of the Ancient Monuments of Cyprus, but when he requested an increase in the tiny amount given to him for the preservation of the island's antiquities, in particular for the repair and preservation of the Bellapais monastic dormitory, he was told by the British authorities that its stone 'would come in handy for road-metal'. It did not do that. The weathered sandstone was far too soft.

The **Abbey** is built on a rock escarpment whose north edge drops vertically for more than 30m. The main entrance is on the south side through a fortified gateway with a high machicolation. This replaces the former drawbridge. If the door to the 13C **church** is locked, ask the custodian to open it for you. Like other Gothic churches in Outremer, it has a flat roof. Its curious appearance is accentuated, rather than disguised, by the quaint belfry, above the entrance. Only one bell remains *in situ*. Note the remains of a modern wall painting in the **porch**. The church has a broad nave flanked by two aisles, a square choir and a sacristy. Its dark musty interior, with open service books and half melted candles, seems to be in mourning for the priest and congregation that have long departed. The vaulting of three sides of the **cloisters** remains in place. Note the **lavabo** on the north side where the canons performed their ablutions. This is made of two antique sarcophagi. Water flowed from the upper sarcophagus, which has a decoration of swages, lion heads and putti, into the lower, undecorated sarcophagus and thence through a channel to the cloister garden. Three stairs from the cloisters provide access to the roof. The **Treasury** was over the north aisle of the church.

To the south east of the cloisters is the square **Chapter House**. Its vault was once supported by the single marble column which was re-erected by George Jeffery. Note the **corbels**. The meaning of their carvings—a man carrying a double ladder, a man between two maidens, a man holding a shield under a pear tree—is not known. They may be repre-

Bellapais Abbey

sentations of long forgotten proverbs. The roofless **Common Room**, where the canons worked and studied, lies to the north.

The best preserved part of the abbey is the **Refectory**, 30m long and 10m wide, which is on the north side of the cloisters. The roof of this magnificent chamber is supported by seven columns which appear to grow out of the side walls. Six windows on the north wall give breathtaking views over the surrounding countryside and of the sea in the far distance. There is a fine rose window high in the east wall. Note the projecting pulpit on the north wall. At mealtimes a lector read from the scriptures or the lives of the saints here. The refectory is now used for concerts, recitals of classical music and lectures. Stairs lead to the **undercroft** which occupies the whole area under the refectory. Note the decorative ceiling bosses. The **Cellarium** and **Kitchens** were sited to the west of the refectory—appropriately within a few metres of the outdoor tables of the Kybele Restaurant!

An old track leads from Bellapais by Mt Alonagra 935m to Aşağı Dikmen (Kato Dhikomo). From there the road continues southward across the featureless plain of the Mesaoria to Nicosia.

Girne ~ Kyrenia to the Karpas

Highlights
Sourp Magar, Alevkaya, Antiphonitis, Boğaz, Cnidos, Kanakaria, Paleovikla tomb, Sipahi (Ayia Trias), Dipkarpaz, Ayios Philon, Blue Sea Hotel, Monastery of Apostolos Andreas

During the holiday season there are day excursions to the principal places of interest in the Karpas peninsula. This is sometimes referred to—bizarrely and incorrectly—as the 'Panhandle'. However, to explore this beautiful part of the island properly and enjoy its uncrowded, secluded beaches, you will need your own transport. There are several car hire firms in Kyrenia. Details of current daily and weekly rates may be obtained from your hotel reception or the Tourist Information Office. Taxis may be hired on a daily basis from the rank near the Dome Hotel. Agree the price before departure and take a picnic lunch.

Just east of the town is the small sandy beach of **Karakum**. (Its name means 'black sand'.) Signposted off the main road is the **tekke** of Hz. Ömer. An officer in the army of Muawiya, the Arab governor of Syria and later first caliph of the Umayyad dynasty, Ömer and six of his friends were killed here during one of the Arab raids of the 7C. A shrine and mosque were erected after the Ottoman conquest. The shrine is also venerated by the Greek Cypriots who call it **Ayii Phanotes**.

At **Çatalköy (Ayios Epiktitos–Vrysin)** archaeologists have found a Neolithic II site on a crumbling, wind swept peninsula. This appears to have been occupied between 4410 BC and 3750 BC. The first settlers built their shelters below ground, perhaps to escape the cold winter winds from Anatolia. Later

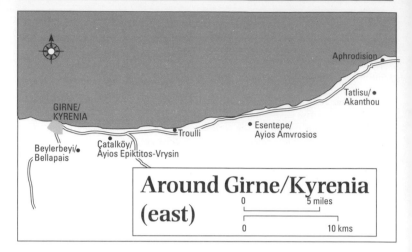

Around Girne/Kyrenia (east)

0   5 miles

0   10 kms

more substantial windowless dwellings were constructed. The bones of goats, sheep, dogs and cats were found and evidence of the cultivation of lentils, barley, wheat, olives, figs and grape vines discovered. The dead were buried beneath the floors of the houses. The inhabitants made and decorated pottery. There are some examples in the museum at Güzelyurt (Morphou).

Surrounded by sand dunes **Turtle Beach** remains relatively uncrowded even during the holiday season. Archaeologists found two separate layers of occupation on the **Troulli peninsula** at the east end of the beach. Now built over, there were settlements here during the Neolithic I and II periods. The discovery of imported materials, including obsidian from Çiftlik in central Anatolia suggest that it may have been a trading post established by the first immigrants.

The abandoned 19C Armenian monastery of **Sourp Magar**, which nestles in a secluded ravine, was a favourite pilgrimage place for Armenians en route to the Holy Land. It was first a Coptic monastery dedicated c 1000 AD to the Egyptian hermit St Makarios the Great (300 to 390). Venerated by the universal church, he was exiled for some time because of his defence of the Catholic faith against attacks by Arians. Later the dedication was changed to the Blessed Virgin Mary. Note the inscription in Armenian on a pillar on the east side of the complex. This dates from 1933.

The **forestry station** at **Alevkaya** welcomes visitors every day between 08.00 and 16.00. There is a small herbarium, a picnic area and a bar which also serves food. A number of mountain tracks start at the forestry station.

The disused Greek Orthodox monastic church of **Antiphonitis** is hidden away in a beautiful, pine-clad glen, where in summer only the murmur of insects disturbs the silence. Dating from the end of the 12C, its name means, 'Christ who responds'. The design is somewhat unusual for Cyprus. A vaulted 15C narthex leads to an octagonal nave. The centrally placed dome is supported by eight columns. There is a rounded apse at the east end. In the dome there is a fine early 15C fresco of Christ Pantokrator. Below are representations of the Blessed Virgin and St John leading a procession of saints and angels to a throne that awaits the Risen Lord. Alas, mindless barbarians have damaged these paint-

A turning on the right from the main road leads to the **Deniz Kizi** hotel complex (see accommodation Kyrenia) where there is a sheltered, well maintained sandy beach. The village of **Alsancak (Karavas)** is in the centre of an important citrus growing area. It is said that some of its lemon trees are almost 100 years old and can produce as many as 5000 lemons each year. The lemon groves are irrigated with water from a mountain spring above the village.

The picturesquely sited **Akhiropietos Monastery Church**—its name means 'built without hands'—was founded in the 12C, rebuilt in the 14C and much changed later by the addition of a huge apse. This is seven sided externally but internally forms a semi-circle. The church has two domes over the transept. It was surrounded by arcaded cells which, according to Osbert Lancaster, were 'formerly inhabited by stray shepherds, farm animals and English intellectuals'. An ancient Cypriot legend states that the monastery was brought over by the Blessed Virgin from Asia Minor during the course of single night to prevent it from being desecrated by the heathens—hence its name. It had a wonder working icon of the Holy Veil of St Veronica and, it is asserted, once held the Holy Shroud of Christ which is now in Turin Cathedral. The complex has been converted into a military warehouse and rest centre and is not, at present, open to the public.

A short distance to the west is the site of **Lambousa**. Probably established by the Phoenicians in the 8C BC, it was for many centuries an important trading centre. Pottery was a major export. The town was walled, had a harbour and a lighthouse. From 295 to 227 BC it was the capital of one of four Ptolemaic Districts. Lambousa achieved its greatest prosperity during the periods of Roman and Byzantine rule. A bishopric was established here in AD 61. The city was destroyed by Arab raids in the 7C and virtually abandoned. Much of its stone was used to build Lapta (Lapithos). Revived in the Middle Ages, it was known as 'La Fief de la Pison'.

All that remains today are a part of the city wall, the foundations of the lighthouse and some rock cut fish tanks. The first scientific excavations at the site were made between 1913 and 1917. An early 7C AD silver dinner service, the famous **Lambousa Treasure**, which was hidden, perhaps from the Arabs, was found near the chapel of Ayios Evlambios c 1905. Some of the plates are in the Cyprus Museum, Nicosia. The rest is divided between the British Museum and the Metropolitan Museum, New York. The dishes in Nicosia show the Marriage of David. On the backs appear the earliest known silverware hallmarks.

The village of **Lapta (Lapithos)**, surrounded by lemon and orange groves and stands of medlars, is a short distance south of the main road. There are two foundation legends. Strabo (fl. 1C AD) says it was established by Spartans under Praxander. According to Thubron '...it was famous, apparently, for its amphorae and homosexuals'. Another account says it was settled by Phoenicians led by Belus, King of Tyre. Fresh blood was introduced c AD 654 when refugees from Lambousa, which had been sacked by the Arabs, sought refuge here. In 1307 it belonged to Echive d'Ibelin and from c 1464 to the Constable of Cyprus, Sor de Naves. Its citrus groves were famous even then. Cotton was grown after the Ottoman conquest. Now onions, sesame and vegetable marrows are also cultivated. During the Byzantine period Lapta was the see of an Orthodox bishop. This was suppressed by the Latins in 1222. There are several rather uninteresting 19C churches in the village.

The **Club Lapethos** holiday complex (see Accommodation Kyrenia) is on the main road just after the turning to Lapta village. Some 6km to the west, under the shadow of **Mt Kornos** (946m), the westernmost peak of the Kyrenia range, is the village of **Karşıyaka (Vasilia)** where there is an **Early Bronze Age cemetery** (2500 to 2075 BC). The settlement to which it belonged appears to have been occupied by immigrants from Anatolia who lived in harmony with the indigenous people and formed part of the so called Philia Culture. A number of monumental chamber tombs have been found here. There is a popular **fish restaurant** at **Güzelyalı (Vavilas)** which is on the coast a short distance to the north of the main road.

Continue on the minor road which passes through the villages of Kayalar and Sadrazamköy and ends at Koruçam Burnu. This land is wild and lonely. Here and there goat tracks wind among tangled thorn bushes. The road twists and bends, now climbing to the top of a small rise, then dropping steeply to pass within a few yards a tiny sandy beach. There are few people and '...every prospect pleases'.

Shortly after Kayalar (Orga) is the little bay of **Ayios Yeoryios**. Today nobody prays in the deserted church, the old carob warehouse is home only to night birds, and the sand, unsullied, unmarked, awaits the touch of human feet. This indeed is Paradise!

At **Sadrazamköy (Liveras)** the church dedicated to SS Constantine and Helena stands empty. The village is now the home of immigrants from Anatolia. There are the ruins of a square medieval **Venetian watchtower** nearby. From here to the cape the road is rough, so leave your car and continue on foot. It is said that the sturdy lighthouse at the tip of **Koruçam Burnu (Cape Kormatiki)** is built on the site of a Roman temple. This is reputed to be one of the best fishing grounds in Northern Cyprus. If the day is clear, look to the north. You should be able to see Cape Anamur in Turkey. It is only 66km, 41 miles away.

A pretty side road climbs up from Sadrazamköy through the woods to **Koruçam (Kormakiti)**. However, it is best to approach this Maronite village from the main road, as it is in a restricted area and permission to visit it (a formality) must be obtained from the police station in Çamlibel.

The Maronites are Eastern Rite Christians, Arabs in origin, who fled to Cyprus from the Orontes valley in Syria in the 7C to escape persecution. They trace their origins back to St Maron, a late 4C or early 5C Syrian hermit and to St John Maron, Patriarch of Antioch in the late 7C. For some time they followed the heresy of Monothelitism which said that Christ has two distinct natures, divine and human, but one will and activity. This was first promulgated by the Byzantine emperor Heraclius c 624 in an attempt to end the controversy between the Arians and the main body of the Church. Monothelitism was condemned by the third Council of Constantinople in 680. In the 12C the Maronites re-established communion with the Catholic Church. They recognise

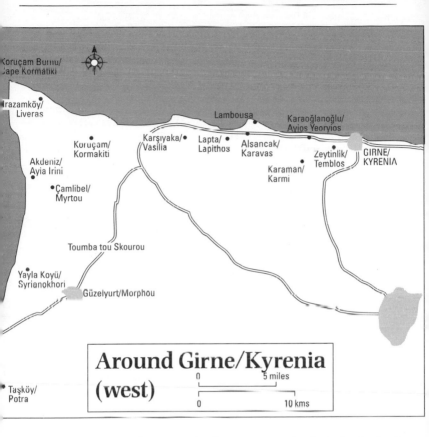

Around Girne/Kyrenia (west)

```
0          5 miles
0          10 kms
```

Koruçam Burnu/
Cape Kormatiki

Irazamköy/
Liveras

Koruçam/
Kormakiti

Karşıyaka/
Vasilia

Lapta/
Lapithos

Alsancak/
Karavas

Lambousa

Karaoğlanoğlu/
Ayios Yeoryios

Akdeniz/
Ayia Irini

Zeytinlik/
Temblos

GIRNE/
KYRENIA

Karaman/
Karmi

Çamlibel/
Myrtou

Toumba tou Skourou

Yayla Koyü/
Syrianokhori

Güzelyurt/Morphou

Taşköy/
Potra

the supreme authority of the pope, but have their own head, the Patriarch of Antioch and All the East, who lives near Beirut. They have a considerable degree of autonomy and use the Antiochene rite in Syriac for their services. There are c 1.3 million Maronites in the world with communities in the Lebanon, Cyprus, Syria, Palestine and North and South America.

In the centre of the village is a big modern **church** dedicated to **St George**. Note the paintings of both Maronite and Catholic saints and patriarchs. This church replaced an earlier 15C building which is still standing. Both churches are in use and are usually open. Up the hill a small international **community of nuns** occupies a house surrounded by flower gardens. Nursing sisters, they live an austere life of poverty and prayer caring for the sick of all religious beliefs in the village and surrounding countryside. The sisters welcome visitors and are happy to show them their beautiful ancient chapel.

The river valleys in the Güzelyurt/Morphou plain appear to have been thickly populated in early prehistoric times. Pottery from Chalcolithic III, the so called Philia Ware, has been found near Morphou and Ambelikou.

Just before **Çamlibel (Myrtou)** a turning on the right leads the **Late Bronze Age site of Pighades**. Here in a grove of cypress and cedar trees is an ancient

shrine. The principal deity in the Aegean and Eastern Mediterranean in the Bronze Age appears to have been female. Referred to sometimes as **Potnia, the Lady**, she is often represented with raised arms. The **Horns of Consecration** and shrine chamber found here are similar to those at Knossos in Crete and Beycesultan in Turkey. So far only the shrine has been investigated. It is likely that an ancient town or city awaits discovery.

Çamlibel is an ancient village. The **Monastery of Ayios Panteleemon** was a residence of the Bishop of Kyrenia from 1571 to 1921. In the early part of this century it was drastically restored and now is of little interest.

From **Tepebaşı (Dhiorios)** there are good views of Morphou Bay and of the Troodos range to the south.

At one time **Akdeniz (Ayia Irini)** had good access to the sea. Now the area is being slowly covered with sand, even though efforts are being made to halt the process by reafforestation. In 1930 a large number of terracotta figurines, mostly male, were found in an Iron Age temple at nearby **Paleokastro**. These are now in the Cyprus Museum, Nicosia. Italian archaeologists excavated a Bronze Age cemetery on the seashore in 1970 and discovered jewellery, bronze tools, an ostrich egg and a Late Minoan or Late Helladic II cup decorated with the Minoan double headed axe. There is a carved Roman cippus in the church-yard.

At **Toumba tou Skourou**—the name means the Mound of Darkness—to the north of Güzelyurt, a hoard of Lusignan coins was found in 1904. The site was known to the authorities in 1936 when there were extensive mud brick walls resting on a stone foundation. Inexplicably, permission was given to local farmers to clear the site so that they could plant citrus trees. It is believed that 800 loads of stone were taken away and the mound, that gives the site its name, was rased down to the rock foundations. In 1963 Late Cypriot (1650 to 1050 BC) artefacts were discovered here and in 1973 a Harvard University Expedition found a variety of objects including Minoan pottery, cylinder seals from Syria and ostrich eggs. Houses and tombs have been laid bare in the southern part of the site. In a shaft grave there were niches on the sides for the burial of infants. Examples of the distinctive white painted pottery found here are in Güzelyurt Museum. Evidence of the city's extensive trading connections is provided by the discovery of a Tell-el-Yahudiya small jug decorated with Nilotic birds and lotus flowers. The city, which was originally much more easily accessible from the sea, was probably established c 1600 BC. It continued to be occupied until the Late Bronze Age.

Güzelyurt ~ Morphou

Very little is known about the history of Güzelyurt (Morphou). The area around the town appears to have supported a substantial population in prehistoic times. There is evidence that during the Byzantine period it was well irrigated and farmed efficiently. An anti-pirate coast-watch was operated in the 10C from the town. Its inhabitants took an active part in the revolt of the peasant 'King Alexis' in 1426.

In the Lusignan period the main crops grown in this area were sugar, cotton and, later on, flax. They have been largely replaced by citrus production, straw-berries—two crops annually—vegetables and cereals. When the town was connected by rail to Nicosia and Famagusta in 1907 the export of its produce was greatly facilitated. It was visited by Alexander Drummond, H.M. Consul at

Aleppo, in the mid 18C. He described it as 'a very cheerful place', but was critical of some of the beliefs associated with St Mamas.

The **Monastery of Ayios Mamas** is the town's principal monument. Its first church, which may have been built on the site of a temple dedicated to Aphrodite, was Byzantine in style. At some time in the Middle Ages this was replaced by a Gothic structure which, in turn, was almost completely reconstructed in 1725 when the central dome was added. In fact, all that remains of the Gothic building are the north and south doorways, the columns in the nave, two marble columns in the west window, part of the Iconostasis and the Shrine of Ayios Mamas. In the monastic buildings, which were erected in 1779, there are some columns and capitals from the Gothic church. The modern wing was the residence of the Bishops of Kyrenia. The west door of the church is covered with ancient graffiti. Look for the name of M. Porey, the French consul, who came here in 1738, and an inscription of 1753 which records the visit and cure of a man from Moscow.

The impressive iconostasis is a mixture of both styles and periods. The four marble columns with Gothic capitals and the lower panels of marble date from c 1500. The panels are, perhaps, the most interesting examples of Venetian minor art remaining in Cyprus. Grapes, acorns and figs are carved in high relief and the shields on the corners once bore painted coats of arms. The gilded and painted woodwork of the iconostasis, the two small Holy Doors on the extreme left and the baldachino above the altar date from the late 16C. The altar is supported by five marble columns. Two of these have Byzantine capitals. The only old icon is one of the Blessed Virgin. This dates from 1745. The painted pulpit is from 1761.

The **Shrine of Ayios Mamas** is in an arched recess on the north side of the church. The Gothic stone work has been spoiled by carelessly applied oil paint. The white marble, reused Roman or Byzantine, sarcophagus, the authorities are not sure which it is, is built into the thickness of the wall, so that it can be seen from inside and outside the church. Containing the relics of the saint, this was opened by the Ottomans in search of treasure. Two holes in the sarcophagus are said to sweat a miraculous ichor which can effect cures. Drummond was scathing about this belief. 'I know the Greeks, who are naturally credulous, gave faith to traditional miracles; but if I rightly remember, this is the first I have ever known them impose upon mankind...' he wrote.

The story of Ayios Mamas, one of the most popular in Cyprus, appears frequently on icons. The saint lived austerely in a cave and refused to pay the poll tax levied by the Byzantine Duke who ruled the island. Arrested for his refusal, he and his armed escort were passing through a wood when a lion leaped out from the undergrowth in pursuit of a lamb. Ayios Mamas held up his hand and the lion promptly abandoned the chase. The saint gathered the lamb into his arms, and feeling rather tired, got up on the lion's back and rode it to Nicosia and into the Duke's palace. The Duke, amazed by this sight, immediately exempted Mamas from all taxes for the rest of his life.

Another version is given in the Chronicle of Makhairas. According to this, Ayios Mamas lived in Alaiye (modern Alanya in Southern Turkey). Able to catch, tame and milk lions, he fed the poor with cheese which he made from the lions' milk. Martyred for his faith, his body was placed in a coffin which was set adrift in the sea. This reached a beach near Morphou where it was found by a carter and his sons. They carried the coffin with a team of oxen to this place but could not get the animals to move it any farther. Later the first shrine in honour of the saint was built here.

In the Western Church the feast of St Mamas is celebrated on 17 August. According to the standard martyrologies he was a shepherd of Caesarea in Cappadocia who was martyred under Aurelian. His *Acta* are considered to be unreliable.

Near the monastery there is a small **museum** devoted to the archaeology and natural history of Cyprus. It has some Middle or Late Cypriot period ceramics, including examples of the distinctive white painted pottery from Toumba tou Skourou, a small worn and battered 2C AD statue of Ephesian Artemis found in the sea off Salamis, Hellenistic earrings, two fine black figure Attic *lekythoi*, Roman glass and medieval *sgraffito* ware. On the ground floor there are geological specimens, stuffed birds, mammals and fish.

The pretty village of **Yayla Koyü (Syrianokhori)** is surrounded by orange groves. As its Greek name suggests, it was probably founded by Syrian settlers. It has a pleasant little café. According to the locals, the marshes around Morphou Bay still provide good snipe shooting.

Yeşilyurt (Pendayia) was an important town in Byzantine and medieval times. In the Middle Ages Pendayia gave its name to one of the 12 baronies of Cyprus. To the north, surrounded by Roman tombs, are the ruins of the church of **Ayios Yeoryios**. The nearby **Monastery of Xeropotamo** was attached to Kykko. Around its church, which was dedicated to SS Cosmas and Damian, are architectural fragments—marble Corinthian capitals and granite columns from Soloi. To the south are the ruins of the Byzantine monastery of **Ayii Seryios and Bacchos**.

The village of **Taşköy (Petra)**, near the Attila Line, was once the personal property of Peter II. In 1375 he gave it to Sir Thibald Belfarage for services rendered against the Genoese. The former church of St Basil was converted into a mosque. It is said that its ancient frescoes are still on the walls beneath a coat of whitewash.

Gemikonağı (Karavostasi) is an unattractive place of rusty processing plant and abandoned ore conveying equipment for the Skouriotissa Mine. Until 1974 it was the main port for the shipping of copper and asbestos. In 1441 Helena Palaeologus made her landfall in Cyprus here. Described by Pope Pius II as being 'treacherous and sagacious, an adept in Greek treachery, hostile to the Latin religion, and an enemy of the Roman church,' she came to the island to marry John II. A determined woman, she dominated her husband and introduced Greeks to the court to the detriment of Latin influence. Of a very jealous disposition, she bit off the nose of Mary of Patras, the king's mistress and mother of the bastard James II, the last King of Cyprus.

Lefke (Lefka), one of the principal baronies in the Middle Ages, was, like Morphou, a centre of the peasant uprising of 1426. It is surrounded by a large Hellenistic and Roman necropolis. Fine glass objects, ' of quite unusual variety and beauty, especially needle-like toilet pencils and finger rings of variegated glass', have been found in the tombs. These date from the period when the Romans worked the copper mines. Bronze Age artefacts have also been found here.

The **Orta**, ie, Middle and **Piri Osman Paşa** mosques are said to stand on the sites of ancient churches. There is the Rococo tomb of **Vezir Osman Paşa**, who died in 1839 in the graveyard and inscribed Roman cippi abound. Lefke is full of fine examples of Ottoman architecture. It recently acquired a university.

Bağlıköy (Ambelikou) to the north west is surrounded by Roman tombs. Chalcolithic remains have also been found here. A Corinthian marble capital from Soloi and other fragments may also be seen.

Within walking distance of ancient Soloi is the **Soli Inn** which offers accommodation and food. Set in pleasant gardens, it has a swimming pool.

Soloi

Very little remains of ancient Soloi. What may be the earliest reference to the place appears in a list of enemy towns in a temple of Ramesses III (1194 to 1162 BC) at Medinet Habu in Egypt. In 707 BC seven kings of Cyprus paid a tribute of gold and silver to Sargon II of Assyria. It is believed that one of them was the king of Soloi. Names on the prism of Esarhaddon (613/2 BC) include Sillua (Salamis) and Sillu (Soloi). According to Strabo Soloi was built by the Athenians, Phaleros and Acamas and had a harbour, a river and a temple of Aphrodite and Isis. When the English traveller Richard Pococke visited what he believed to be the site of Soloi in 1738, he found the remains of a fortification which ran from the hills to the sea, a substantial section of a semi circular wall which could have belonged to a temple or a church and three piers adorned with pilasters on which there were fine Corinthian capitals. Alexander Drummond, who came to Cyprus in 1745, recalled the apocryphal foundation story of the city. According to this Solon, the Athenian law-giver, c 580 BC persuaded his friend, the king Philocypros, to build a new capital in a more fertile location. This city was so successful that it was named Solon after the lawgiver.

Whatever the truth about its establishment, the city had a good harbour, a plentiful water supply and it was located in an excellent trading position. Soloi resisted the attempts of Evagoras of Salamis to bring it under his control. As a reward for helping Alexander the Great, Stasanor of Soloi was made satrap of several provinces of the new empire. The discovery of a late 4C BC representation of an Amazonomachia testifies to the presence of Greek temples in the city at that time.

Soloi had a flourishing trade in copper during the Roman period. It is said to have had the first public library on the island. Its theatre was probably constructed in the 2C AD and its Christian basilica in the 5C AD. It was a residence of the Orthodox Bishop of Nicosia in the 13C after the issue of the **Bulla Cypria** by Pope Alexander IV which reduced both the position and authority of the Orthodox Church. By that time the place was virtually abandoned. It had been in decline since the Arab raids in the 7C AD.

Swedish archaeologists, led by Professor Einar Gjerstad, excavated the theatre in 1930. In 1932 they uncovered the 1C BC temple of Isis and the mid 3C BC temple of Aphrodite. A 1C BC nude statute of Aphrodite found here is in the Cyprus Museum in Southern Nicosia. This is in the style known as the Aphrodite of Cyrene. The goddess turns her head slightly to the left; her braided hair hangs over her shoulders. The arms of the statue have been broken off at the shoulder, the legs at the knee. The archaeologists also found a mid 6C AD temple dedicated to Serapis. All the temples have been reburied.

Other deities worshipped at or near Soloi included Athena. A fine terracotta showing her mounting a chariot is now in the Medelhavsmuseet, Stockholm. An

Antonine period, larger than life, bronze head of a youth found at Soloi is exhibited in the Cyprus Museum, Southern Nicosia.

The **Roman theatre**, high up on the hillside, has been so restored that it has lost all feeling of antiquity. It has a diameter of c 52m and a seating capacity of c 3500. The *cavea* was cut into the hillside. Nothing of the stage building remains.

At the bottom of the hill on the right are the extensive remains of the **Christian basilica**. The outer courtyard was ringed by colonnades paved with *opus sectile*. Note the fragmentary mosaics depicting animals in the centre of the courtyard. Entrance to the basilica was by three doors. The roof of the nave was supported by huge pillars of local yellow stone. Only the bases and a few capitals remain. Note the variety of geometric mosaics which cover the floor of the nave. There is a charming representation of a white swan surrounded by lotus flowers. At the east end of the basilica there are substantial parts of the *synthronon* on which the officiating clergy sat during services.

Palace of Vouni

The approach to the imposing site of the **Palace of Vouni** is by a narrow, twisting road which will not commend itself to nervous drivers. The palace was built by the pro-Persian city of Marion (see Polis) after the failed revolt in 499 BC by the Ionian Greeks against the Persian Empire. Its purpose was to overlook Soloi which had supported the Greek cause. It was remodelled and enlarged when a pro-Greek king ruled Marion.

A temple dedicated to Athena was erected on the summit of the hill at this time. This had a cella with the cult statue and a large courtyard. Near the courtyard there were several rooms in which offerings to the goddess were placed. Among those found by the archaeologists were a bronze cow and statuettes of Athena wearing a Corinthian helmet. This distinctly Greek style structure must have been visible from a considerable distance. It is believed to have inspired the development of the cult of Athena in the surrounding area.

The palace was finally destroyed c 380 BC. It was probably at this time that the so called Treasure of Vouni was buried by its terrified occupants. The Swedish archaeologists found a collection of Persian objets d'art—gold bracelets, bowls and coins from cities which supported the Persian cause, in a fire blackened pot.

The main entrance to the palace was on the south west side. Later blocked off, this led to the megaron. The state apartments were off the megaron. A flight of seven steps descended to a peristyle court surrounded by rooms. Below this court is a cistern. On the seaward side of the well stands a stone block designed to support a windlass. The baths, with a vaulted furnace, were towards the north west.

The Swedish team also explored the small island of **Petra tou Limniti** which lies to the west of Vouni. There they found Neolithic I implements. This early Neolithic phase appeared to have had no pottery, but the presence of obsidian, which is not found in Cyprus, suggests trade contacts with Anatolia.

The Castles of the Gothic Mountain Range

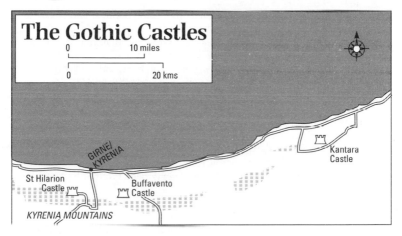

The mountain range that runs along the north coast of Cyprus is called Beşparmak in Turkish and Pentadaktylos in Greek. Both words mean the same thing, 'the five fingers', and strictly speaking should be restricted to five rocky spurs east of Girne. Some years ago Rose Macaulay and Lawrence Durrell gave the range a more romantic name. They called it the 'Gothic Range'.

For Durrell, it is unquestionably Gothic 'for it is studded with crusader castles pitched on the dizzy spines of the mountains ... The very names smell of Gothic Europe: Buffavento, Hilarion ...' A more recent visitor to the island, Colin Thubron, continued this strain of hyperbole, '... Pendactylos like a mailed fist ... (goes) ... on and on for a hundred miles, castled by the Lusignans with a fairy tale madness on their razor peaks.' Whatever one may think of these rather florid descriptions, there is no doubt that the Kyrenia mountains are entrancing. Their three castles, St Hilarion, Buffavento and Kantara, belong to that place of dreams which mortals may sometimes visit.

St Hilarion Castle

Leave the Girne–Nicosia motorway by a signposted minor road. This climbs steeply to the main entrance of the Castle of St Hilarion.

■ Open daily from 08.30 to 17.00.

Rose Macaulay called St Hilarion, 'a picture-book castle for elf kings' and it is, indeed, a wild dramatic maze of fortifications, vaulted chambers and crumbling towers that sprawl over a confused mass of jagged rock. At a height of 732m, it is an eagle's nest that commands the Kyrenia range and offers stunning views of the fertile coastal plain that lies far below.

There is a tradition that an anchorite named Hilarion, who was born in Gaza, came here in the 4C in search of solitude. A disciple of St Antony the Great, Hilarion founded a number of monasteries in Palestine and worked many miracles before fleeing from the crowds that followed him everywhere. He died here at the age of 80. A monastery, dedicated to his memory, was established in this lonely place in the 10C or 11C.

The upper part of the first fortified structure stood between two peaks, so it was sometimes called 'Didymos', the Greek word for 'twins'. This was built by the Byzantines c 1110 on the orders of Alexius I Comnenus. In its heyday the Castle of St Hilarion played an important part in the defence of the island. It could communicate by flares at night with Kyrenia and Buffavento and through the latter with Nicosia and Kantara. As a result of a romantic, linguistic confusion 'Didymos' was transmuted into 'Dieu d'Amour' or 'Dio d'Amore' and so for the Lusignan chroniclers and troubadours it became the castle of Cupid, that naughty wilful son of Venus!

The earliest reference to the place is from 1191 when it was besieged by Guy de Lusignan on behalf of Richard Coeur de Lion. It is believed that Isaac Comnenus, the self styled Emperor of Cyprus, fleeing from the wrath of Richard, had taken refuge here. In 1228 the Regent, Jean d'Ibelin brought his family and the boy-king Henry I to St Hilarion. He improved the fortifications and was able to hold out against the supporters of the German Emperor Frederick II Hohenstaufen who was attempting to establish his suzerainty over Cyprus. In 1229 Frederick's followers were in turn besieged in the castle by Jean d'Ibelin. That soldier, poet and chronicler Philipo di Novarra took part in the siege. While lying wounded in the castle, he taunted the besieged with satirical verses which annoyed and discomfited them. When, through lack of food, they slaughtered an emaciated donkey, he congratulated them on their long eared Pascal Lamb and wished them a happy Easter! Philipo spent most of his life on the island. The author of a history of the war, the *Gestes des Chyprios*, he died c 1265.

After a siege lasting almost a year the castle surrendered in 1230 to d'Ibelin. On 15 June 1232 the young king Henry I, who had just reached his majority, raised a siege of the castle by the imperial troops. He defeated them at Aghirda which is located south west of the pass that leads to Kyrenia. They took refuge in Kyrenia castle, but were forced to capitulate in the following April. This ended the attempts of Frederick to rule Cyprus.

Modified and improved during the 14C St Hilarion was frequently used as a summer residence by the Lusignan court which was glad to escape from the oppressive heat of Nicosia. They passed the time with tournaments and pageants. Hugh IV came here in 1348 to avoid the plague which was decimating the island's population. John, Prince of Antioch, uncle to the young King Peter II, sought safety in St Hilarion during the Genoese invasion. It was here that the grim episode of the murder of the Bulgarian mercenaries took place. In a fit of insanity, John believed that the Bulgarians were planning to assassinate him and he had them precipitated one by one from the topmost tower into the abyss. It is said that only one mercenary survived and that he was badly injured by the fall.

In spite of its strategic importance the castle was neglected by the Venetians. In 1489 they had it dismantled in case it should fall into the hands of their enemies. Abandoned and overgrown, it became the haunt of wild animals, the nesting place of birds of prey.

However, even in its ruined state St Hilarion has continued to play a part in

St Hilarion Castle

martial affairs. In 1964 it was occupied by Turkish Cypriot militia and its garrison of boys successfully repelled an attack led by the Greek Cypriot Minister of the Interior. As a result the Turkish Cypriots were able to keep control of the main Kyrenia to Nicosia road.

Access to the castle is by an outer gateway which admits to the barbican. The restored gate house is on the right. From the barbican the main gate, flanked on the left by the barbican tower and on the right by a Byzantine Tower leads into the **Lower Ward**. The garrison and their mounts were quarted here. There were two cisterns to the left of the main gate.

A path ascends passing the stables on the right. It continues to the upper gate-house and gate tower. From here a passage leads to the **Middle Ward**. On the right is the once domed, late 10C Byzantine church which was restored in 1959 to prevent the collapse of its vaults. During the Lusignan period Mass was cele-brated in this chapel. The small room with a Hospitallers' cross was probably the sacristy. There are traces of 12C paintings on the south wall. Steps descend to a vaulted passage and the 14C great hall which replaced the monastery's refec-tory. Behind are the kitchen quarters and the latrines. To the right is a vaulted loggia or belvedere from which there are fine views of the countryside and coast. On the north east side a palatial suite of rooms was occupied by the royal family before the erection for them of more extensive accommodation in the Upper Ward.

A path to the **Upper Ward** passes a huge water tank. On the west side of the Upper Ward are the royal apartments which served as the summer quarters of the Lusignans. Three of the fine Gothic windows, which lit the elegant upper storey, survive. They offer superb views over the coast. One of them has deep stone seats. This is known as the 'Queen's Window'.

The ascent to the isolated 'Prince John's Tower' is for the bold and the agile. It stands alone in the centre of the fortress. There are sheer precipices on three sides. From here, it is said, the unlucky Bulgarian mercenaries were thrown to their deaths on the order of their insane employer.

'But in happier times—and they were longer than would seem—' Colin Thubron muses, 'the Lusignans preened away their summers with pageants and tournaments in the glade below, while under the cool belvedere the officers and chamberlains, within sight of the hostile mountains over the sea, reclined on samite cushions and drank their sherbet and forgot the morrow.'

Buffavento Castle

■ Open at all times.

Buffavento is appropriately named. Occupying a more exposed position than either St Hilarion or Kantara, it is still buffeted by winds, but now they blow around abandoned towers and through empty halls. The castle may be reached by a track which bears west from the highest point of the Girne/Değirmenlik road. In view of its isolated position and ruinous condition, it would be prudent to confine visits to daylight hours. This track is just passable by car. A more pleasant alternative to a bumpy car ride is a leisurely 90 minutes walk through pine woods to the base of the castle. A zig-zag path leads upwards to the summit of the peak (954m) on which the ruins are perched. Buffavento is the highest of the three great castles of the Kyrenia range.

The earliest reference to the castle is found in the *Gesta Regis Henrici II et Ricardi I*, a chronicle attributed to Benedict, Abbot of Peterborough from 1177 to 1193. After the daughter of the self-styled Emperor of Cyprus, Isaac Comnenus, had thrown herself on the mercy of Richard Coeur de Lion, 'the exceeding strong castle of Buffavent (was delivered to Richard) and after that all the towns and fortresses of the Empire (of Cyprus) were surrendered' to him. When the Emperor Frederick II Hohenstaufen attempted to establish his authority over Cyprus in 1232, he was opposed by Jean d'Ibelin, Regent of the young king Henry I. Eschive of Montbeliard, wife of Balian d'Ibelin, disguised herself as a Franciscan friar and made her way from Nicosia to Buffavento. The imperial troops did not follow her and made no attempt to capture the castle.

Buffavento was sometimes used as a prison. King Henry II (1285 to 1324) suspected his brother, the Constable of Cyprus, and the Prince of Galilee of plotting his downfall. He had them incarcerated in Buffavento. Perhaps the most unfortunate occupant of the dungeons of Buffavento was Sir John Visconti. A loyal friend of the unstable King Peter I (1359 to 1369), he told him that his queen Eleanor of Aragon had been unfaithful with the Count of Rocha while he had been abroad fighting the Saracens '...your lamb has gone astray and been with the ram.' Peter held an enquiry, but the Court supported the queen. The king believed that Visconti had lied and he was imprisoned in Kyrenia castle. Later Peter ordered his gaolers to '...take him from the dungeon at Kyrenia and (send) him to the Castle of Buffavento: then they threw him into a dungeon, and there he stayed without food till he died' (*Chronicle of Leontios Makhairas*). Peter then embarked on an orgy of torture. Not even his family was safe. On 16 January 1369, with the tacit agreement of his brother, John, Prince of Antioch, he was assassinated by some of his nobles.

The last prisoners of quality in Buffavento were the brothers Parot and Wilmot de Montolif who were imprisoned by King James I (1382 to 1398) for political reasons. They decided to escape and Parot succeeded in doing so, suffering nothing more serious than a sprained ankle. He sought refuge in the church of St Antony in Kyrenia, but was brought back to the castle. He and his brother were then confined with 'two wooden beams across their feet, one to each of them.' Later they were beheaded, their bodies were placed in a chest and conveyed on mule back to Cava where they were buried. It is said that the mule fell dead after the chest was removed from its back!

The bloodletting did not end with the execution of the Montolif brothers. Makhairas relates how James had Peter de Carzie and two other soldiers beheaded on the roof of the bread market near the Jew's bridge '...and the blood (ran) down the gutter upon the bread, and spoiled the bread below'.

As in the case of St Hilarion, the Venetians had no use for Buffavento. They removed its armaments and also most of the roof.

In 1683 Cornelius van Bruyn, a native of the Hague, visited the castle. He found it a frightening experience. 'The ascent is as difficult and dangerous as ever I made. The greater part of the time we had to climb with our hands as well as our feet, and whichever way we turned our gaze we saw only what made our hair stand on end.'

From Buffavento Castle it is possible to see the Mesoria to the south and the short stretch of sea which separates Cyprus from Turkey to the north. Watchers could detect hostile movements on the plain and the approach of enemy shipping. Messages were sent by fire signals to Nicosia, to Kyrenia and to the other castles on the mountain range.

A steep path leads up to the gateway of the castle. It passes the ruined stables on the left and a large reinforced cistern on the right. Byzantine masonry on the south wall of the Lusignan gatehouse indicates that this replaced an earlier structure. The two vaulted buildings to the left of the stairs appear to have had a double function. They could be used as quarters for the soldiers and in the defence of the castle. To the west are the remains of a large two storeyed Byzantine building and a rectangular building whose purpose and function are not known.

In the centre of the **Upper Ward** is the keep. This and the buildings on the west side of the castle were the areas of last resistance. The keep may also have served as the place where prisoners of state were held. The ruined building to the east of the keep was probably another barracks.

Kantara Castle

The quiet village of Kantara is cooled by refreshing breezes. A few hill bungalows—reminders of the period of British rule—conjure memories of Simla! Refreshments are available in a small café. There are fine views over the Mesaoria to the south.

It is a pleasant 3.5km walk along a mountain track to Kantara Castle. At a height of 630m, it has splendid views eastwards over the Karpas peninsula, south over the Mesaoria and north over the narrow coastal plain.

■ Open from early morning to dusk.

The castle's name is believed to be derived from the Arabic word for a high building. Kantara is the lowest in height and perhaps the least important of the three castles on the Gothic range. The first structure erected here was a watch tower. This kept a look out for the Arab corsairs who raided and frequently sacked the cities of Cyprus and Southern Anatolia in the 7C and 8C. A more substantial fortification was erected during the reign of Alexius I Comnenus (1081 to 1118). The self styled emperor of Cyprus, Isaac Comnenus, took refuge here. After his eventual surrender to Richard Coeur de Lion, Isaac was taken, fettered in silver chains, to the Hospitaller's castle at Margat, near Tripoli in Syria, where he died a few years later.

'The galley harbour has been wholly destroyed', he wrote 'I saw about two hundred cannon, not one of them serviceable. I never saw so many true aloes as on the ramparts... the town is in far worse condition than the fort; all the houses built by the Venetians are utterly demolished or deserted. There are but three hundred inhabitants, chiefly Turks, who occupy the miserable remains of the famous city...'.

The Christians lived in the village of Maraş (Varosha) to the south west of the Land Gate. At the beginning of the 19C about one hundred houses stood here among orchards, orange groves and mulberry trees which supported the local silk industry. Later in the century the intervening space was built over and during the early 20th century a new town was laid out overlooking the sandy beach stretching to the south.

The British. When the British arrived in 1878 they found a number of state prisoners incarcerated in the town. They included Subh-i-Ezel, the successor of Mirza Ali Mohammed of Shiraz, founder of the Babi sect. Subh-i-Ezel had two wives living in separate houses and he divided his time between them, 24 hours with one, then 24 hours with the other. He died at the age of 82 in 1912. Babism incorporated elements of Sufism, Gnosticism and Shiite Islam. Its principal doctrine was a belief in the coming of the Promised One. Its founder proclaimed himself the Bab or gate in 1844. The movement seceded completely from Islam in 1848 and its adherents were expelled from Persia in 1863. One of the principals of the sect, Baha Ullah, founded Baha'ism.

The harbour was so silted up that it was not until 1906 that it began to be used again commercially. Later it became the island's main port and was further extended in 1962. Famagusta was the eastern terminus of the island's railway. Begun in 1905, this was abandoned in 1951. Part of the old railway track was followed by the highway between Famagusta and the capital which was completed in 1962.

1974. In 1974 most of the the area around Famagusta was occupied by Greek Cypriots and many Turkish Cypriots sought refuge within the walled city. This was shelled by the Greek Cypriots until the Turkish air force intervened. Subsequently, the northern part of Maraş (Varosha) was occupied by Turkish Cypriots. The remainder is an eerie urban jungle of abandoned high rise apartments and empty hotels.

The City

The **wall** surrounding the **Old City** is the most complete fortification remaining on the Mediterranean littoral. On average 15m high and in some places as much as 8m thick, it has 15 bastions. It was built by the Venetians on existing Lusignan fortifications. The east side overlooks the harbour. The other three sides rise from a fosse partly excavated from the rock. On the south west side there is a rather sad, dusty garden. The sea gate, now closed, is not far from the citadel, sometimes called Othello's Tower. The land gate is in the south west corner of the walls facing the modern Victory Monument.

The 1930 edition of the *Handbook of Cyprus* states that golf was played 'over the ramparts'. This required 'an accuracy of direction which makes up for the comparative shortness of the holes'. Thus our Empire-builders relaxed! Admittedly it was only a nine-hole course.

The **Land Gate** adjoins the original gateway which the Venetians called the *Porta di Limasso*. The 9m high arch of this gateway remains. To the west rises the huge **Rivettina Bastion** the **Ravelin** which dates from 1544. This was the scene of some of the fiercest fighting during the great siege of 1570 to 1571. It is made up of a complex of dungeons and guardrooms.

The four bastions along the west side of the enceinte are the *Diocare, Moratto, Pulacazaro*, originally *Podocataro*, and *San Luca*.

In the counterscarp west of the first two bastions and also near the Land Gate a series of loopholes was discovered during road construction in 1982. From these the Ottoman besiegers could fire on the Venetians attempting to remove the debris which was being used to fill up the moat.

Jutting out like a broad arrow-head to the north west is the immense **Martinengo Bastion**. The Turks judged this to be impregnable and did not attempt to take it. Shafts to allow the escape of gunpowder smoke may still be seen in its vaulted casemates. The walls are between 4 and 6m thick. The bastion dates from c 1550 and is said to have been designed by Giovanni Girolamo Sammicheli, the best military engineer of the day. It was named after Hieronimo Martinengo who died off Corfu on his way to command Venetian troops in Cyprus in 1570.

The northern section of the walls was defended by the *Del Mezzo Bastion* and the *Diamante Bastion*, once washed by the sea. Between them there is an entrance to the city. Next comes the small *Signoria Bastion*. The imposing 14C **citadel**, with a round tower at each corner, was once almost surrounded by a sea moat. It was remodelled in 1492 by Nicolo Foscarini who reduced the height of the towers. It has an imposing **great hall** 28m long. Note the Venetian winged lion over the entrance.

The citadel is also known as **Othello's Tower**.

■ It is usually **open** daily from 08.00 to 17.00.

A certain Christophoro Moro, Venetian Lieutenant Governor of Cyprus between 1506 and 1508, had a coat-of-arms of three mulberries sable. This gave rise to the story that he was a Moor—*Moro* means mulberry and Moor. It may also have given Shakespeare the principal character for his play. There is, however, another theory. The Moor may have been Francesco de Sessa, a professional soldier from Calabria employed in the Venetian service in Cyprus. Because of his dark complexion he was known as 'Il Moro' or 'Il Capitano Moro'. In 1544 de Sessa was put on trial for an unspecified offence and banished.

For a magical experience stand on the summit of Othello's Tower in the quiet of

The Citadel or Othello's Tower

the evening, when the sounds of the city are reduced to a murmer, and watch the sun descent behind the cathedral of St Nicholas, now the Lala Mustafa Camii, the building that more than any other epitomises Famagusta's tumultuous past.

Behind a late 19C entrance is the **Sea Gate**, the Venetian *Porta del Mare*, built in 1496 by Nicolo Prioli. Its iron portcullis remains. The iron clad wooden doors date from the Ottoman period. Note the huge carved lion.

The sea wall extends to the **Cambulat Gate** and **Bastion** in the south east corner of the walls. Between here and the Land Gate extend the bastions of *Camposanto, Andruzzi* and *Santa Napa.* During the siege the fiercest fighting took place in this area.

A 19C bridge over the dry moat provides access to the city via the **Land Gate**. The Ottoman gatehouse is now a post office. A rather smelly ramp ascends under an arch in the Ravelin. Note the faded heraldic shields on the walls. There is a good view from the top of the bastion. You can walk along the walls as far as the *Pulacazara Bastion*, which marks the beginning of a restricted area, and south east to the Cambulat Bastion. It is also possible to walk on the bed of the moat from the Cambulat Bastion to the *Del Mezzo Bastion*.

The triple apsed **Nestorian Church** or **Ayios Yeoryios Xorinos**, St George the Exiler, got its name from the superstition that anyone wishing to get rid of an enemy had only to collect some dust off the church floor and leave it in the house of his bête noire. The recipient of this unwanted gift would either die or leave the island within the year. A well-built edifice, it dates from c 1359. The Nestorians were followers of Nestorius (382 to 451), archbishop of Constantinople from 428 to 431. They rejected the doctrine proclaimed by the Council of Ephesus in 431 that Christ was one single person and that consequently that Mary should be called the Mother of God. Although for some time in the past it had been used as a stable for camels, the church was a Greek Orthodox place of worship as recently as 1963.

Since 1974 a number of churches in the old city have been put to secular use. There are some in the northern restricted area. These include **Ayia Anna**. This has a high western façade topped by acroteria and a single nave. There are some murals and Latin inscriptions. Nearby is the **Tanners' Mosque** which appears to have been a 16C church. There are acoustic vases in the vault and traces of painting on the walls.

The **Carmelite Church of St Mary** dates from the mid 14C. Its priory has disappeared. The body of the Latin Patriarch of Constantinople, Blessed Peter de Thomas, who died of wounds received at the siege of Alexandria in 1366, was buried at the entrance of the choir, 'so that all, even goats and dogs, might walk over it'. On the north wall there are some 14C and 15C paintings of patriarchs and bishops and coats of arms of England, France and other countries.

Nearby is the mid 14C **Armenian Church**. Earthenware jars were built into the vault to improve the acoustics. There were fragmentary wall paintings of scenes of the Passion of Christ and of apostles and saints with inscriptions in Armenian. The Armenians had settled in Cyprus before the arrival of the Lusignans. Their bishop resided in Nicosia, but for a time there was a second prelate in Famagusta. The Armenians claim to be the first nation to convert to Christianity. St Gregory the Illuminator baptised King Tiridates III in 303. They refused to accept the decision of the Council of Chalcedon in 451, which stated that Christ has both a divine and human nature which exist inseparably within him, and formed a separate church.

The **Martinengo Bastion** is also in the restricted area. Two huge subterranean chambers, discovered in 1966, were provided with ventilation shafts. The bastion could accommodate 2000 persons and may have been a place of refuge during the great siege of 1570 and the events of 1974.

The roofless late 13C church of **St George of the Latins** is south of the Citadel in Cafer Paşa Sokak. It was once fortified, a fact which suggests that it antedated the city walls. It had a single nave with four bays and a triple apse. Some of the fine carving remains—the lion lying down with the lamb on the north tower, the gargoyles of a greyhound and a dragon projecting from the apse and the capital showing a cluster of bats. Bombardment from an Ottoman battery mounted on an offshore reef reduced the church to its present condition.

The **Cathedral of St Nicholas**, previously known as Aysofya, has been renamed **Lala Mustafa Camii** after the Ottoman conqueror of Cyprus. A remarkable example of early 14C French Gothic architecture, it is the most important single monument in Famagusta. The approach to the cathedral, by a series of narrow streets, leaves one quite unprepared for the sight of its glorious façade. Suddenly there is this magnificent vision of soaring, honey coloured stone. The 'Latin cathedral, modelled on the purity of Rheims ...rises with a miraculous intricacy from the waste. The window of six lights, the counterpoint of gable and flying buttress and traceried tower, are like a lucid and perfect dialectic.' (Colin Thubron.)

The cathedral, possibly after the design of a Frenchman named Jean Langlois, is 55m long and 23m wide. It has a nave, two side aisles, no transepts and a triple apse. As is customary in the Eastern Mediterranean the roof is flat. It was consecrated in 1326. The only additions to the original structure are the two chapels on the south side and one on the north. Until 1372 the Lusignan kings of Cyprus came here to be crowned King of Jerusalem, an empty honour after the loss of Acre in 1291. Here James II the Bastard and his posthumous infant son James III, the last two Lusignan sovereigns, were buried in 1473 and 1474 respectively. Here Caterina Cornaro, widow of James II, renounced her royal rights in 1489 and ceded Cyprus to Agostino Barberigo, Doge of Venice, before retiring to Asolo.

The cathedral was much damaged during the bombardment of 1571 and again by an earthquake in 1735. During its conversion to a mosque after the conquest a *mihrab* was constructed on the south east side and all representations of the human figure in its decoration, furnishings, stained glass and ornaments were destroyed. Its frescoes were covered with whitewash. Its altars were demolished. Just a few medieval tombstones survive in the north aisle. However, spared the Baroque additions and 19C restorations which have damaged the unity of many European cathedrals, it remains an unusual example of pure Gothic architecture. Even with '...the furniture of a mosque superimposed, the ascent of Gothic stone is scarcely troubled...' (Thubron).

The **parvis**, shaded by an ancient *Ficus sycomorus*, was once much larger. Here St Bridget of Sweden is said to have preached against the profligacy of Famagustan society. After the capture of the city by the Ottomans, Bragadino, the Venetian commander of the garrison, was flayed alive here. Note the west front, with its three shallow porches, the centre one wider than the others. Each is surmounted by richly carved straight sided gabled canopies. Over the centre porch there is a superb six light window and above that a rose window. Over the side doors are tall blind double light windows. The glass in the rose window is an early 20C restoration. Only the lower sections of the twin towers, which have been compared to those at Rheims, survive. A slender minaret has been added to the north tower.

The Archbishop's Palace was on the north side of the cathedral. A Venetian style loggia, which has lost its upper storey, now houses a fountain for Moslem ritual ablutions. The central doorway is flanked by two circular windows above which there are Venetian coats of arms sculpted in marble. Below the window nearer the cathedral is a fragmentary marble frieze, probably from the cornice of a Roman temple, representing animals chasing each other through foliage. Outside the loggia benches of Roman marble offer welcome places of rest.

On the west side of the square nothing now remains of the Lusignan palace occupied by the kings of Cyprus until the reign of Peter II (1369 to 1382). It was replaced by the Venetian **Palazzo del Provveditore**. The imposing façade of the palazzo has three arches supported by four columns from Salamis. Above the arches there was a balcony. Over the central arch are the arms of Giovanni Renier, Captain of Cyprus in 1552. The area behind the façade has been excavated. It is now a garden—and a car park—and is littered with architectural fragments. The guard house on the west side was used as a prison during the Ottoman period. In the mid 19C Mehmed Namik Kemal (1840 to 1888), sometimes called the Shakespeare of Turkey, was imprisoned here because he had defied the sultan. A bust has been erected in his memory and the square has been named after him.

The ruined 13C church of **St Francis** is almost all that remains of the Franciscan friary which Martoni described in 1394 as being '...with a fair cloister, a dormitory, many cells and other rooms, with a fine garden and a quantity of conduits, and cisterns'. The Genoese added two mortuary chapels to form a transept. In the southern chapel there are tombstones dating from 1314 to 1474. During the Ottoman period a hammam was built nearby. This is now a disco.

Almost opposite the church of St Francis are the twin churches of the **Knights Templar** and of the **Knights Hospitaller**. The dark church of the Templars, which dates from the early 14C, was restored earlier this century. It is now the Atatürk Cultural Centre. The Knights Hospitallers added the smaller church and then acquired the church of Templars when that order was suppressed at the beginning of the 14C.

On the left hand side of Naim Effendi Sokağı, leading north from the cathedral, there is a house in the Italian Renaissance style. A short distance beyond is an elaborate doorway known as **Biddulph's Gate** after the British High Commissioner who saved it from destruction in 1879.

The church of **St Peter and St Paul** dates from c 1360. It suffered some damage from the earthquakes of 1546 and 1548. The Gothic north door was probably moved here from another church. Note the carving of the angels, one holds a censer, the other is bearing souls to paradise. The buttresses, which support the nave roof, are unusual. The high west front and round windows are features reminiscent of the churches of Provence. Turned into a mosque, it was known as **Sinan Paşa Camii**. Later the British stored potatoes in it. Now it is used for the presentation of plays, for concerts and for exhibitions.

The ruined church of **St George of the Greeks** was once the Orthodox cathedral of Famagusta. Fragments of paintings remain in the arches and the founders' tombs are preserved on the side wall. To the south are the ruins of the original Byzantine cathedral dedicated to Ayios Symeon. Two of the apses of this smaller structure survived the Turkish bombardment of 1571. It is claimed that the body of St Epiphanios (310 to 406), Archbishop of Salamis, was buried here at one time. It was taken to Constantinople c 900.

Two semi circular apses and part of the south aisle of the church of **Ayios Nikolaos** remain. Nearby is **Ayia Zoni**, a 14 to 15C building in the Byzantine style. The walls were covered with paintings, slight traces of a large representation of Archangel Michael survive.

Cambulat Bastion, formerly known as the **Arsenal**, is named after a celebrated Turkish hero of the siege of 1571. Cambulat led the attack through a breach made by explosives and held the walls for five hours before being forced to retreat. The Venetians then brought a terrifying war engine to defend the gap in their defences. This was a huge wheel fitted with rotating, razor sharp knives. Cambulat spurred his horse against the terrible instrument. It ripped him and the animal to pieces, but his bravery inspired the whole Ottoman army to make fresh efforts to take the city. Cambulat was buried where he fell. His restored tomb is the centerpiece of a display of armour, weapons, costumes, calligraphy and embroi-

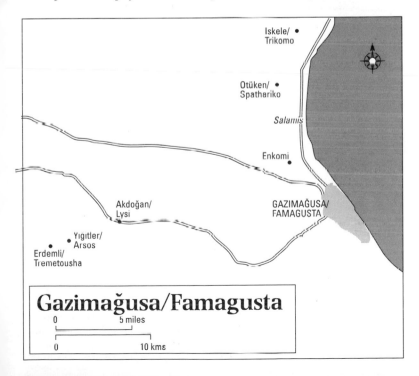

Iskele/ •
Trikomo

Otüken/ •
Spathariko

Salamis

Enkomi
•

Akdoğan/
Lysi

GAZIMAĞUSA/
FAMAGUSTA

Yiğitler/
Arsos
•

Erdemli/
Tremetousha
•

Gazimağusa/Famagusta

0   5 miles

0   10 kms

dery. There is also an outstanding collection of Iznik pottery which was largely pieced together from fragments found when the bastion was restored.

Before the restoration Cambulat's tomb stood in the open and was shaded by a large fig tree. Childless and pregnant women hung rags on this tree in the hope that they would bear sons as brave as Cambulat.

North and west of Gazimaǧusa

Highlights
Salamis, the Tombs of the Kings, the Monastery of Ayios Varnavas, Enkomi

Salamis

Ancient Salamis is c 8km north of Famagusta. Parts of the site are very overgrown and covered with thick, spiny scrub. If you intend to wander off the paths and explore all the ruins, wear a stout pair of shoes and long thornproof socks. The remains are spread over a wide area and to see everything requires at least one day. However, Salamis is an excellent place for picnics. It has a clean sandy beach which is usually uncrowded. There is a small restaurant and the Park Hotel with all its facilities is just 300m away.

■ Open daily from 08.00 to 19.00 (17.00 in winter).

History of the site

According to an ancient myth the city was founded by Teucer, the half brother of Ajax and the son of Telamon, king of Salamis, an island in the Saronic Gulf. Banished by Telamon for failing to protect Ajax at the siege of Troy, Teucer went to Syria. There he was welcomed by King Belus who was about to embark on the conquest of Cyprus. The king took Teucer and his companions with him. Teucer established a settlement in Cyprus and named it after his island home.

However, the discovery of a mid-11C BC tomb at Salamis proved what had long been suspected, that it had succeeded the Late Cypriote Period city of Enkomi (see below) which existed from c 1550 BC. It would appear that following a disastrous earthquake the inhabitants of Enkomi began to leave their city c 1075 BC. They established a new home where the Pedieos river flowed into Salamis bay.

Nothing is known about the history of Salamis from the mid-11C BC until 709 BC when it is listed on an Assyrian stele as one of the cities of Cyprus paying tribute to Sargon II. Judging by the so called Royal Tombs (see below) Salamis was a prosperous place in the 8C and 7C BC. About 560 BC Evelthon of Salamis became the first Cypriot king to issue his own coinage. At the beginning of the 5C BC Evagoras, who may have been a member of the Teucrid dynasty, killed Abdemon of Tyre, who had been placed on the

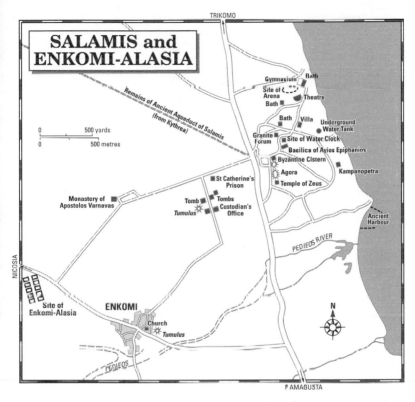

TRIKOMO

SALAMIS and ENKOMI-ALASIA

Remains of Ancient Aqueduct of Salamis
(from Kythrea)

0   500 yards
0   500 metres

Gymnasium Bath
Site of ⟨ ⟩
Arena   Theatre
Bath

Bath   Villa   Underground
                Water Tank
Granite   Site of Water Clock
Forum
        Basilica of Ayios Epiphanios
        Byzantine Cistern
                Kampanopetra
            Agora
        Temple of Zeus

St Catherine's
Prison

Monastery of   Tombs
Apostolos Varnavas   Tomb   Custodian's
            Tumulus   Office

                        Ancient
                        Harbour

PEDIEOS RIVER

NICOSIA

Site of
Enkomi-Alasia   ENKOMI
            Church
                Tumulus   N

PEDIEOS

FAMAGUSTA

throne of Salamis by the Persians, and took his place. Evagoras tried to unite the Cypriot kings against the Persians. He welcomed Greek poets and philosophers to his court and in an overt act of defiance introduced gold coinage, a right which the Great King of Persia reserved for himself. Defeated by the Persians at the naval battle of Kition, Evagoras was obliged to abandon his ambitious plans and accept the Great King as his overlord. In 306 BC the walls of Salamis were destroyed by the catapults and war machines of the formidable Demetrius Poliorcetes whose name means, 'the besieger'.

Ptolemy I Soter took possession of Cyprus in 294 BC and the island remained under Ptolemaic rule until 58 BC when the Romans made it part of the province of Cilicia. With its good harbour and long established trading connections Salamis flourished, though it was replaced by Paphos as capital. Hadrian and Trajan contributed funds for the construction, and reconstruction, after earthquakes, of its public buildings. About AD 45 St Paul met and converted the Roman ruler of Cyprus, the proconsul Sergius Paulus at Salamis. Shortly after that event he changed his name from the Semitic Saul to the Roman Paul to mark its importance. St Barnabas was a native of Salamis, which had a considerable Jewish population in the 1C, and he suffered martyrdom here at their hands.

There followed a long period of decay. During the Jewish Revolt of AD 116 to 117 against the Romans Salamis was largely destroyed. Frequent earthquakes contributed to its further decline. Then c AD 350 the city was rebuilt on a smaller scale. To help its recovery the Emperor Constantius II remitted taxes for four years and the grateful inhabitants renamed their city **Constantia**. It was an episcopal see. The Bishop of Constantia, with two other Cypriot bishops, attended the Council of Nicaea in 325.

In the mid 7C Constantia was sacked and largely razed to the ground by the Arabs under Mu'âwiya, the first Ommayad caliph. As a consequence it was abandoned by its inhabitants who fled to nearby Famagusta. The ruins are mentioned by Christopher Fürer of Nurenberg who came to Cyprus in 1566 and they were visited by Richard Pococke in 1738. The ancient city was stripped of its cut stone by the people of Famagusta who used it for the construction and decoration of their churches and public buildings and for the strengthening of the city walls. The first of a number of modern archaeological expeditions to excavate the site took place in 1880. The most recent exploration was by a team from the University of Lyon.

The City

A ruined section of the **city walls** of Constantia and parts of the **aqueduct**, which brought water 50km from Kythrea (Değirmenlik), are visible from the approach road to the site.

You enter the imposing remains of the **palaestra** from the south. Originally built during the Hellenistic era, it was altered during the period of Roman rule. Most of the marble columns, re-erected between 1952 and 1955, came from the theatre which was not rebuilt after it was damaged by an earthquake. They were placed here in the early 4C AD when the palaestra was used as a Christian meeting place. In an annexe in the south west corner there was a semi circular communal latrine which could accommodate 44 persons at one time.

The fluted columns of the wider eastern portico came from another ruined building. At each end of this portico there are annexes containing rectangular pools. Behind the portico two *frigidaria* with octagonal tanks flank the central *sudatorium*, the steam room. There is a late 3C AD fresco here of the encounter of Hylas, the handsome young lover of Hercules, with the water nymphs. This shows the boy hiding behind a hill in an attempt to escape from the deadly sirens who want to draw him down into their pool. In the southern *sudatorium* there are two wall mosaics, also 3C AD. One shows the river god Eurotas watching Zeus, who has assumed the form of a swan, copulate with Leda. The second mosaic shows the revenge of Leto.

Salamis

Angered by Niobe's claim that she was superior to Leto as she had more children, Leto asked her offspring, Apollo and Artemis, to kill Niobe's brood. Apollo is in the centre of the mosaic, Artemis on the left. Below is an exquisite female head in the centre of a garland of fruit and flowers. The mosaics were covered over during the early Christian period.

The headless statues around the swimming pool in the northern *sudatorium* may have been mutilated at the same time, as representations of pagan deities were anathema to the early Christians. Note those of Asclepius, the god of medicine, Persephone, the goddess of the underworld, and Clotho, one of the Moirae or Fates. It was believed that the three sisters, Atropus, Clotho and Lachesis regulated the length of each person's life by means of a thread. Atropus spun it, Clotho wound it up and Lachesis cut it. Note the spindle in Clotho's hand. Other statues found here are now in the Cyprus Museum, Southern Nicosia.

The eastern end of the central bath has an apse similar to that of the northern *sudatorium*. The rooms are connected by two tunnels built into the thickness of the walls. The outer wall of the northern *sudatorium* was supported by three buttresses.

A short distance south of the gymnasium is the site of an unexcavated **amphitheatre**.

The **theatre** of Salamis, built during the reign of Augustus, was restored and remodelled during the reigns of Hadrian and Trajan. The orchestra, 27.5m in diameter, could be flooded for the staging of mock sea battles. The *scaenae frons* rose 2m above the orchestra. There was an elaborately decorated stage building. A statue of Apollo, which ornamented it, was found among the debris. The stone *cavea* was supported by arches. It had 55 rows of white limestone seats and an estimated seating capacity of 15,000. Twenty rows have been rebuilt. There are a few of the original seats in the lower rows. In the sixth row there was a box for city dignitaries. Destroyed during the earthquakes of the 4C, the theatre was used later as a quarry for the reconstruction of other buildings.

Due south of the theatre are the scant remains of a modest **Roman villa**. Paved in stone, this had a small atrium. The living quarters were arranged around an inner courtyard. Part of a decorative fresco remains. The mill in the atrium was used during the Middle Ages.

There are the ruins of a partially cleared Byzantine **cistern** near the basilica of Ayios Epiphanios. Note the section of the aqueduct which brought water to the city. The **granite forum** gets its name from a number of columns of Egyptian granite from Aswan each c 5.5m in length.

Only the foundations of the 4C **Basilica of Ayios Epiphanios** remain. This was 58m long and 42m wide. Its nave was separated by columns from two side aisles. The semi circular apse had a synthronon, raised benches for the clergy, in the 6C. At the east end of the south aisle there is a marble lined tomb, presumably that of St Epiphanios, whose remains were transferred to Constantinople at the beginning of the 10C. (See Famagusta.)

The basilica was largely destroyed during the Arab raids and a new church was built c 698. Extending east from the tomb, it had a nave and two side aisles separated by square piers which probably supported a wooden roof. This building was reconstructed in the 9C and the roof over the central nave was replaced by three domes. It continued as a place of worship until the 14C.

Entrance to the Early Christian basilica known as **Kampanopetra** was on the

St Epiphanios

St Epiphanios was born in Palestine. He entered the religious life at an early age and became abbot at Eleutheropolis. The 'oracle of Palestine', Epiphanios wrote and preached against heresy, principally against Arianism. He became bishop of Salamis/Constantia in 367 where he continued his vigorous defence of the Catholic faith. In his old age Epiphanios was considered to be somewhat headstrong and unpredictable.

west side by way of a large paved courtyard. In the centre of the courtyard a pink and white column overlooked a well which was used for lustral purposes. The basilica had a nave and two aisles separated by rows of columns. In the 10C a chapel was built over the northern and central apses. Note the sarcophagus in the northern apse which was reused as an altar. The aisles were flanked by side passages where catachumens, ie, those under instruction and awaiting baptism, could follow the Mass but not take part in it. There is a fine *opus sectile* pavement and a number of sarcophagi in the southern passage.

The building to the east of the basilica was probably the episcopal palace. Note the fine *opus sectile* floor, with a design of con-centric circles, and the five standing columns.

The rectangular **agora** of Salamis measured 230m by 55m. Now almost completely covered by scrub, it is difficult to imagine its grandeur when it was restored c 22 BC. Only one of the forest of columns that once lined its colonnades still stands. At the southern end a mound marks the position of the **Temple of Zeus** which appeared on the city's coinage and was founded, so it is said, by Teucer.

A pleasant walk south along the beach will bring you to the sheltered bay of Salamis which was protected by a great breakwater. Today the harsh cries of seabirds replace the chants of the ancient sailors as they raised the lateen sails of ships bound for Palestine, for Syria, for Egypt, for Rome.... ships laden perhaps

> 'With a cargo of ivory,
> And apes and peacocks
> Sandalwood, cedarwood, and sweet white wine...'

Necropolis of Salamis

The extensive necropolis of Salamis lies to the west of the ancient city and occupies an area of c four square miles. Here nine so called **Royal Tombs** were excavated in recent years. Because of their size, striking architectural features and the rich grave goods found in some of the tombs, the epithet 'royal' has been applied, somewhat indiscriminately, to them. Certainly important people were laid to rest here. Who they were and what position they held in Salamis are matters of conjecture. The tombs date from the 8C and 7C BC.

Each tomb was approached by a large entrance ramp. In these *dromoi* offerings to the dead—amphorae filled with wine, oil and sometimes honey—were laid carefully on the ground. The animals, which had drawn the funeral cart, were butchered here and their bodies, still wearing harness, were placed with the carts before the entrance to the tomb.

Tomb 50, sometimes called **St Catherine's Prison**, dates from the 8C BC. At some time during the Roman period the steps of the portico were removed and a wall was built across the façade of the burial chamber. The association of the tomb with St Catherine of Alexandria dates from the Middle Ages. It is thought that a local woman named Catherine may have been imprisoned in the tomb and in time she became identified with the saint. The skeletons of two horses were found by archaeologists in the *dromos* which measures 28m by 13m.

Tomb 47 dates from the end of the 8C or beginning of the 7C BC. It was robbed in antiquity, probably during the Roman period. The tomb was used for two separate burials. In the *dromos*, which measures 20m by 13.5m, the skeletons of two horses from the first burial were found. The funeral cart was placed with the body inside the burial chamber

Tomb 2 contained some human remains.

In the **museum** near the custodian's hut there are modern reproductions of the funeral carts and some of the original horse harness found in the *dromoi*. There are also some interesting iron artefacts, including a bundle of tarnished spear heads. Drawings and photographs illustrate the activities of the archaeologists who worked on the site.

Tomb 77 is located on the south west outskirts of the modern village of Tuzla (Enkomi). No evidence of a burial was found here, but there were the remains of a pyre on a large rectangular stepped platform of mudbrick. It is believed that this was a funerary monument created by the people of Salamis in memory of Nicocreon, the last king of their city. With members of his family Nicocreon commited suicide to escape capture by Ptolemy I Soter and he was buried under the ruins of his palace. The archaeologists found charred gold and copper wreaths, decorated scent bottles, weapons and the remarkable clay portraits of a woman and four men. The monument has been tentatively dated to 306 BC.

Apostolos Varnavas

The Monastery of Apostolos Varnavas is pleasantly sited in a grove of eucalyptus trees. St Barnabas, a native of Cyprus, was not one of the original 12, but has always been honoured as an apostle. The friend of St Paul, his missionary work is set out in detail in the Acts of the Apostles. It is said that he was killed by the Jews of Salamis. Barnabas is usually depicted holding a book and standing on a mound of stones.

In the latter part of the 5C the patriarch of Antioch made strenuous efforts to bring the Church of Cyprus under his jurisdiction. Anthemios, the bishop of Constantia, had a dream in which he was told to dig under a carob tree in the necropolis of Salamis. There he found the tomb of St Barnabas. The saint was holding his own handwritten copy of the Gospel of St Mark clasped in his arms. Anthemios took the book to Constantinople and presented it to the Emperor Zeno. In return the emperor gave the bishop the right to carry a sceptre and to use purple ink, two imperial prerogatives. More importantly, at a synod arranged by Zeno the independence of the Church of Cyprus was formally recognised.

The restored **mausoleum**, appropriately shaded by carob trees, has an empty stone tomb which, it is said, once held the remains of St Barnabas. A monastery erected nearby was destroyed by Arab raiders. The present mid 18C **church** has parts of its 5C predecessor—two columns, a section of wall and part of an *opus* *sectile* pavement—near the outside wall of the apse. The church was damaged by an earthquake in 1941. The campanile was erected in 1958. Note the modern wall painting of the discovery of the tomb of St Barnabas, the work of three brothers, monks of this monastery. There is a collection of 19C icons.

The last monks left the monastery in 1977. The monastic buildings now house a small **museum**, which has some exhibits from Salamis and Enkomi, and a café offering light refreshments.

Enkomi

A short distance to the south west is the site of Enkomi. This is sometimes called Enkomi-Alasia because of some references in the El Amarna tablets to a place called Alasia which sent copper to Egypt and was commissioned to build ships for its rulers. The tablets record correspondence between two 18th dynasty pharaohs, Amenophis III (1417 to 1379 BC) and Amenophis IV the heretic Akhenaten (1379 to 1362 BC), and the king of Alasia. However, most scholars now believe that the name 'Alasia' refers to the island of Cyprus and not to its capital.

Enkomi was nearer the sea than at present and was linked to it by a navigable channel. The earliest artefacts discovered so far date from the Middle Bronze Age (1900 to 1650 BC) when it was a small pastoral community. About 1550 BC, during the invasions of the Hyksos, who so disrupted life in the Eastern Mediterranean, a fortress was erected at Enkomi. It was destroyed not long afterwards. At that time Enkomi was a copper processing centre. The mines were probably at Khalkovouni near Lysi c 19km to the south west. Enkomi continued to flourish as an emporium for the export of minerals and had trading relations with many countries on the Eastern Mediterranean and in lands to the west. Particularly close commercial contacts were established with Ugarit, modern Ras Shamra, 145km across the sea near Latakia in Syria. Grave goods from that time include Mycenaean vases and gold trinkets from Egypt and the Aegean. Enkomi reached its apogee towards the end of the 13C BC. Cyclopean walls were built and a grid plan imposed on the northern part of the city. During the following two centuries it was ravaged by the so-called Sea People. Consumed by fire, what remained of the partly rebuilt town was razed to the ground by an earthquake in the 12C BC. Enkomi was finally abandoned c 1050 BC and its inhabitants moved to Salamis. Later the remains of the city were partially submerged by silt from nearby rivers.

The first exploration of the necropolis of Enkomi was undertaken by a British Museum expedition in 1896. A Swedish team excavated a number of tombs in 1930. French archaeologists under the direction of Professor Claude Schaeffer began work on the city in 1934. In 1946 and 1947 a stretch of its outer fortifications was discovered.

Although of great interest to the expert, the site has limited appeal for the layman as comparatively little survives above ground.

The main buildings so far excavated are, from north to south, a fortress like structure adjoining the North Gate. In the **Sanctuary of the Horned God** the famous 12C bronze statue was found during the 1948 to1951 excavations. This may be a representation of Apollo Keraeatas, a god of herdsmen, whose worship was brought from Arcadia in Greece to Cyprus. It is believed that horned

Mylonas, Nicodemus 155
Mylouthkia 126
Myriantheus, Makarios 155
Myrtou 203

N

Nea Paphos 108
Neophytos 148
Nestorius 224
Neta 195
Nicocles 110, 133
Nicocreon 233
Nicosia 152
  American Center 173
  Arab Ahmet Mosque 176
  Arablar Mosque 164
  Archbishop Makarios III Cultural
    Foundation 165
  Archbishop's Palace 165
  Atatürk Meydanı 175
  Augustinian Church of St Mary
    164
  d'Avila Bastion 163
  Ayios Antonios 165
  Ayios Ioannis 166
  Ayios Kassianos 167
  Barbaro Bastion 163
  Bedesten 179
  Büyük Hamam 176
  Büyük Han 177
  Byzantine Museum 165
  Caraffa Bastion 162
  Cathedral of Ayia Sophia 177
  Central Post Office 163
  Church of St Catherine 180
  Church of St Paul 159
  Church of the Holy Cross 163
  Costanza Bastion 162
  Cyprus Museum 159
  Ercan Airport 173
  Ethnographic Museum 165
  Famagusta Gate 162
  Flatro Bastion 163
  Folk Art Museum 167
  Garaffa Bastion 162
  Haydar Paşa Mosque 180
  Holy Cross Church 174
  House of the Dragoman Haji

Nicosia cont.
  Georghakis Kornessios 164
  International Airport 170
  Jeffery's Museum 180
  Kaimakli Gate 163
  Kumarcılar Hanı 176
  Kyrenia Gate 163, 174
  Laiki Geitonia 163
  Lapidarı Müzesi 180
  Ledra Palace Hotel 159
  Leventis Municipal Museum 163
  Library of Sultan Mahmut II 179
  Loredano Bastion 163
  Louki Pierides Library 160
  Mansion of Derviş Paşa 176
  Mausoleum of the Şeyhs 175
  Mevlevi Tekke 175
  Mosque of the Standard-bearer
    162
  Mula Bastion 163
  Museum of Barbarism 181
  Museum of National Struggle 167
  Panayia Khrysaliniotissa 167
  Panayia Phaneromeni 164
  Pancyprian Gymnasium 167
  Paphos Gate 163
  Plateia Vasileos Georgiou II 162
  Ömerye Mosque 164
  Porta del Provveditore 163, 174
  Porta Domenica 163
  Post Office 173
  Quirini Bastion 163
  Roccas Bastion 163
  St George of the Latins 176
  Saray Önu Mosque 175
  Sellmiye Mosque 177
  Sourp Asdouadzadzin 176
  Stavrou tou Missiricou 164
  Sultan Mahmut Kütüphanesi 179
  Tourist Office 163
  Tripoli Bastion 163
  Walls 162
  Yeni Cami 180
Nikoklia 136
Nisou 168
Nissi Beach 71
Nitovikla 195
Novarra, Philipo di 210

O

Olympos, Mt 140
Ömer, Prophet 164
Omodhos 136
Onesilos 88
Ormidhia 69
Orounda 172
Osman, Chil 154
Otüken 235
Ovid 151
Özanköy 188

P

Palaealona 200
Palaepaphos 103, 110
  Château de Couvoucle 107
  Leda and the Swan, mosaic 106
  North East Gate 106
  Palaepaphos Museum 107
  Sanctuary of Aphrodite 104
  Siege Ramp 106
Palekhori 147
Paleokastro 204
Paleomylos 140
Paleovikla tomb 195
Panayia Amasgou Monastery 134
Panayia Angeloktistos, Kiti 78
Panayia tou Araka Monastery 147
Panayia Aspromoutti 68
Panayia Eleousa Agrou Monastery 146
Panayia Eleousa Monastery, Troodos 196
Panayia Eleousa, Podithou 144
Panayia Evangelistria, Klirou 149
Panayia Galaktotrophousa Monastery 75
Panayia Galoktisti, Kato Pyrgos 132
Panayia Khryseleousa, Emba 125
Panayia Khryseleousa, Lyso 130
Panayia Khryseleousa, Strovolos 170
Panayia Khrysiotissa, Aphendrika 198
Panayia Khrysokoudhaliotissa, Monastery 146
Panayia Khrysopolitissa, Erimi 94

Panayia Khrysorroyiatissa Monastery 133
Panaya Khrysospiliotissa Monastery, Lagoudhera 170
Panayia Phorviotissa, Asinou 145
Panayia Theotokos, Podithou 144
Panayia, church of the, Galata 144
Pani Panayia, Kannaviou 133
Pano Arkhimandrita 136
Pano Arodhes 129
Pano Lefkara 149
Pano Platres 137
Paphos 108
  Agora 120
  Amazon (mosaic) 124
  Archaeologoical Park 120
  Asclepieion 119
  Ayia Kyriaki/Khrysopolitissa 117
  Ayios Antonios 117
  Ayios Lambrianos 115
  Ayios Misitikos 115
  Ayios Yeoryios 116
  Cami Kebir Mosque 112
  Catacombs of Ayia Solomoni 115
  Daphne and Apollo (mosaic) 122
  Dioscouroi (mosaic) 121
  Fabrica Hill 115
  First Bath of Achilles (mosaic) 124
  Four Seasons (mosaic) 122
  Frankish Baths 116
  Gothic Church 117
  Hellenistic Theatre 116
  Hercules and the Nemean Lion (mosaic) 124
  House of Aion 122
  House of Dionysos 120
  House of Orpheus 124
  Icarius and Dionysos (mosaic) 121
  International Airport 103, 109
  Kato Paphos 115
  Ktima 108, 112
  Latin Cathedral 116
  Monochrome Mosaic 124
  Mosque 116
  Moulia Rocks 125
  Narcissus (mosaic) 121
  Neptune and Amymone (mosaic) 121
  North Gate 115

Paphos cont.
Odeion 119
Ottoman Castle 125
Panayia Limeniotissa 118
Panayia Theoskepasti 116
Paphos District Archaeological
Museum 112
Petra tou Digheni 114
Phaedra and Hippolytus (mosaic)
121
Pillar of St Paul 118
Poseidon and Amphitrite (mosaic)
124
Pyramus and Thisbe (mosaic) 121
Rape of Ganymede (mosaic) 121
Roman City Wall 115
Sanctuary of Apollo Hylates 118
Saranda Kolones 118
Scylla Mosaic 120
Theseus and the Minotaur (mosaic)
123
Tombs of the Kings 114
Triumph of Dionysos (mosaic) 120
Turkish Baths 112
Villa of Theseus 123
Paradhisi 235
Paralimni 70
Pausanias 104, 109
Pedhoulas 142
Pedieos River 159
Pelendria 143
Pendalia 134
Pendayia 206
Pentadactylos, Mt 215
Perukhorio 75
Perapedhi 135
Peristerona 171
Pernera 70
Pesaro, Jacobo 116
Peter I 78, 141, 168
Peter II 153, 184, 226
Petra tou Digheni 114
Petra tou Limniti 208
Petra tou Romiou 107
Peyia 127
Phaneromeni 94, 96
Phasouri Plantations 91
Phikardhou 149
Philip IV of France 83

Philocyprus 207
Phini 138
Phinikas 93
Phrenaros 69
Phterykoudhi 148
Pighades 203
Pissouri 101
Plakoti, Cape 195
Plataniskia 101
Platanistasa 147
Pyla, Cape 69
Pococke, Richard 141, 190, 199,
207, 219
Poditou 144
Podocatoros family 78
Polemi 132
Polis 130
Politiko 151
Polystipos 146
Poor Knights of Christ 82
Potamia 168
Potamos tou Liopetrou 71
Prodhromos 140
Prophitis Elias Monastery, Pano
Lefkara 150
Protaras 70
Psomolophou 171
Ptolemy I Soter 130, 198, 228, 229,
233
Ptolemy II Philadelphus 101, 217
Ptolemy of Cyprus 110
Pyla 68
Pyrga 73
Pyrgos 90

Q

Le Quid 78

R

Radipe 72
Randi Forest 107
Richard Coeur de Lion 82, 89, 92,
126, 135, 184, 199, 210, 213, 235
Rimbaud, Arthur 68, 138
Rizokarpaso 196

S

Sadrazamköy 202
St Andrew 198
St Auxentios, church, Büyükkonuk 193
St Barnabus 88, 89, 96, 143
St Epiphanios 231, 232
St Eutychios 133
St Helena 74
St Heracleidios 143, 150, 151
St Hermogenes 95
St Hilarion Castle 209
St John the Almoner 89
St John Chrysostomos 215
St John Lampadistis 143
St John Maron 202
St Luke 141
St Makarios the Great 192
St Maron 202
St Mavra 135
St Mnason 150, 151
St Neophytos 126
St Nicholas 133
St Paraskevi 148
St Paul 89, 111, 143
St Sozomenos 169
St Spyridon 236
St Theodore Tyro 141
St Trifyllios 153
St Tykhonas 87, 89
Salamis 228
  Agora 232
  Amphitheatre 231
  Aqueduct 230
  Basilica of Ayios Epiphanios 231
  Bay of 232
  Cistern 231
  City Walls 230
  Fresco of Hylas 230
  Granite forum 231
  Kampanopetra 232
  Mosaics 230
  Museum 233
  Necropolis 232
  Palaestra 230
  Roman villa 231
  Royal Tombs 232
  St Catherine's Prison 233

Salamis cont.
  Temple of Zeus 232
  Theatre 231
  Tomb 2 233
  Tomb 47 233
  Tomb 50 233
Salt Lake 76, 92
Sarandi 147
Savorgnano, Ascanio 162
Savorgnano, Giulio 162
Selim II, Sultan 93, 218
Serayia 95
Sergius Paulus 118
Sessa, Francesco de 223
Silikou 134
Simon of Cyrene 184
Sipahi 195
Skales 107
Smith, Haji 102
Smith, Sir William Sidney 102, 111
Soloi 207
Solon 207
Sopater of Paphos 120
Sotira 70, 96, 135
Sourp Magar Monastery 192
Souskiou 136
Spathariko 235
Spilia tou Mavrou 126
Spilla 146
Stasanor of Kourion 96
Stasanor of Soloi 207
Stavros Mithas, Monastic Church 129
Stavros tis Psokas, Forest Station of 130
Stavros tou Ayiasmati Monastery 147
Stavros Monastery 136
Stavrovouni Monastery 74
Stazousa 76
Steni 130
Strabo 96, 100, 104, 109, 151, 201, 207
Strovolos 170
Süleyman the Magnificent 82
Syrianokhori 206

T

Tacitus 104
Tala 125
Tamassos 1
Taslica 195
Tatlisu 193
Tavernier, J.
Tekke of (H
  77, 78
Temblos 2
Tembria 1
Templos 9
Tepebaşı 2
Terra 129
Teucer 22
Theodosiu
Thubron,
Timi 103
Toumba t
Trajan 1
Tremetou
Trikomo
Trikoukk
Trimitho
Tris Elies
Troodos
Troulli v
Troulli p
Tripylos
Tsadha
Turner,
Turtle I
Tuzla

V

Varots
Vasa
Vasilia
Vavila